Corporate Financial Statements under Ind AS

About the Authors

Sudhir S. Jaiswall is an Associate Professor in the Finance & Control group of IIM Calcutta. He specializes in teaching MBA and Ph.D. level courses on Corporate Financial Reporting, Cost Management, Financial Statement Analysis, Analysis of Cash Flows & Earnings Quality, and Shareholder Value Creation.

He is a Deloitte / J. Michael Cook Doctoral Consortium Fellow of the AAA. He has an MBA from IIM Ahmedabad, M.S. from the University of Rochester, and M.Com. (Gold Medalist) & Ph.D. from the University of Calcutta. He has also received various professional certifications including FRM (GARP), CFA (ICFAI), Grad CMA (ICMAI), and Grad OR (ORSI).

Dr. Jaiswall is a life member of the Indian Accounting Association (IAA). He has held membership of the American Accounting Association (AAA), American Finance Association (AFA), Global Association of Risk Professionals (GARP), Operational Research Society of India (ORSI), and Institute of Cost & Management Accountants of India (ICMAI). His research papers on Executive Compensation, Corporate Governance, and Financial Policy have been published in reputed scholarly journals in India and abroad.

Asish K. Bhattacharyya is a Distinguished Professor in Department of Finance, Accounting, and Control at Shiv Nadar Institution of Eminence (Deemed to be University, formerly known as Shiv Nadar University), Greater NOIDA (Delhi NCR). He obtained D. Phil degree from the University of Allahabad. He is also the Founder of Nonlinear Insights, which operates in the space of online executive education in business management domain.

Earlier, he worked as a Professor at IIM Calcutta, SPJIMR Mumbai and IMT Ghaziabad. He is a Fellow of the Institute of Chartered Accountants of India, a Fellow of the Institute of Cost Accountants of India, and an Associate of the Chartered Institute of Management Accountant (CIMA, UK).

Dr. Bhattacharyya also served IMT Ghaziabad and IMI Kolkata as the Director and as the Technical Director of the Institute of Chartered Accountants of India.

Corporate Financial Statements under Ind AS

Sudhir S. Jaiswall
Associate Professor,
Finance & Control Group,
IIM Calcutta

Asish K. Bhattacharyya
Distinguished Professor,
Finance, Accounting, and Control,
Shiv Nadar Institution of Eminence,
Greater NOIDA, Delhi NCR

McGraw Hill Education (India) Private Limited

Published by McGraw Hill Education (India) Private Limited,
Registered Office: Anjana Complex No: 5/90 A, Butt Road, St. Thomas Mount, Chennai – 600016, Tamil Nadu, India.

Fifth reprint 2025

Print-Book Edition
ISBN-13: 978-93-5532-459-7
ISBN-10: 93-5532-459-6

Print-Book Edition
ISBN-13: 978-93-5532-456-6
ISBN-10: 93-5532-456-1

06 07 08 09 10 RAJ 29 28 27 26 25

Typeset at The Composers, 260, C.A. Apt., Paschim Vihar, New Delhi 110 063 and printed and bound in India at Rajkamal Electric Press, Kundli, Haryana.

Cover Designer: Neeraj Dayal

Visit us at: www.mheducation.co.in
Toll free in India: 1800 103 5875
Write to us at: support.india@mheducation.com
CIN: U80302TN2010PTC111532

Dedicated to

My mother Smt. Vidya Jaiswall
and My visionary teachers,
Prof. Bhabatosh Banerjee and Prof. Asish K. Bhattacharyya

—Sudhir S. Jaiswall

My grand-daughter Mrinalini Bhattacharya

—Asish K. Bhattacharyya

Dedicated to

Preface

The importance of Financial Statements is well known. These statements convey the performance achieved and risk inherent in an enterprise and help assess its future earnings and cash flow prospects. It is vital for business managers, professionals, executives, and aspiring directors to not only grasp the information conveyed by income statements, cash flow statements, and balance sheet but also use the information in their careers.

This book is for management professionals, executive programme participants, and business school students keen to learn about financial statements prepared following Ind AS, the IFRS-based new accounting standards in India. With the help of the book, one can comprehend the contents of financial statements and analyze them to assess the operating and overall performance, efficiency, liquidity, and solvency of Indian companies.

This book has several outstanding features as listed below:

- First, this book does not require any prior accounting and finance knowledge.
- Second, we discuss the concepts in brief and simple language and emphasize their importance and application.
- Third, this book has under 200 pages that can be quickly covered.
- Fourth, the chapters present the essential material, whereas appendices have advanced materials, which can be skipped.
- Fifth, with the help of a mini case, the book explains in detail how transactions affect financial statements and how one can easily prepare financial statements from transactions.

This book has five chapters. *Chapter 1* covers the fundamental concepts helpful in understanding financial statements. It also has a mini-case, illustrating the effect of transactions on financial statements and the preparation of financial statements. The following three chapters are for understanding and analysis of income statement (*Chapter 2*), balance sheet (*Chapter 3*), and cash flow statement

(*Chapter 4*). They begin with several questions that can be answered using their content. Next, they explain the contents of reported statements. Finally, they discuss how to analyze the financial statement information to assess a firm's performance and risk. These three chapters also have appendices to explain advanced concepts. Finally, *Chapter 5* is for financial ratio analysis. It explains 25 crucial financial ratios for assessing profitability, efficiency, liquidity, and solvency.

Acknowledgements

We acknowledge the contribution of our teachers, peers, and students from whom we have learned much.

We hope you will enjoy learning and benefiting from this book. We invite you to email your constructive feedback on this book to *sj.book.feedback@gmail.com*.

Sudhir S. Jaiswall

Asish K. Bhattacharyya

Contents

CHAPTER ONE

Overview of Financial Statements

This chapter provides an overview of business activities, business goals, financial reporting, generally accepted accounting principles (GAAP), financial statements, and the Accounting Equation. A mini-case illustrates the accounting equation for analyzing transactions and preparing a simple balance sheet, income statement, and cash flow statement. The concepts covered in this chapter are fundamental to gaining a deeper understanding of the financial statements in later chapters.

I. Business & Activities

A business is an economic unit that invests, lends money, or sells goods and services to customers to generate an adequate rate of return for its owners.[1] Business owners start and operate a business to serve customer needs for a price and to make a profit. To achieve their goals, firms transact with various parties. A transaction is an exchange of money, goods, or services which affects the firm's financial position. Financial position changes due to a change in assets (resources a firm controls), liabilities (the firm's obligations), and equities (owner's claim on assets).

A transaction can arise from financing, investing, or operating activity. Firms raise funds (financing activities). They use the funds to acquire fixed assets (investing activities) and working capital (operating activities) needed to start the operations. They carry out procurement, production, sales, service delivery, and administration of the business (operating activities).

[1] To vary exposition, the terms – business, firm, entity, enterprise, company, and corporation – are used synonymously throughout this book to refer to a for-profit company. Any legal differences among these terms have been ignored.

(a) Financing Activities

Financing activities involve raising external funds and servicing them. These activities include raising money from an issue of equity and preference shares, short-term and long-term borrowings, acquiring assets on long-term lease arrangements, paying dividends on equity and preference shares, paying interest on borrowings and leases, buying back equity shares, redeeming preference shares, repaying borrowings and lease liabilities, etc. Financing activities affect interest expenses and dividends.

(b) Investing Activities

Investing activities involve acquiring fixed assets and investments. They are essential for creating capacity (for production, retail, and service delivery), building business networks (through investments in subsidiaries, joint ventures, associates, suppliers, customers, etc.), and deploying surplus funds in short-term investments. These activities include purchasing, constructing, and disposing of fixed assets, purchasing and selling investments, and earning income (interest, rent, or dividend) from investments. Examples of fixed assets are property, plant, and equipment (such as land, building, machinery, computers, vehicle, furniture, etc.) and intangible assets (such as computer software, patents, copyrights, trademark, goodwill, etc.), among others. Examples of investments are fixed deposits, loans (given), investments in liquid mutual funds, investments in equity shares issued by other companies, etc. Investing activities result in interest income, dividend income, and gains/losses on the sale of fixed assets and investments.

(c) Operating Activities

Operating activities involve everything else. They are required to carry out day-to-day work. These activities include employing workers and managers; using fixed assets; buying raw materials, components, and packing materials; producing and selling finished goods; buying and selling stock-in-trade; providing service; collecting from customers; paying employees and suppliers of goods and services; paying taxes to the government; hiring auditors; conducting board meetings; and organizing community service, among others. Operating activities result in sales, cost of sale (or cost of goods sold), selling and distribution expense, general and administration expense, and research and development expense, thereby contributing to profit or loss. Operating activities also cause changes in the value of various assets (such as inventory, trade receivables, prepaid expenses, security deposits, etc.) and liabilities (for example, trade payable, expenses payable, tax payable, etc.), thus changing the composition of assets and liabilities.

II. Business Goals

A business may have several goals, including those related to its sustainability. However, the three most important goals are maintaining liquidity and profitability, and achieving growth.

(a) Liquidity

Liquidity refers to the ability to pay short-term obligations when they become due and arrange cash quickly. Liquidity comes from having adequate cash and assets that can be converted into cash easily and quickly. With adequate liquidity, a business operates efficiently. For example, consider a retailer who buys goods, stores them in its store, and sells them for cash; if its sales are erratic or its goods become obsolete, it will have difficulty selling and generating money; its liquidity will suffer, and it will not be able to carry on its business for long. As another example, a firm with enough liquidity pays cash for all purchases and enjoys a lower purchase price than a financially-constrained firm (with inadequate liquidity) needing a more extended credit; as a result, cash purchases lower its costs and increase its profits. Note that liquidity is a hygiene factor, and firms should have sufficient liquidity to operate smoothly. Too less liquidity would result in a firm struggling to pay its dues and making inefficient operating decisions. Too much liquidity could also result in wasteful expenditures and agency problems.

We should avoid confusing liquidity with solvency and using them interchangeably. Liquidity is about paying short-term obligations (within one year), whereas solvency is about fulfilling long-term obligations (beyond one year) and continuing to thrive in the future.

(b) Profitability

Profitability is the ability to generate adequate return on the capital invested in the business by earning revenue higher than expenses, i.e., by earning profit. Net Profit is computed as total revenue minus total expenses.[2] Firms must price their products above cost and control their operating and financing costs to achieve profit. By making a profit, they generate a positive rate of return for their owners. The exact rate of return a firm must generate varies depending on the owners' expected return on investment. An entity may be for-profit or not-for-profit enterprise. A for-profit enterprise strives to earn profits. That is not the case for not-for-profit enterprises (such as charities) because they operate for reasons

[2] Profit and earning are often used synonymously.

other than providing goods or services at a profit or profit equivalent. However, for long-term survival, even these firms must generate surplus by ensuring their revenue and income exceed expenses and losses.

(c) Growth

Growth refers to an increase in the size of the business. Size can be measured in sales revenues, total assets, or market value. Growth is achieved by investing funds into productive assets supporting profitable revenue increases.[3] Thus, a firm invests in new assets, grows its sales, and increases its market value. Among the various growth measures of a firm, sales growth and growth in market value are the favourites of the media, investors, and analysts.

III. Financial Reporting

Financial Reporting is the process of providing decision-makers with financial information useful for decision-making. Users of financial information can be internal (such as managers and employees) or external (such as current and potential investors, lenders, and other creditors, as well as everyone else). Stakeholders need financial information to assess how a firm's operating, investing, and financing activities contribute to its profitability, liquidity, and growth. Financial reporting is vital in providing that information. Companies provide financial statements and other disclosures to fulfil financial reporting requirements. Therefore, financial statements are the means, whereas financial reporting is the end.

According to the Conceptual Framework for Financial Reporting under Indian Accounting Standards (Ind AS), the objective of financial reporting is to provide information about an entity that is useful to the primary users of information (namely, current and potential investors, lenders, and other creditors) in making decisions on providing resources to the entity.[4] These decisions are mainly related to the purchasing, holding, and selling a company's equity and debt securities, granting and collecting loans and other forms of credit to the company, and voting in the company board meetings and general meetings to affect the use of its resources. As per Ind AS 1, the objective of

[3] As an exception, firms may build market share in the short run by pursuing unprofitable sales growth. Furthermore, companies in the start-up phase or winner-takes-all industries may pursue unprofitable sales growth to become large.

[4] The Institute of Chartered Accountants of India. 2020. The Conceptual Framework for Financial Reporting under Indian Accounting Standards (Ind AS). para 1.2, page 8. https://www.icai.org/post/conceptual-framework-financial-reporting-indas

financial statements is "to provide information about the financial position, financial performance, and cash flows of an entity that is useful to a wide range of users in making economic decisions."

A firm must comply with the financial reporting requirements to benefit the users of financial statements. Compliance ensures the relevance and reliability of the information contained in the financial statements.[5] Information is *relevant* if it can help predict future information (for example, earnings or cash flows) and confirm present or past forecasts of information (for example, earnings or cash flows). Information is *reliable* (or faithfully representative) if it is neutral (or unbiased), complete, and free from material error. Furthermore, compliance ensures the financial information has several enhancing qualitative characteristics, such as being *consistent* and *comparable* across years, *comparable* across firms in the industry, *verifiable* (by auditors, for example), *understandable* (by informed users), and *timely*.[6] Auditors are required to check the compliance of financial statements with financial reporting requirements and report if there is any deviation.

IV. Generally Accepted Accounting Principles (GAAP)

Financial statements must be prepared based on GAAP, a common set of accounting principles, methods, and standards issued by regulators. For example, companies listed on an Indian stock exchange (other than banking and insurance companies and those listed on the SME Exchange) must comply with the Indian Accounting Standards (Ind AS).[7] Ind AS is a new set of accounting standards in India since 1st April 2016. It is fully converged with the International Financial Reporting Standards (IFRS). India has not adopted IFRS. It has added a few principles (called, carve in) and eliminated a few (called, carve out). Therefore, it is said that India has taken the convergence route.

---

[5] Relevance and reliability are the two fundamental qualitative characteristics of useful financial information. Useful financial information also has several enhancing qualitative characteristics.

[6] Companies must file their financial statements with the Indian stock exchange on which they are listed: quarterly financial statements within 45 days of the end of the quarter, and annual financial statements within 60 days of the end of the financial year. These statements can be downloaded from the stock exchange's website.

[7] In addition, unlisted entities whose net worth is at least ₹250 crores must adopt Ind AS. Furthermore, if an entity is required to adopt Ind AS, its subsidiaries, parent, joint-venture, and associate companies must also follow Ind AS. For all other entities (including banking and insurance companies and those listed on SME exchanges), it is not mandatory to use Ind AS, and they may use the old AS accounting standards.

In India, accounting standards are prepared by the Accounting Standards Board of the Institute of Chartered Accountants of India and notified by the Ministry of Corporate Affairs.[8] The Indian government constituted the National Financial Reporting Authority (NFRA) in October 2018 to recommend accounting and auditing standards for adoption by the government, monitor and enforce compliance with these standards, and oversee the quality of service of auditors. The Securities and Exchange Board of India (SEBI) provides additional disclosure requirements, including filing quarterly, half-yearly and annual financial statements, for companies listed on Indian stock exchanges.

Although a deep understanding of accounting standards is *not necessary for most users* of financial statements, we will refer to the relevant standards in brief wherever appropriate. We discuss below the following fundamental accounting principles and concepts underlying GAAP, which are needed for understanding and analyzing financial statements.

(a) Economic Entity Assumption

A business is assumed to be separate from its owners and other entities while recording transactions and preparing financial statements. Transactions of a firm's owners and other entities are outside the scope of its financial statements unless the firm is one of the parties to the transaction (in such cases, the transaction is recorded). Note that transactions between a firm and its owner are reported as equity transactions. Essentially, the separate economic entity assumption sets a boundary for financial reporting. For a firm's standalone financial statements, the limit is the firm itself (various divisions are not considered separate economic entities). By contrast, for consolidated financial statements, the boundary includes the firm and all subsidiaries in which the firm controls more than 50% of the equity shares or otherwise controls the financial and operating decisions of the investee.

(b) Going Concern Assumption

The firm is assumed to live forever unless there are reasons to believe it intends to or will be forced to liquidate next year. Its management must assess the going concern assumption, and auditors must agree. If this assumption is not valid, the same must be reported, and assets must be restated at their liquidation value.

[8] In the United States of America (U.S.), the Securities & Exchange Commission (SEC) requires companies listed on a U.S. stock exchange to follow the U.S. GAAP issued by the Financial Accounting Standards Board (FASB). The Public Companies Accounting Oversight Board (PCAOB) oversees the auditors in the U.S.

(c) Periodicity Assumption

The periodicity assumption allows dividing the life of a business into smaller periods (for example, one financial year or one calendar year) so that financial statements can be prepared for each period.

(d) Monetary Unit Assumption

The monetary assumption requires that financial statements be based only on transactions that can be measured in terms of money. The number of factories (or employees, products, markets, brands, patents, etc.), employee morale, productivity, production capacity, capacity utilization, quantity sold, etc., may be helpful information to stakeholders. Still, such information is disregarded in the preparation of financial statements. However, firms are free to disclose them voluntarily, along with other essential items not measured in money, in the notes to financial statements.

(e) Historical Cost Principle

Historical Cost refers to the original cost/amount at which an asset/liability was initially recorded. For example, the historical cost of a car is the purchase price (including taxes) for that car. The historical cost principle is one of the several measurement bases used in preparing financial statements. It has been in use for a long time as it offers several advantages. For example, historical cost information is reliable, verifiable, consistent, and comparable. Although historical costs provide a confirmative value, they may only offer predictive value in some cases. The historical cost of trade payable (a current liability) has predictive value about how much cash will be paid to the suppliers of goods and services.[9] By contrast, the historical cost of property, plant, and equipment (a non-current asset) may have little predictive value about how much it will cost to purchase the asset at the end of its life or how much cash will be generated using the asset.[10] Most current assets and liabilities have high predictive value, whereas most non-current ones have low predictive value due to their long life and the effect of inflation.

(f) Fair Value Principle

The fair value is the other measurement basis for preparing financial statements. Fair value refers to the price in an orderly (or arm's length) transaction between

[9] A current liability is payable within the next year, whereas a non-current liability is due after the next year.

[10] A non-current asset is expected to be used over (or sold after) several years, whereas a current asset is expected to be realized into cash within the next year.

market participants. It is the amount expected to be received from the sale of an asset or to be paid to transfer a liability on a specific date. The fair value principle ensures that the assets are shown on the balance sheet at their recoverable amounts (at the end of the year) and liabilities at their exit price, and any estimated losses or gains (from a change in the value) are reflected on the income statement.

(g) Full Disclosure Principle

The full disclosure principle requires companies to disclose all events, circumstances, and financial information that are *material.* For example, a company must disclose when an earthquake has damaged its only factory. Similarly, a company that has won a disproportionately large sales order must disclose the event. A company also must disclose items carrying large amounts without clubbing them with other things. Note that the concept of materiality is essential here. Items are considered *material* if they could (either individually or collectively) influence the economic decisions that users make based on financial statements. It is important to emphasize that materiality depends on the item's size and nature and must be judged based on specific circumstances.

(h) Conservatism or Prudence Principle

The conservatism principle requires that bad news (for example, losses) is reflected immediately on the financial statements, but the recognition of good news (such as revenue, income, and gains) is delayed until the amount is realized (see realization principle below). Thus, losses, whether incurred or estimated, are included on the income statement, but only realized income or gains are presented on the income statement. In other words, unrealized gains are not taken to the income statement. Consequently, the "true profit" is greater than or equal to the reported "net profit" on the income statement. Since net profits is included in equity, "true value" of equity is expected to be greater than the reported value of equity on the balance sheet. Consequently, the "true value" of assets is expected to be higher, and that of liabilities is expected to be lower than what appears on the balance sheet.

(i) Accrual Basis

Business entities follow the accrual basis by applying the realization and matching principles (discussed below). They record revenues, incomes, and gains when these are realized (irrespective of when cash is received) and record expenses and losses in the period to which these are related (regardless of when money is paid).

(j) Realization Principle

The realization principle helps determine when to recognize revenue and income. A company should recognize revenue when it has fulfilled all the terms and conditions of its contract with a customer and is reasonably sure it can collect the amount from the customer. For example, sales revenue is realized when the control of the goods is transferred or services are delivered to the customer, and there is no reasonable uncertainty about the customer not paying the sales consideration. By contrast, sales revenue should not be recognized when receiving a full or partial advance from a customer if the control of the goods is yet to be transferred or the service is yet to be rendered.

(k) Matching Principle

The matching principle helps determine when to recognize expenses. Costs are recognized as expenses in the periods their benefits are consumed, irrespective of when the costs are paid. For example, a company buys 200 units of merchandise @ ₹100 each in the financial year 2021–22 and sells 76 units in 2021–22 and 124 units in 2022–23. It will expense ₹7,600 (= 76 units × ₹100 per unit) as the Cost of Sales in 2021–22 and ₹12,400 (= 124 units × ₹100 per unit) in 2022–23. Until these goods are sold, product costs remain as inventory (an asset). As another example, a company pays a full advance of ₹30 lakh for print advertisements, of which one-third will appear in 2021–22 and the remaining in 2022–23. It will recognize ₹10 lakh as advertising expenses in 2021–22 and the remaining ₹20 lakh as advertising expenses in 2022–23. Until the advertising costs are expensed, they remain prepaid expenses (an asset).

V. Financial Statements

Financial statements play an essential role in economic decision-making by a firm's multiple stakeholders. They are used in fundamental analysis, debt contracting, and executive compensation contracting, among others.

Analysts, investors, and creditors do fundamental analyses utilizing information from financial statements (among others) and assess a firm's operating and financial strengths and weaknesses. For example, analysts use financial statements to analyze a firm's financials, forecast its future earnings, assess its intrinsic value, and offer recommendations on its stock (such as strong buy, buy, hold, sell, or strong sell).

Lenders use financial statements in debt contracting. For example, a lender assesses borrowers' solvency and credit risk using information from their financial statements. It decides whether to grant a loan, how much interest to charge, and what minimum level of equity cover borrowers must maintain for the borrowings.

Boards of directors use performance metrics (obtained from financial statements) in executive compensation contracts. Boards assess their firm's performance to decide how much bonus to give to their top executives. For example, Jaiswall and Raman (2021) show that CEO compensation in large Indian firms is tied to the firm's sales growth and profitability.[11]

There are four financial statements: Balance Sheet (B/S), Income Statement (I/S), Cash Flow Statement (CFS), and Statement of Changes in Equity (SOCE). Of these, the first three are the most widely used (and discussed below), and a statement of changes in equity is often considered an extension of a balance sheet. Note that a balance sheet provides information at a point in time (just like a picture). In contrast, the remaining three statements provide information over a period of time (just like a video). All four financial statements provide information for both current and previous periods.

(a) Balance Sheet

A Balance Sheet provides information about the financial position of a firm. It discloses assets, liabilities, and equities of the firm, by description and value, at the end of a financial period. A firm's balance sheet helps understand the types of assets a firm owns and how it has funded them. We can ascertain the magnitude and the mix of equity, debt, and operational liabilities used to finance assets. We can also analyze the importance of assets that can be converted into cash within a year and the obligations due within a year. Statement of changes in equity is considered an extension of the balance sheet. As the name suggests, a statement of changes in equity shows the changes in equity accounts (equity share capital and various reserves and surplus items) during a financial period.

(b) Income Statement

Income statement provides information about a firm's financial performance. It shows the revenues, expenses, incomes, gains, profits, and losses during a financial period. A firm's income statement helps us assess its profitability and the performance of its various activities. We can find different sources of revenue, income, and gains. We can also find out the nature of expenses and

[11] Jaiswall, S.S., and Raman, K.K. 2021. Sales Growth, CEO Pay, and Corporate Governance in India. *Journal of Accounting, Auditing, and Finance*. Volume 36 (2), pages 249–277.

losses. Accordingly, we can assess the profitability of its production/retail/service (using gross profit), its operations (using operating profit), or its entire business (using net profit). We can scrutinize the quality and sustainability of its earnings.

(c) Cash Flow Statement

Cash flow statement shows the cash flows from operating, investing, and financing activities during a financial period. A firm's cash flow statement helps understand the sources and uses of cash and the ability to generate cash flows. We can find cash flows related to operating activities before taxes, income taxes, capital expenditure, investments, investment income, borrowings, interest, equity, and dividends, among others.

VI. Accounting Equation

The accounting equation is at the core of the way accounting is done. It helps apply the accrual basis of accounting. The equation must always hold, and its validity is evident in a Balance Sheet. The accounting equation states that the total assets of an entity must always be equal to the sum of its equity and total liabilities.

$$\textit{Assets} = \textit{Liabilities} + \textit{Equity}$$

When a company is started, it has no asset, liability, or equity, i.e., Total Assets 0 = Total Liabilities 0 + Equity 0. Thereafter, although every transaction changes some asset, liability, or equity, the accounting equation must hold, and the change in assets must also equal the change in liabilities plus the change in equity.

$$\Delta\ \textit{Assets} = \Delta\ \textit{Liabilities} + \Delta\ \textit{Equity}$$

The application of how transactions affect these two equations is illustrated in Appendix 1A: Mini-Case.

Appendix 1A: Mini Case: Pet Shop Ltd.

Pet Shop Ltd., a merchandiser, started its business on January 1, 2022. Subsequently, it had the following transactions in the month of January 2022. Explain the effect of these transactions on assets, liabilities, and equity using the Accounting Equation. After that, prepare a table showing the impact of each transaction on cash, other assets (mention the name of the asset), liabilities (mention the name of the liability), equity share capital, and income & expense (mention the name of the income or expense). Based on this table, prepare a simple income statement, balance sheet, and cash flow statement.

1. On 01-01-2022, Issued equity shares and received ₹10 lakh.
2. On 02-01-2022, Rented a store for a monthly rent of ₹50,000. Gave a security deposit of ₹75,000, which is refundable when the one-year rental agreement expires. Rent will be paid in arrears at the beginning of next month.
3. On 03-01-2022, Borrowed from the bank ₹9 lakh. Interest is payable @ 1% per month on March 31.
4. On 04-01-2022, Bought store equipment for ₹5 lakh. It will be used for five years and then sold for ₹20,000.
5. On 05-01-2022, Bought a store management software license for ₹252,000. It will be used for three years, and after that, it will be of no use.
6. On 06-01-2022, Purchased stock-in-trade ₹200,000 cash and 300,000 payable next month.
7. On 06-01-2022, Paid freight outward ₹10,000 to send goods to a customer.
8. On 07-01-2022, Sold goods (costing ₹400,000) for ₹800,000. ₹300,000 is cash sales. The remainder will be collected next month.
9. On 15-01-2022, Paid ₹1,92,000 premium for a 24-month fire insurance policy starting 16-01-2022.
10. On 16-01-2022, Purchased supplies by paying cash for ₹5,000.
11. On 27-1-2022, Received bills for utility expenses of ₹15,000 payable next month.
12. On 30-01-2022, Received ₹20,000 as an advance from a customer, Jayant, for the supply of goods next month.
13. On 31-01-2022, Paid staff salaries for the month ₹65,000.
14. On 31-01-2022, Earned Interest income on Bank Balance ₹1,000, which is receivable on 31-03-2022.

15. On 31-01-2022, the monthly rent of ₹50,000 is due.
16. On 31-01-2022, the monthly depreciation for store equipment is ₹8,000.
17. On 31-01-2022, the monthly amortization for software is ₹7,000.
18. On 31-01-2022, the Cost of supplies consumed is ₹3,000.
19. On 31-01-2022, the monthly Interest Expense accrued is ₹9,000.
20. On 31-01-2022, the Insurance expense for the half month is ₹4,000.

Solution

1. On 01-01-2022, Issued equity shares and received ₹10 lakh.

   In this transaction, the company has raised cash by issuing equity capital. Hence, its cash has increased by ₹10 lakh, and equity share capital has increased by ₹10 lakh.

   - Δ Cash (Assets) = +10 lakh; Δ Equity Share Capital (Equity) = +10 lakh
   - 10 lakh Δ Assets = 0 Δ Liabilities + 10 lakh Δ Equity
   - After this transaction, Total Assets 10 lakh = Total Liabilities 0 + Equity 10 lakh.

---

2. On 02-01-2022, Rented a store for a monthly rent of ₹50,000. Gave a security deposit of ₹75,000, which is refundable when the one-year rental agreement expires. Rent will be paid in arrears at the beginning of next month.

   The company has rented a store and paid a security deposit in this example. Paying a security deposit is a transaction. Cash has decreased by ₹75,000. As this amount is refundable, the security deposit is an asset, which has increased by ₹75,000. Thus, this transaction affects two assets and does not affect any liability or equity.

   - Δ Cash (Asset) = –75,000; Δ Security Deposit (Asset) = +75,000.
   - 0 Δ Assets = 0 Δ Total Liabilities + 0 Δ Equity
   - After this transaction, Total Assets 10 lakh = Total Liabilities 0 + Equity 10 lakh.

---

3. On 03-01-2022, Borrowed from the bank ₹9 lakh. Interest is payable @ 1% per month on March 31.

   In this transaction, the company borrowed cash from the bank. Hence, its cash (asset) has increased by ₹9 lakh, and bank borrowings (liability) have increased by ₹9 lakh.

- Δ Cash (Asset) = +9 lakh; Δ Bank Borrowings (Liability) = +9 lakh.
- 9 lakh Δ Assets = 9 lakh Δ Total Liabilities + 0 Δ Equity. Thus, total assets and liabilities have changed due to this transaction.
- After this transaction, Assets 19 lakh = Liabilities 9 lakh + Equity 10 lakh.

---

4. On 04-01-2022, Bought store equipment for ₹5 lakh. It will be used for five years and then sold for ₹20,000.

In this transaction, the company has paid cash to purchase equipment. Hence, its cash has decreased by ₹5 lakh. The company owns the equipment and will use it for several years. Thus, equipment is an asset that has increased by ₹5 lakh. This transaction affects two assets and does not affect liability or equity.

- Δ Cash (Asset) = –5 lakh; Δ Equipment (Asset) = +5 lakh.
- 0 Δ Assets = 0 Δ Total Liabilities + 0 Δ Equity. Thus, this transaction does not change total assets, liabilities, or equity.
- After this transaction, Assets 19 lakh = Liabilities 9 lakh + Equity 10 lakh.

---

5. On 05-01-2022, Bought a store management software license for ₹252,000. It will be used for three years, and after that, it will be of no use.

The company has paid cash to purchase the software. Hence, its cash has decreased by ₹252,000. The company owns the software license and will use it for several years. Thus, the software is an asset that has increased by ₹252,000. This transaction affects two assets and does not affect liability or equity.

- Δ Cash (Asset) = –252,000; Δ Software (Asset) = +252,000.
- 0 Δ Assets = 0 Δ Total Liabilities + 0 Δ Equity. Thus, this transaction does not change total assets, liabilities, or equity.
- After this transaction, Assets 19 lakh = Liabilities 9 lakh + Equity 10 lakh.

---

6. On 06-01-2022, Purchased stock-in-trade ₹200,000 cash and 300,000 payable next month.

In this transaction, the company has purchased stock-in-trade (asset) ₹5 lakh for resale. It has paid cash ₹2 lakh and owes ₹3 lakh to suppliers. Thus, its stock-in-trade inventory (asset) has increased by ₹5 lakh, cash (asset) has decreased by ₹2 lakh, and trade payable (liability) has risen by ₹3 lakh. This transaction affects two assets, one liability, and no equity item.

- Δ Stock-in-Trade (Asset) = +5 lakh; Δ Cash (Asset) = −2 lakh; Δ Trade Payable (Liability) = +3 lakh.
- After this transaction, Assets 22 lakh = Liabilities 12 lakh + Equity 10 lakh.

---

7. On 06-01-2022, Paid freight outward ₹10,000 to send goods to a customer.

The company has incurred an expense and paid it in cash. Thus, its cash has decreased by 10,000. Its expenses have increased, which causes equity to fall by 10,000.

- Δ Asset (Cash) = −10,000; Δ Equity (Freight Outward Expense) = −10,000 (the negative sign for equity denotes that the expense has caused a decrease in equity).
- After this transaction, Assets 21.9 lakh = Liabilities 12 lakh + Equity 9.9 lakh.

---

8. On 07-01-2022, Sold goods (costing ₹400,000) for ₹800,000. ₹300,000 is cash sales. The remainder will be collected next month.

We will deal with this transaction in two steps.

First, the company sold goods. Sales Revenue has increased by ₹8 lakh. Since revenues increase equity, equity has risen by ₹8 lakh. The company has collected ₹3 lakh cash from cash sales and will receive ₹5 lakh next month from its customers. Thus, cash has increased by ₹3 lakh, and trade receivables have increased by ₹5 lakh. Therefore, there is an effect on two assets, one equity, and no liability item.

- Δ Cash (Asset) = 3 lakh; Δ Trade Receivables (Asset) = 5 lakh; Δ Equity (Sales) = 8 lakh.

Next, the goods costing ₹4 lakh in inventory were sold. These goods are no longer with the company. Therefore, inventory has decreased by ₹4 lakh. Furthermore, the cost of merchandise sold ₹4 lakh is now an expense. Thus, the Cost of Sales (Expense) has increased by ₹4 lakh. Since expenses decrease equity, equity has decreased by ₹4 lakh. Therefore, this transaction affects one asset, one equity, and no liability item.

- Δ Stock-in-Trade Inventory (Asset) = −4 lakh; Δ Equity (Cost of Sales) = −4 lakh (the negative sign for equity denotes that the expense has caused a decrease in equity).

- After these effects (sales and cost), Assets 25.9 lakh = Liabilities 12 lakh + Equity 13.9 lakh.

---

9. On 15-01-2022, Paid ₹1,92,000 premium for a 24-month fire insurance policy starting 16-01-2022.

   In this transaction, the company has paid the insurance premium in cash. Hence, cash (an asset) has decreased by ₹1,92,000. The insurance premium is paid in advance, and the benefit will be consumed over several months. Therefore, the amount paid is an asset (known as Prepaid Expense). Thus, Prepaid Insurance (an asset) has increased by 1,92,000. This transaction affects two assets and does not affect liability or equity.

   - Δ Cash (Asset) = –1,92,000; Δ Prepaid Insurance (Asset) = +1,92,000. Thus, total assets, liabilities, or equity have not changed due to this transaction.
   - After this transaction, Assets 25.9 lakh = Liabilities 12 lakh + Equity 13.9 lakh.

---

10. On 16-01-2022, Purchased supplies by paying cash for ₹5,000.

    The company has made cash purchases of supplies (an asset). Thus, supplies have increased by ₹5,000. As it has paid cash, its cash (asset) has decreased by ₹5,000. This transaction affects two assets, no liability, and no equity.

    - Δ Supplies (Asset) = +5,000; Δ Cash (Asset) = –5,000. Thus, this transaction does not change total assets, liabilities, or equity.
    - After this transaction, Assets 25.9 lakh = Liabilities 12 lakh + Equity 13.9 lakh.

---

11. On 27-1-2022, Received bills for utility expenses of ₹15,000 payable next month.

    The utility bill is an intimation (by the utility provider) of the service consumed and the amount payable by the consumer to the provider. In this transaction, the company has received utility bills. Thus, Utility Expense has increased by ₹15,000, which has caused equity to decrease by ₹15,000. As the amount is unpaid, Utility Expense Payable (a liability) has risen by ₹15,000. This transaction affects no asset, a liability, and an equity.

    - Δ Liability (Utility Expense Payable) = +15,000; Δ Equity (Utility Expense) = –15,000 (the negative sign for equity denotes that the expense has caused a decrease in equity).

- After this transaction, Assets 25.9 lakh = Liabilities 12.15 lakh + Equity 13.75 lakh.

---

12. On 30-01-2022, Received ₹20,000 as an advance from a customer, Jayant, for the supply of goods next month.

    In this transaction, the company has received cash for a supply of goods at a future date. Thus, Cash (an asset) has increased by ₹20,000. As the goods will be supplied at a future date, the company has not earned an income yet and has an obligation (or a liability) to provide the goods to Jayant. Therefore, Advance from Customer (a liability) has increased by ₹20,000. This transaction affects one asset, one liability, and no equity.

    - Δ Asset (Cash) = +20,000; Δ Liability (Advance from Customer) = +20,000.
    - After this transaction, Assets 26.1 lakh = Liabilities 12.35 lakh + Equity 13.75 lakh.

---

13. On 31-01-2022, Paid staff salaries for the month ₹65,000.

    As the company has paid salaries, Cash (an asset) has decreased by ₹65,000. Salaries are paid to employees for the service they have rendered; therefore, salaries are an expense. Salaries Expense has increased by ₹65,000, which causes equity to decrease by ₹65,000. This transaction affects one asset, no liability, and one equity.

    - Δ Asset (Cash) = –65,000; Δ Equity (Salaries Expense) = –65,000.
    - After this transaction, Assets 25.45 lakh = Liabilities 12.35 lakh + Equity 13.10 lakh.

---

14. On 31-01-2022, Earned Interest income on Bank Balance ₹1,000, which is receivable on 31-03-2022.

    The company has earned interest income on its cash balance with the bank. Therefore, Interest Income has increased by ₹1,000, which causes equity to increase by ₹1,000. This amount is also an asset because the company will receive it later. Thus, Interest Receivable (an asset) has risen by ₹1,000. This transaction affects an asset, no liability, and an equity.

    - Δ Asset (Interest Receivable) = +1,000; Δ Equity (Interest Income) = +1,000.
    - After this transaction, Assets 25.46 lakh = Liabilities 12.35 lakh + Equity 13.11 lakh.

---

15. On 31-01-2022, the monthly rent of ₹50,000 is due.

Note that the company had rented a store (transaction number 2) for a monthly rent of ₹50,000, payable in arrears at the beginning of the following month. Thus, on 31-01-2022, the company incurred rent expense, which remains unpaid. As a result, Rent Expense has increased, which causes equity to decrease by ₹50,000. This amount is also a liability because it must be paid on a future date. Thus, Rent Payable (a liability) has increased by ₹50,000. This transaction affects no asset, one liability, and one equity.

- Δ Liability (Rent Payable) = +50,000; Δ Equity (Rent Expense) = −50,000.
- After this transaction, Assets 25.46 lakh = Liabilities 12.85 lakh + Equity 12.61 lakh.

---

16. On 31-01-2022, the monthly depreciation for store equipment is ₹8,000.

Note that the company had purchased store equipment (transaction number 4), which is an item of property, plant, and equipment (PPE).[12] At the end of January, the company incurred monthly depreciation for store equipment. Thus, Depreciation Expense has increased by ₹8,000, which causes equity to decrease by ₹8,000. Furthermore, Accumulated Depreciation (a contra-asset) has risen by ₹8,000, which causes total assets to reduce by ₹8,000. Thus, this transaction affects one asset, no liability, and one equity.

- Δ Asset (Accumulated Depreciation) = −8,000; Δ Equity (Depreciation Expense) = −8,000.
- After this transaction, Assets 25.38 lakh = Liabilities 12.85 lakh +Equity 12.53 lakh.

---

17. On 31-01-2022, the monthly amortization for software is ₹7,000.

Note that the company had purchased software (transaction number 5), an intangible asset.[13] At the end of the month, the company has incurred monthly amortization for the software. Thus, Amortization

[12] For a PPE, depreciation expense is incurred every period. As a result, there is an increase in Depreciation Expense (an expense) and Accumulated Depreciation (a contra-asset). The PPE is reported net of Accumulated Depreciation. We will discuss these concepts in detail in Chapter 2 (Income Statement) and Chapter 3 (Balance Sheet).

[13] For an intangible asset (such as computer software), amortization expense is incurred every period. As a result, there is an increase in Amortization Expense (an expense) and Accumulated Amortization (a contra-asset). The intangible asset is reported net of Accumulated Amortization. We will discuss these concepts in detail in Chapter 2 (Income Statement) and Chapter 3 (Balance Sheet).

Expense has increased by ₹7,000, which causes equity to decrease by ₹7,000. Furthermore, Accumulated Amortization (a contra-asset) has risen by ₹7,000, which causes total assets to reduce by ₹7,000. Thus, this transaction affects one asset, no liability, and one equity.

- Δ Asset (Accumulated Amortization) = –7,000; Δ Equity (Amortization Expense) = –7,000.
- After this transaction, Assets 25.31 lakh = Liabilities 12.85 lakh + Equity 12.46 lakh.

---

18. On 31-01-2022, the Cost of supplies consumed is ₹3,000.

The company had purchased supplies (transaction number 10). Supplies are meant for consumption; once used up, they are no longer an asset, and their cost becomes an expense. In this example, at the end of the month, the company has determined that supplies costing ₹3,000 has been consumed. Thus, Supplies Expense has increased by ₹3,000, which causes equity to decrease by ₹3,000. Furthermore, Supplies (an asset) have fallen by ₹3,000. Thus, this transaction affects one asset, no liability, and one equity item.

- Δ Asset (Supplies) = –3,000; Δ Equity (Supplies Expense) = –3,000.
- After this transaction, Assets 25.28 lakh = Liabilities 12.85 lakh +Equity 12.43 lakh.

---

19. On 31-01-2022, the monthly Interest Expense accrued is ₹9,000.

Note that the company had taken a bank borrowing (transaction number 3), for which interest is payable @ 1% per month on March 31. Thus, on 31-01-2022, the company incurred interest expense, which is unpaid. Therefore, Interest Expense (or Finance Cost) has increased, which causes equity to decrease by ₹9,000. This amount is also a liability because it must be paid on a future date. Thus, Interest Payable (a liability) has increased by ₹9,000. This transaction affects no asset, one liability, and one equity.

- Δ Liability (Interest Payable) = +9,000; Δ Equity (Interest Expense) = –9,000.
- After this transaction, Assets 25.28 lakh = Liabilities 12.94 lakh +Equity 12.34 lakh.

---

20. On 31-01-2022, the Insurance expense for the half month is ₹4,000.

Note that the company had taken a 24-month fire insurance policy (transaction number 9) on 15-1-2022. As time passes, the policy will remain effective for fewer months. Thus, on 31-01-2022, a half-month of insurance protection expired, and the company incurred an expense. Insurance Expense has increased, which causes equity to decrease by ₹4,000. Furthermore, Prepaid Insurance (an asset) has reduced by ₹4,000. This transaction affects one asset, no liability, and one equity.

- Δ Asset (Prepaid Insurance) = –4,000; Δ Equity (Insurance Expense) = –4,000.
- After this transaction, Assets 25.24 lakh = Liabilities 12.94 lakh + Equity 12.30 lakh.

Thus, at the end of January 2022, total assets are ₹25.24 lakh, total liabilities are ₹12.94 lakh, and Equity is ₹12.30 lakh.

The effects of these twenty transactions are summarized in Table 1A.1. Although we could have had just three columns (one each for asset, liability, and equity) in the table, we have five columns – one each for cash, all other assets, liabilities, equity share capital, and income & expenses. This choice makes it easier to prepare a simple balance sheet (lists assets, liabilities, equity & their amounts), a simple income statement (lists revenue, expenses, & their amounts, information in column 5), and a simple cash flow statement (lists cash receipts and payments in column 1 grouped into operating, investing, and financing activities).

Analysis of Transactions using Accounting Equation

Table 1A.1 Analysis of Transactions using Accounting Equation

Sl. No	Date 2022	Transaction (Column)	Assets			Liabilities		Equity		
			Cash (1)	Other Assets (2)	Description of Other Assets	Amount (3)	Description of Liabilities	Share Capital (4)	Income & Expense (5)	Description of Income & Expense
1)	01-Jan	Issued equity shares and received ₹10 lakh.	1,000,000					1,000,000		
2)	02-Jan	Rented a store for a monthly rent of ₹50,000. Gave a security deposit of ₹50,000, which is refundable when the one-year rental agreement expires. Rent will be paid in arrears at the beginning of next month.	–75,000	75,000	Security Deposit					
3)	03-Jan	Borrowed from the bank ₹9 lakh. Interest is payable @ 1% per month on March 31.	900,000			900,000	Bank Borrowings			
4)	04-Jan	Bought store equipment for ₹5 lakh. It will be used for five years and then sold for ₹20,000.	–500,000	500,000	Equipment					
5)	05-Jan	Bought store management software license for ₹252,000. It will be used for three years, and after that, it will be of no use.	–252,000	252,000	Software					
6)	06-Jan	Purchased stock-in-trade ₹200,000 in cash and 300,000 payable next month.	–200,000	500,000	Stock-in-Trade Inventory	300,000	Trade Payable			
7)	06-Jan	Paid freight outward ₹10,000 to send goods to a customer.	–10,000						–10,000	Freight Outward
8)	07-Jan	Sold goods (costing ₹400,000) for ₹800,000. ₹300,000 is cash sales. The remainder will be collected next month.	300,000	500,000	Trade Receivable				800,000	Sales

Sl. No	Date 2022	Transaction (Column)	Assets			Liabilities		Equity		
			Cash (1)	Other Assets (2)	Description of Other Assets	Amount (3)	Description of Liabilities	Share Capital (4)	Income & Expense (5)	Description of Income & Expense
8)	07-Jan	Sold goods (costing ₹400,000) for ₹800,000. ₹300,000 is cash sales. The remainder will be collected next month.		–400,000	Stock-in-Trade Inventory				–400,000	Cost of Sales
9)	15-Jan	Paid ₹144,000 premium for a 24-month fire insurance policy starting 16-01-2022.	–192,000	192,000	Prepaid Expense					
10)	16-Jan	Purchased supplies for ₹5,000	–5,000	5,000	Supplies Inventory					
11)	27-Jan	Received bills for utility expenses of ₹15,000 payable next month				15,000	Utility Payable		–15,000	Utility Expense
12)	30-Jan	Received ₹20,000 as an advance from a customer, Jayant, for the supply of goods next month.	20,000			20,000	Advance from Customer			
13)	31-Jan	Paid staff salaries for the month ₹65,000	–65,000						–65,000	Salaries Expense
14)	31-Jan	Earned Interest income on Bank Balance ₹1,000, which is receivable on 31-03-2022.		1,000	Interest Receivable				1,000	Interest Income
15)	31-Jan	The monthly rent of ₹50,000 is due.				50,000	Rent Payable		–50,000	Rent Expense
16)	31-Jan	The monthly depreciation for store equipment is ₹8,000.		–8,000	Accumulated Depreciation – Equipment				–8,000	Depreciation Expense
17)	31-Jan	The monthly amortization for software is ₹7,000		–7,000	Accumulated Amortization – Software				–7,000	Amortization Expense
18)	31-Jan	The cost of supplies consumed is ₹3,000		–3,000	Supplies				–3,000	Supplies Expense

Sl. No	Date 2022	Transaction (Column)	Assets			Liabilities		Equity		
			Cash (1)	Other Assets (2)	Description of Other Assets	Amount (3)	Description of Liabilities	Share Capital (4)	Income & Expense (5)	Description of Income & Expense
19)	31-Jan	The monthly interest expense accrued is ₹9,000.				9,000	Interest Payable		–9,000	Interest Expense
20)	31-Jan	The insurance expense for the half month is ₹4,000.		–4,000	Prepaid Expense				–4,000	Insurance Expense
	31-Jan	Total	9,21,000	16,03,000		12,94,000		10,00,000	2,30,000	Net Profit
		Total of Liabilities & Equity 25,24,000	Total Assets 25,24,000			Liabilities 12,94,000		Equity 12,30,000		

Note: Instead of just three columns – one each for asset, liability, and equity – five columns have been created to ease the preparation of the cash flow statement and income statement. Column (1) will be used for preparing a simple cash flow statement, Column (5) for a simple income statement, and Columns (1) to (5) for a simple balance sheet.

Balance Sheet

Here is a simple Balance Sheet prepared at the end of 31-1-2022 (amounts are in ₹Lakh) using Column (1) total (for Cash), Column (4) total (for Equity Share Capital), Column (5) total (for Retained Earnings), and the information contained in Columns (2) and (3) of Table 1A.1 (for assets other than cash and for liabilities):

Table 1A.2 Balance Sheet

Balance Sheet as at 31-1-2022		**₹ Lakh**
Assets:		
Equipment	5.00	
Less Accumulated Depreciation – Equipment	–0.08	4.92
Software	2.52	
Less Accumulated Amortization – Software	–0.07	2.45
Stock-in-Trade Inventory (5.00 – 4.00)		1.00
Supplies Inventory (0.05 – 0.03)		0.02
Trade Receivable		5.00
Cash		9.21
Interest Receivable		0.01
Security Deposit		0.75
Prepaid Insurance (1.92 – 0.04)		1.88
	Total Assets	25.24
Equity:		
Equity Capital		10.00
Retained Earnings (Net Profit)		2.30
	Total Equity	12.30
Liabilities:		
Bank Borrowings		9.00
Advance from Customer		0.20
Trade Payable		3.00
Utilities Payable		0.15
Rent Payable		0.50
Interest Payable		0.09
	Total Liabilities	12.94
	Total Liabilities & Equity	25.24

The simple balance sheet shows that the company has an equity of 12.3 lakh. Total assets are 25.24 lakh, whereas total liabilities are 12.94 lakh. Thus, the company has enough assets to meet its obligations (liabilities). Cash, Trade Receivables, and Fixed Assets (Store Equipment and Software) are the top three assets, whereas Bank Borrowings, Trade Payable, and Rent Payable are the top three liabilities.

Income Statement

Here is a simple Income Statement prepared for the month ending on 31-1-2022 (amounts are in ₹Lakh) using the information contained in Column (5) of Table 1A.1:

Table 1A.3 Income Statement

Income Statement (for Jan 2022)	₹ Lakh
Revenues, Income, & Gain:	
Sales Revenue	8.00
Interest Income	0.01
Total Revenue, Income, & Gain	8.01
Expenses & Losses:	
Cost of Sales	4.00
Freight Outward	0.10
Utility Expense	0.15
Salaries Expense	0.65
Rent Expense	0.50
Depreciation Expense	0.08
Amortization Expense	0.07
Supplies Expense	0.03
Insurance Expense	0.04
Interest Expense	0.09
Total Expenses & Losses	5.71
Net Profit	2.30

The simple income statement shows that the company has made a net profit of 2.30 lakh. It achieved sales of 8 lakh (operating activities) and interest income of 0.01 lakh (investing activities). It incurred interest expense of 0.09 lakh (financing activities) and other expenses totaling 5.62 lakh (operating activities). Since revenue from operating activities (8 lakh) exceeds expenses other than interest (5.62 lakh), the company earned an operating profit of 2.38 lakh (= 8.00 – 5.62). Thus, its operating activities are profitable. The company sold goods costing 4 lakh for 8 lakh and generated a gross profit of 4 lakh (= 8 – 4), indicating its trading activities are profitable. The company successfully priced its product, managed its product mix, and controlled its procurement cost.

Cash Flow Statement

Here is a cash flow statement for the month ended 31-1-2022 (amounts are in ₹Lakh) using the information contained in Column (1) of Table 1A.1:

Table 1A.4 Cash Flow Statement

Cash Flow Statement (for Jan 2022)	₹Lakh
Cash Flow from Operating Activities:	
Cash Sales	3.00
Advance Received from Customer	0.20
Cash Purchase of Stock-in-Trade	–2.00
Freight Outward Paid	–0.10
Security Deposit Given	–0.75
Insurance Premium Paid	–1.92
Cash Purchase of Supplies	–0.05
Salaries Paid	–0.65
Net Cash Flow from Operating Activities	–2.27
Cash Flow from Investing Activities:	
Store Equipment Purchased	–5.00
Software Purchased	–2.52
Net Cash Flow from Investing Activities	–7.52
Cash Flow from Financing Activities:	
Issues of Equity Share Capital	10.00
Bank Borrowings Taken	9.00
Net Cash Flow from Financing Activities	19.00
Net Cash Flow in January 2022	9.21
Beginning Cash on 01-01-2022	Nil
Ending Cash on 31-01-2022	9.21

From the simple Cash Flow Statement, we learn that the operating activities are yet to generate net cash inflow and required funding. The company raised 19 lakh from financing activities, out of which it has deployed 7.52 lakh in investing activities in purchasing fixed assets (store equipment and software) and 2.27 lakh to fund cash used in operating activities. It had 9.21 lakh in cash at the end of January 2022.

CHAPTER TWO

Statement of Profit and Loss

Statement of Profit and Loss (P&L), henceforth Income Statement, provides information useful to assess the firm's operating and overall performance. Income statements are prepared for a financial period and contain revenue, expenses, incomes, gains, and losses that occurred during the period. Here are 10 sets of questions about a company's performance that can be answered from income statements and notes:

1. How much are its sales during the financial period? Are the sales growing?
2. Is the company's business overall profitable? How much net profit has it generated during the financial period? How much net profit, on an average, is contributed by a rupee of sales? Does the company effectively manage its sales and control its costs? At what rate did net profit grow during the current and previous financial periods?
3. What would be the profit before tax if the company did not have other operating income and non-operating income/gains/losses? What percentage of profit before tax is *not* contributed by other operating income and non-operating income/gains/losses? Do the principal revenue-producing activities contribute to a positive profit before tax?
4. How much is its gross profit? For every one rupee of sales, what is the average gross profit? Does the company effectively manage its production/purchase/service? Does it effectively price its products, choose its product mix, control its production/purchase/service costs, and generate profits from its production/retail/service operation? At what rate did gross profit grow during the current and previous financial periods?

5. How much is the operating profit during the financial period? How much is the operating profit, on an average, contributed by a rupee of sales? Does the company effectively manage its operations? At what rate did operating profit grow during the current and previous financial periods?
6. Does the company grow its sales profitably? Is the profit growth rate higher than the sales growth rate? Why or why not? How do the company's sales and profit growth rates compare with those of its industry in general and those of its rivals in particular?
7. How much earnings before interest and taxes does it have for every rupee of finance cost? By what percentage can the earnings fall (maximum) and still the earnings are sufficient to cover finance cost? Does the company have enough profits to cover its finance cost?
8. What is the degree of operating, financial, and total leverage? If sales were to fall by 1% from the current level, what would be the rate of decrease in operating profit? If operating profit were to rise by 1%, what would be the rate of decline in profit after tax? Does the company effectively control its operating and financial risks given its business model?
9. For every one rupee of profit before tax, what is the average tax expense of the company, i.e., what is the effective tax rate of the company? Is the company efficient in tax planning? How does that compare with those of its industry rivals? What percentage of its total taxes is current taxes? Are deferred taxes originating or reversing on the whole?
10. How much is its Earnings Per Share (EPS)? Is EPS growing? Is the growth driven by rising profits, declining outstanding shares, or both? Will the EPS be the same if additional equity shares are issued for all outstanding convertible securities and stock options? By how much does the Basic EPS differ from Diluted EPS?

I. Key Terms

The Statement of Profit and Loss (or Income Statement) has various items of income, revenue, gain, expense, and loss for a financial period. These items are aggregated and netted to obtain profit, a measure of a firm's financial performance during a financial period.[1] Investors, lenders, and others may be interested in using information about income, revenues, gains, expenses, and losses to forecast the long-term earnings of a company. Let us understand these terms: income, revenue, gain, expense, loss, and profit.

(a) Income

Income is an increase in economic benefits during an accounting period that increases equity. An income arises from an increase in assets and/or a decrease in liabilities and a corresponding increase in equity for reasons *other than* contributions by equity shareholders (subscription to equity shares).[2]

Income includes revenue and gain. Income is earned (and expenses are incurred) either at a point in time or over a period of time. For example, a retailer earns sales revenue at a *point in time* when the control of the goods is transferred to the buyer, usually at the point of shipment or delivery based on the contractual terms or when services are rendered to the satisfaction of the buyer. Similarly, gain (or loss) on the sale of investments arises at a point in time when an investor sells an investment. Furthermore, dividend income from a subsidiary occurs at a point in time when the subsidiary declares a dividend. By contrast, interest income is earned over a *period of time* a loan is outstanding. Similarly, service revenue is earned over a period of time, whether services are delivered over several days (for example, home décor) or a few hours (for example, cinema).

(b) Revenue

Revenue is the income arising from the ordinary activities (or main business) of a company. Depending on the nature of the business, revenues may be from sales, fees, royalties, interests, dividends, etc. For example, manufacturers, retailers, and traders earn revenue from the sale of goods since their main business is selling goods. They may also have interest income from investments, but earning interest income is not their main business. By contrast, for banks, interest earned from loans and fees charged to customers for various financial services are revenue

---

[1] Aggregation is the adding of items (of assets, liabilities, equity, income, or expenses) having shared characteristics and the same classification. Netting is deducting any income with related expenses arising on the same transaction (such as for determining net proceeds from the sale of equipment), deducting carrying amount from net sale proceeds (such as for determining gain or loss on sale of equipment), or setting off a liability with an asset of similar nature (such as the setting off deferred tax assets and liabilities).

[2] The Institute of Chartered Accountants of India. 2020. The Conceptual Framework for Financial Reporting under Indian Accounting Standards (Ind AS). para 4.68, page 37. https://www.icai.org/post/conceptual-framework-financial-reporting-indas

because a bank's main business is granting loans and providing financial services to customers. Similarly, dividend income is revenue for holding and investment companies but not revenue for manufacturers, retailers, and banks.

(c) Expense

Expense is a decrease in economic benefit during an accounting period that results in a decrease in equity. It arises from an increase in liabilities or a decrease in assets and a corresponding decrease in equity for reasons other than distributions to equity shareholders (in the form of dividends or equity share buybacks).[3] It is important to emphasize that expenses are not distributions to shareholders in the form of dividends and share repurchases. As you can see, the concept of expense is just the opposite of income.

Expenses that arise in the ordinary activities of a business are material cost, employee benefits, depreciation & amortization, power & fuel, repairs & maintenance, insurance, auditor's remuneration, etc. These examples are of expenses aggregated by their nature. Alternatively, expenses may be aggregated by function into the cost of goods sold or cost of sales, selling & distribution expense, administrative & general expense, research & development expense, etc.

Expense and expenditure are not the same. *Expenditures* are the outflow of resources. They can be revenue expenditure or capital expenditure. *Revenue expenditures* are incurred for generating revenue (such as purchases of raw material, packing material, stock-in-trade, etc.) or running the business (such as selling & distribution, general & administration, research & development, etc.). Revenue expenditure is also called operating expenditure (or Opex). By contrast, *capital expenditure* (or Capex) is incurred for the purchase of long-lived assets (such as property, plant, & equipment). While revenue expenditure becomes an expense sooner (when its benefit expires), capital expenditure for fixed assets is expensed over a longer period as depreciation & amortization expense over the period the asset is used in the business. Whether expenditures are revenue or capital, we expense them using the matching principle (discussed in Chapter 1).

(d) Gain or Loss

Gain is accretion in the value of an asset, decline in the value of a liability, the excess of net sales proceeds from an asset over its carrying amount, or the excess

[3] The Institute of Chartered Accountants of India. 2020. The Conceptual Framework for Financial Reporting under Indian Accounting Standards (Ind AS). para 4.69, page 37. https://www.icai.org/post/conceptual-framework-financial-reporting-indas

of the carrying amount of a liability over the amount paid to settle it. Here are examples, one for each type of gain:

i. A gain of ₹35 crore arises when the price of 1 crore shares owned has increased from ₹460 to ₹495.[4]

ii. A gain of ₹50 arises when the value of a liability of $100 has declined from ₹7,800 to ₹7,750 due to a decline in the USD/INR conversion rate from INR 78 to 77.50 per USD.

iii. A gain of ₹40 arises when an investment (bought at ₹180) is sold for ₹220.

iv. A gain of ₹12 arises when a trade payable of ₹567 is fully settled by paying only ₹555.

Gains represent items that meet the definition of income but may or may not arise from the ordinary activities of a business. For a manufacturer, gains on investment do not arise from ordinary activities, whereas such gains are from the ordinary activities of a bank or an investment company. Note that gains could be realized (such as gain on sale of investment or a gain on settlement of a liability) or unrealized (such as a holding gain, i.e., an increase in the market value of an investment that a company continues to hold or a decline in the market value of a liability). In the examples given above, the first two gains are unrealized, whereas the third and fourth gains are realized. Note that unrealized gains may reverse in the future and may turn into a loss.

The concept of loss is just the opposite of gain. When the amount of a gain is negative, we call it a loss. Therefore, a loss could arise from accretion in the value of a liability or a decline in the value of an asset. Alternatively, it could arise because the net sales proceeds from an asset were below its carrying amount or because the amount paid to settle a liability was more than its carrying amount. Like expenses, losses signify a decline in economic benefits and may or may not arise from ordinary activities. For a manufacturer, losses on foreign currency might or might not arise from its ordinary activities, whereas such losses are from the ordinary activities of a foreign exchange dealer. Just like gains, losses may be realized (such as a loss on the sale of investments) or unrealized (such as a holding loss, i.e., a decrease in the market value of an investment that a company continues to hold).

(e) Profit

Net Profit is total income minus total expenses. It is a measure of an entity's overall financial performance and tells us how well it has managed all of its

[4] ₹ is the currency sign for the Indian Rupee or INR. 1 crore = 10 million.

income and expenses and maintained its nominal invested capital during the financial period and how much return it has generated for its shareholders. Note, we are referring to net profit when we use the term profit without any prefix (such as operating profit or gross profit). The concept of loss is just the opposite of profit.

There are various measures of profit, each revealing a specific aspect of a firm's performance. Not all these profit measures are on a reported income statement, but we can prepare a multi-step income statement (discussed later in this chapter) to show these measures of profits for insights into the performance drivers.

i. Gross Profit

Gross Profit is the portion of sales value left after deducting just the cost of sales (i.e., without deducting the operating expense). Thus, Gross Profit is the amount available to recover all other costs incurred by the company. This profit measure reveals how well a company has set the price of its products, optimized its sales mix, and managed its cost of sales.

$$\text{Gross Profit} = \text{Sales} - \text{Cost of Sales}$$

ii. Operating Profit

Operating Profit is the portion of total revenue from operations left after deducting the cost of sales and operating expenses. Therefore, Operating profit is the amount available to recover all non-operating costs incurred by the company. This measure of profit speaks about the overall performance of its operating activities: how well a company has generated gross profit, earned other operating income, and controlled its selling and distribution expenses, general & administration expenses, research & development expenses, etc.

$$\text{Operating Profit} = \text{Gross Profit} - \text{Operating Expenses} + \text{Other Operating Income}$$

iii. Profit Before Interest & Tax (PBIT)

Profit Before Interest & Tax (PBIT) or Earnings Before Interest & Tax (EBIT) informs us about the performance of its operating and investing activities (and before considering financing costs and taxes). From PBIT, we learn how well a company has generated operating profit and investment income.

$$\text{PBIT} = \text{Operating Profit} + \text{Non-Operating Income \& Gains} - \text{Non-Operating Losses}$$

iv. Profit Before Tax (PBT)

As the name suggests, Profit Before Tax (PBIT) or Earnings Before Tax (EBT) are the profits a company has made before deducting tax expenses. PBT speaks about the performance of its operating, investing, and financing activities (before considering taxes).

$$PBT = PBIT - Finance\ Costs$$

v. Profit After Tax (PAT)

Profit After Tax (PAT), Earnings After Tax (EAT), or Net Profit measures a firm's overall financial performance. It tells us how well the company has managed all incomes and expenses.

$$PAT = PBT - Tax\ Expenses = Total\ Income - Total\ Expenses$$

II. Reported Income Statements

A reported income statement has two sections: (1) Profit and Loss section (P&L) and (2) Other Comprehensive Income (OCI). The P&L section provides information on revenue, income, gains, expenses, losses, and net profit. This section is the most significant one for understanding the operating and financial performance of a firm. Therefore, we will discuss this section in detail in this chapter.

As per Schedule III of the Companies Act, 2013, companies must disclose by way of notes various additional information, including income or expense that exceeds ₹100,000 or 1% of revenue from operations, whichever is higher. Therefore, we should also review the notes to gain a deeper understanding of the financial performance of a company.

The Other Comprehensive Income section has a few items related to unrealized fair value gains or losses. Therefore, we will not discuss Other Comprehensive Income in this chapter.

(a) Total Income

Total Income arises from two main sources: (1) Revenue from Operations, which is comprised of (a) Sales (sale of products & services) and (b) Other operating income, and (2) Other Income.

$$Total\ Income = Revenue\ from\ Operations + Other\ Income$$

$$Revenue\ from\ Operations = Sales + Other\ Operating\ Income$$

$$Sales = Sale\ of\ Products\ (Finished\ Goods\ \&\ Stock\text{-}in\text{-}Trade) + Sale\ of\ Services$$

Table 2.1 Total Income

Amounts are in ₹ crore	Asian Paints		Avenue Supermarts		Infosys	
Year ended 31st March	2022	2021	2022	2021	2022	2021
Sale of Products	24,936	18,252	30,258	23,729	Nil	Nil
Sale of Services	67	28	Nil	Nil	103,940	85,912
Sales	25,003	18,280	30,258	23,729	103,940	85,912
Other Operating Income	186	237	94	58	Nil	Nil
Revenue from Operations	25,189	18,517	30,352	23,787	103,940	85,912
Other Income	452	366	141	209	3,224	2,467
Total Income	25,640	18,883	30,493	23,996	107,164	88,379

Source: 2022 Annual Reports of Asian Paints Ltd., Avenue Supermarts Ltd., and Infosys Ltd.[5]

In its 2021–22 Income Statement, Asian Paints discloses three main sources of its total income of ₹25,640 crore: revenue from contracts with customers (i.e., Sales) of ₹25,003 crore, other operating revenue ₹186 crore, and other income (i.e., non-operating income) of ₹452 crore. The company also provides the details of revenue from operations in note 22 and other income in note 23.

Avenue Supermarts discloses a total income of ₹30,493 crore in 2021–22, which comprised Revenue from operations of ₹30,352 crore (sales ₹30,258 crore and other operating income ₹94 crore) and Other income of ₹141 crore.[6] A detailed disclosure of these two sources of total income is provided in note 23 for revenue from operation and note 24 for other income.

Infosys reported total revenue of ₹107,164 crore in 2021–22, which was made up of ₹103,940 crore of Revenue from operations (sale of services) and ₹3,224 crore of Other income. The details are reported in notes 2.18 and 2.19. The company did not have other operating income.

i. Sales

Sales is the net revenue earned by an entity from sale of finished goods, stock-in-trade, and services. Sales is also referred to as turnover and topline.

[5] All financial statement information, here and elsewhere in this book, is obtained from or computed based on information in the publicly available 2022 Annual Report of the companies, except when mentioned otherwise.

[6] Reported amounts (in this and other chapters) have been rounded off to ₹ crore unless mentioned otherwise. Due to rounding off, the sum of the amounts given in a table/list in this book may slightly differ from those reported.

Table 2.2 Sales

Amounts are in ₹ crore	Asian Paints		Avenue Supermarts		Infosys	
Year ended 31st March	2022	2021	2022	2021	2022	2021
Sale of Products	24,936	18,252	30,258	23,729	Nil	Nil
Sale of Services	67	28	Nil	Nil	103,940	85,912
Sales	25,003	18,280	30,258	23,729	103,940	85,912
Growth in % Sales	36.7%		27.5%		21.0%	

In 2021–22, Asian Paints reports in note 22A that it had ₹24,936 crore revenue from the sale of products as well as ₹67 crore revenue from the sale of services. Thus, its total sales are ₹25,003 crore. The sales growth rate is quite high, 36.7%. The company provides additional details in note 22B.

In 2021–22, Avenue Supermarts reveals in note 23 that its Sales are ₹33,114 crore (up 27.5% from last year). In addition, the company also reported sales ₹32 crore and cost of sales ₹27 crore from goods on approval basis, which suggests that it generated ₹5 crore gross profit (or 16.5% of sales) from goods on approval basis.[7] Together, these account for ₹33,119 crore and include goods and services tax of ₹2,861 crore. When the tax is excluded, we get Net Sales of ₹30,258 crore.

In 2021–22, Infosys discloses in note 2.18 that its total Sales was ₹103,940 crore (21% higher than last year) consisting of software service revenue ₹103,515 crore and products and platforms revenue ₹325 crore. It also provides qualitative disclosure about its revenue.

Sales are usually derived from the main business and, thus, are related to operating activities (for example, sales revenue for a manufacturer, retailer, or trader). Any returns and allowances are deducted from gross sales. Furthermore, if the sales price includes indirect taxes (such as goods and services tax or export duty), then such taxes must also be deducted from revenue. Similarly, if discounts and rebates are given after the invoice is raised (i.e., these are not reflected on the

[7] For goods sold on approval basis, Avenue Supermarts is an agent of the supplier. In note 1(l) significant policy related to revenue from operations (on page 113 of the 2022 annual report), Avenue Supermarts discloses, "The inventory of third party does not pass to the Company till the product is sold. At the time of sale of such inventory, the sales value along with the cost of inventory is disclosed separately as sale of goods on approval basis and cost of goods sold on approval basis and forms part of Revenue in the Statement of Profit and Loss. Only the net revenue earned, i.e., margin is recorded as a part of revenue." This treatment corresponds to goods sold by a consignee.

invoice and the invoice amount is before deducting discounts and rebates), such discounts and rebates must also be deducted from the revenue. Thus,

Sales = Gross Sales – Returns & Allowances –
Discounts & Rebates – Duties & Taxes

Suppose gross sales were ₹500 and sales returns ₹20. Gross sales and sales return amounts are inclusive of a 10% goods & services tax. Quantity discounts of ₹3 were offered after invoices were raised. In this example, on the income statement, we will report ₹429 as sales (= 500 gross sales – 20 returns – 10% of (500 – 20) goods & services tax – 3 quantity discounts).

The realization principle helps in timing revenue recognition and determining the amount of revenue recognized. According to Ind AS 115 Revenue Recognition, to recognize revenue, a seller must not only fulfil its performance obligation as per the contract with the customer but also have no reasonable uncertainty about the collection of the transaction price. Thus, revenue does not appear on the Income Statement until the seller (1) has satisfied its performance obligation and (2) is reasonably certain about the collection of the transaction price.

Revenue from sales is recognized *at a point in time* when the control of goods is transferred to the buyer, which usually happens when the goods are either shipped or delivered to a customer as per the agreement. Service contracts could be based on either time & material, the unit of work completed, fixed price, or fixed timeframe basis. Therefore, revenue from services is recognized *over a period of time* by measuring progress based on performance obligations fulfilled, milestones reached, time passed, or percentage of work completed.

ii. Other Operating Income

Other operating incomes also arise from operating activities, but these incomes do not arise from the main business. Rather, they arise from activities that are only incidental to the main business (for example, scrap sales by a manufacturer).

In 2021–22, Asian Paints reports in note 22 that Other operating revenues are from processing and service income, scrap sales, and royalties from subsidiaries and associate companies. In 2021–22, Avenue Supermarts reveals in note 23 that its Other operating income amounted to ₹94 crore, a very small portion of its Revenue from operations. The company also discloses that other operating income comprises services provided by the company. Infosys did not have any other operating income in both financial years.

Table 2.3 Other Operating Income

Amounts are in ₹ crore	Asian Paints		Avenue Supermarts		Infosys	
Year ended 31st March	2022	2021	2022	2021	2022	2021
Other Operating Income	186	237	94	58	Nil	Nil

iii. Other Income

Other income includes income generated from non-operating activities (for example, interest income and gain on sales of investment for a manufacturer).

Table 2.4 Other Income

Amounts are in ₹ crore	Asian Paints		Avenue Supermarts		Infosys	
Year ended 31st March	2022	2021	2022	2021	2022	2021
Other Income	452	366	141	209	3,224	2,467

In 2021–22, Asian Paints reports that Other income ₹452 crore is made up of interest income ₹72 crore, dividend income ₹27 crore, other non-operating income ₹266 crore, and other gains and losses ₹87 crore. Furthermore, this last item, other gains and losses, consists of net foreign exchange gain ₹43 crore, net gain on sale of property, plant, and equipment ₹40 crore, and net gain on modification or termination of leases ₹4 crore.

In 2021–22, Avenue Supermarts reports in note 24 that Other income ₹141 crore has several constituents: Interest income ₹104 crore, Rent & amenities service income ₹28 crore, Gain on sale of current investments ₹3 crore, exchange gain (net) ₹3 crore, and miscellaneous income ₹4 crore.

In 2021–22, Infosys reported in note 2.19 the breakup of its Other Income of ₹3,224 crore: interest income ₹1,399 crore (=151 + 668 + 580), dividend income ₹1,219 crore, gain on investments ₹128 crore (=1 + 127), exchange gains ₹294 crore (=189 + 105), and miscellaneous income ₹185 crore.

(b) Total Expenses

Total Expenses comprise several expenses. Among these, often the highest amounts are for the cost of materials consumed in the case of manufacturers, purchases of stock-in-trade for retailers and traders, and employee benefits expenses for service firms. Note that there are still a few expenses and losses (tax expense and any exceptional expense) that are not included in Total Expenses. These are reported separately, as discussed later in the chapter. Part II of Division II – Schedule III to the Companies Act, 2013 requires companies to include the following seven items under Expenses:

1. Cost of materials consumed,
2. Purchases of stock-in-trade,
3. Changes in inventories of finished goods, stock-in-trade, and work-in-progress,
4. Employee-benefits expense,
5. Finance costs,
6. Depreciation and amortization expense, and
7. Other expenses.

i. Cost of Materials Consumed

The first item in the list of expenses is usually the cost of materials consumed. It represents the cost of raw material, components, and packing material consumed in the production of finished goods. Therefore, this item is found on the income statement of manufacturing firms. The cost of materials consumed is obtained by deducting the closing stock of materials from the sum of the opening stock of materials and net purchases of materials.

Cost of Material Consumed = Net Purchases of Materials – Changes in Material Inventory

Table 2.5 Material Cost

Amounts are in ₹ crore	Asian Paints		Avenue Supermarts		Infosys	
Year ended 31st March	2022	2021	2022	2021	2022	2021
Cost of Material Consumed	18,839	8,524	Nil	Nil	Nil	Nil
Cost of Software & others	Nil	Nil	Nil	Nil	2,985	2,058
As a % of Sales + ΔWIP + ΔFG	53.40%	46.37%			2.87%	2.40%

* ΔWIP is change in Work-In-Progress, ΔFG is change in Finished Goods.

For example, Asian Paints reports that the cost of materials consumed in 2021–22 is ₹18,839 crore. As per note 24A, this amount is the sum of (a) the cost of raw materials consumed ₹11,690 crore (= opening stock ₹1,038 crore + net purchases ₹12,596 crore – closing stock ₹1,944 crore) and (b) the cost of packing materials consumed ₹2,149 crore (= opening stock ₹69 crore + net purchases ₹2,166 crore – closing stock ₹85 crore). Furthermore, the material cost has increased substantially in the financial year 2022 when compared to 2021. For every rupee of sales + increases in work-in-progress and finished goods inventories, the material cost has increased from 46.37% in 2021 to 53.40% in 2022, an increase of 703 basis points (bps).[8]

By contrast, Avenue Supermarts and Infosys do not report any cost of materials consumed as they are not manufacturers. Instead, Infosys' Income statement has ₹2,985 crore as the cost of software packages and others, which are either for the company's own use (₹1,062 crore) or for service delivery to clients (₹1,923 crore) as per note 2.20.

ii. Purchase of Stock-in-Trade

Stock-in-trade (SIT) is an item bought for resale. For example, retailers purchase and sell merchandise at their retail stores. Similarly, wholesalers and traders buy and sell SIT. If an item is not bought by a company (for example, finished goods produced by the company), that item cannot be termed SIT. Companies that sell only products they have manufactured or developed do not report any purchase of SIT. Similarly, service firms are unlikely to purchase SIT unless they are also buying and selling such items (for example, budget airline companies sell food items purchased from other companies).

The amount of Purchase of SIT is the invoice amount of stock purchased net of any returns, discounts & rebates, and duties & taxes. Note that the purchase of an item is not an expense. Unless the item is sold, its cost is an asset and included in the inventory. However, when we deduct the change in inventory of stock-in-trade from the purchases of stock-in-trade, we obtain the cost of sales (an expense). As per the format prescribed in Part II of Division II – Schedule III of the Companies Act, 2013, companies report purchases of stock-in-trade separately from changes in stock-in-trade inventory.

Table 2.6 Purchase of Stock-in-Trade

Amounts are in ₹ crore	Asian Paints		Avenue Supermarts		Infosys	
Year ended 31st March	2022	2021	2022	2021	2022	2021
Purchase of Stock-in-Trade	2,979	1,649	26,472	20,614	Nil	Nil

In its 2022 Income Statement, Avenue Supermarts reported purchases of stock-in-trade of ₹26,472 crore, whereas Asian Paints purchased stock-in-trade costing ₹2,979 crore. By contrast, Infosys does not have stock-in-trade purchases on its 2022 Income Statement.

[8] Material cost is a component of work-in-progress and finished goods. When material is consumed but production is incomplete or production is complete but goods are unsold, a portion of material cost is in the ending work-in-progress and finished goods. Therefore, it is less appropriate to scale material cost by sales & service revenue and more appropriate to scale by the sum of sales & service revenue, change in WIP, & change in FG.

iii. Changes in Finished Goods, Stock-in-Trade, and Work-in-Progress Inventory

We calculate change as ending balance (closing stock) minus beginning balance (opening stock). However, the change in inventories reported on the income statement is calculated differently: the opening stock minus the closing stock. What is reported as "changes" is actually the negative of changes, and we must be careful in interpreting the amount reported: a negative number indicates an increase in inventory, whereas a positive number indicates a decline in inventory.

Since total expenses are obtained by summing up various expenses, a negative number for the change in inventories (i.e., an increase in inventory) would lower total expenses. However, that is not the case because the change in inventories is not an expense, just as the Purchase of stock-in-trade is not an expense for a retailer. As discussed later (in an appendix at the end of this chapter), together, Purchases and Changes in the inventory of stock-in-trade result in the cost of sales, which is an expense but does not appear on the income statement. For example, when a retailer buys ₹1,000 inventory more than it sells, its purchases and changes in inventory of stock-in-trade, both are higher by ₹1,000. Since increases in stock-in-trade inventory appear as a negative number, it effectively cancels out the higher amounts of purchases of stock-in-trade.

This is also true for manufacturers but is difficult to observe clearly on their reported income statements. Manufacturers incur manufacturing costs comprising (i) material costs, which is on the income statement as a separate line item, and (ii) conversion costs, which does not appear as a separate line item on the income statement. Instead, conversion cost is included in various expenses, such as employee benefit costs (for production workers), depreciation & amortization expenses (for fixed assets used in their factory), and other expenses (manufacturing costs other than labour cost, depreciation, and amortization). When a manufacturer produces more quantities of finished goods, it incurs a higher amount of conversion costs, which are included in employee benefits expense, depreciation & amortization, and other expenses. When some of these finished goods produced remain unsold, their manufacturing cost is included in ending inventory of finished goods and therefore, in the changes in inventories of finished goods. Since increases in finished goods inventory appear as a negative number, it effectively cancels out the higher amounts of not only material costs but also conversion costs included in employee benefits expense, depreciation & amortization, and other expenses.

Table 2.7 Changes in Inventory of Finished Goods, Stock-in-Trade & Work-in-Progress

Amounts are in ₹ crore	Asian Paints		Avenue Supermarts		Infosys	
Year ended 31st March	2022	2021	2022	2021	2022	2021
Changes in Inventories of FG, SIT, and WIP *	–1,209	-91	–420	–258	Nil	Nil

* Although named "Changes in …", the amount reported is the *negative* of the change and obtained as opening stock minus closing stock (rather than closing minus opening stock). Hence, we must be careful in interpreting the amounts reported. A negative number (reported for this item) indicates an increase, whereas a positive number indicates a decline. FG = Finished Goods, SIT = Stock-in-Trade, WIP = Work In Progress (i.e., under production).

During the financial year 2021–22, Asian Paints' inventories increased by ₹1,209 crore. From its note 24C, we ascertain that this ₹1,209 crore aggregate change is due to an increase in inventory of (a) finished goods ₹855 crore (=2262 closing stock – 1407 opening stock), (b) work-in-progress ₹56 crore (=177 closing stock – 121 opening stock), and (c) stock-in-trade ₹298 crore (=658 closing stock – 360 opening stock).

In its 2022 Income Statement, Avenue Supermarts reports a negative amount of ₹(420) crore for the changes in inventories of stock-in-trade. This does not mean that its stock-in-trade inventory decreased during the year. Rather, the stock-in-trade ending inventory (₹2,587 crore from the balance sheet) was higher than the beginning inventory (₹2,167 crore from the balance sheet) by ₹420 crore.

iv. Employee Benefits Expense

As the name suggests, Employee Benefits Expense is the cost incurred for employees. These costs include salaries & wages, bonuses & incentives, contributions to provident & other funds, staff welfare expenses, expenses for shares & stock options granted to employees, etc. The amounts are for employees on the company's payroll.

Employee Benefits expenses are usually large for a service company. For example, the biggest expense for Infosys in 2021–22 is for Employee Benefits (₹51,664 crore), which is comprised of Salaries & bonuses (₹49,575 crore), Contribution to provident & other funds (₹1,417 crore), Share-based payments to employees (₹372 crore; relates to performance-based grants of restricted stock units), and Staff welfare (₹300 crore). By contrast, the amount is much smaller in the case of Avenue Supermarts (₹548 crore in 2021–22) and Asian Paints (₹1,310 crore in 2021–22). As a percentage of Sales, employee costs have decreased marginally for Asian Paints and Avenue Supermarts but have increased for Infosys.

Table 2.8 Employee Costs

Amounts are in ₹ crore	Asian Paints		Avenue Supermarts		Infosys	
Year ended 31st March	2022	2021	2022	2021	2022	2021
Employee Benefit Cost	1,310	1,129	548	495	51,664	45,179
Cost of Technical Sub-contractors					16,298	9,528
As a % of Sales	5.24%	6.18%	1.81%	2.09%	65.39%	63.68%

It is important to note that a company (say H) may also use the services of labourers and workers contracted from another company (P). Therefore, the cost of these contract workers is included in the Employee Benefits Expense of the employing company (P) on whose payroll they are employed, and not in the Employee Benefits Expense of the company (H) whose work they are doing. Therefore, one must be careful and not assume that all manpower costs of a company (H) are reflected in its Employee Benefits Expense. For example, Avenue Supermarts reports ₹603 crore as Contract labour charge (included in its Other Expense, see note 29) in 2021–22. Similarly, Infosys reports an amount of ₹16,298 crore for the cost of technical sub-contractors, as a separate line item under total expenses on its 2022 income statement.

Furthermore, when analyzing the employee costs of two firms, we must be mindful of their use of contractual workers as this causes a difference in employee benefits costs expressed as a percentage of sales: a company that gets all work done by employees on its payroll and another company that gets only some of the work done by employees on its payroll but is identical to the former in all other aspects. The former firm is likely to have a much higher employee benefits cost as a percentage of sales than the latter.

v. Finance Cost

Finance Cost comprises various interest expenses, preference dividends, and other charges incurred for borrowings, acceptance, and banking services. Companies that have large borrowings report large finance costs. A company may incur interest on bank borrowings, term loans, bank overdrafts, cash credits, debentures, zero-coupon bonds, commercial papers, bills discounted, acceptances, lease liabilities, taxes payable, asset retirement obligations, etc.

Under Ind AS, redeemable preference shares are financial liabilities. Under the Companies Act, 2013, all preference shares must be redeemed within a period of 20 years from the date of issue. Therefore, preference dividends are included in finance cost under Ind AS.

Asian Paints reported ₹70 crore as the finance cost for 2021–22, and this amount comprises interest on lease liabilities (₹49 crore) and interest on bill discounting (₹18 crore), among others. In 2021–22 Avenue Supermarts incurred a finance cost of ₹40 crore, which includes ₹38 crore interest on lease liabilities (as given in note 3). Infosys had a finance cost of ₹128 crore in 2021–22 arising entirely from interest on lease liabilities as per note 2.3.

Table 2.9 Finance Cost

Amounts are in ₹ crore	Asian Paints		Avenue Supermarts		Infosys	
Year ended 31st March	2022	2021	2022	2021	2022	2021
Finance Cost	70	72	40	34	128	126

Note that finance cost excludes any interest and other charges capitalized during a year. Capitalization of an expenditure implies that the amount is included in the cost of a fixed asset and, thus, not expensed. For example, when a company borrows and uses the proceeds to construct a building, it can capitalize the interest and other charges incurred on the borrowings (subject to meeting certain conditions). Neither Asian Paints, Avenue Supermarts, nor Infosys reported any capitalization of interest and other charges in 2021–22. By contrast, Hindalco reported interest capitalized ₹26 crore in 2021–22. In 2012–13 financial year, Hindalco had capitalized interest of ₹1,496 crore and reported ₹436 crore finance cost on income statement.

vi. Depreciation & Amortization Expense

Depreciation and amortization allocate the net cost of fixed assets over the period they are expected to be used. Depreciation is an expense for tangible fixed assets (other than Land), whereas amortization is for intangible fixed assets (other than Goodwill).

To obtain depreciation, we need three inputs: the historical cost, expected residual value, and expected useful life of the asset. A company has several items of fixed assets that it intends to use over several years (*useful life*). For these assets, it has incurred *historical costs* (various costs to acquire/construct the assets and make them ready for use), which are capitalized. It may expect to receive some *residual value* (net proceeds from the disposal of these assets at the end of their useful life). The difference between the historical cost and the residual value is the *depreciable amount* that is systematically allocated (i.e., depreciated) over the useful life.

Due to depreciation charged, accumulated depreciation (a contra-asset) increases. Since accumulated depreciation for an item of PPE is paired with that PPE, an increase in accumulated depreciation reduces the carrying amount of that item of PPE each year. The carrying amount reaches the residual value at the end of the useful life. How to calculate depreciation and amortization under different methods is discussed, for those interested, in the Appendix: Calculation of Depreciation and Amortization.

The Straight-Line Method is the most preferred method for charging depreciation and amortization by companies in India. For example, Avenue Supermarts, Asian Paints, and Infosys, all three companies use SLM and disclose their rationale for the depreciation method and the estimates of useful life in a note.

Table 2.10 Depreciation & Amortization Expense

Amounts are in ₹ crore	Asian Paints		Avenue Supermarts		Infosys	
Year ended 31st March	2022	2021	2022	2021	2022	2021
Depreciation & Amortization	722	697	421	371	2,429	2,321
As a % of Sales	2.89%	3.81%	1.39%	1.56%	2.34%	3.19%

In 2021–22, Asian Paints recorded ₹722 crores for Depreciation & Amortization expense. From its note 28, we learn that this sum comprises ₹500 crore depreciation on Property, Plant, and Equipment (PPE), ₹200 crore depreciation on Right of Use assets (ROU, i.e., assets taken on lease), and ₹22 crore amortization on Other Intangible Assets. We also learn about the depreciation and amortization charged for each class of PPE (in note 2A), ROU (in note 2B), and Other Intangible Assets (in note 4).

In 2021–22, Avenue Supermarts expensed ₹421 crore for Depreciation & Amortization. From its note 28, we learn that ₹309 crore was for depreciation on PPE (further details in note 2), ₹108 crore for depreciation on ROU (note 3), ₹4 crore for depreciation on Investment Property (note 4), and ₹4 crore for amortization on Other Intangible Assets (note 5). It also reveals that ₹4 crore was depreciation capitalized. Depreciation on an item of PPE can be capitalized if the item is used to construct another item of PPE. The amount capitalized is deducted from depreciation and only the net amount is expensed. Furthermore, the amount capitalized is added to Capital Work in Progress, an asset that appears as a separate line item on the Balance Sheet.

In 2021–22, Infosys charged ₹2,429 as Depreciation & Amortization. Its notes reveal that this sum comprises ₹1,914 crore depreciation on PPE (asset-wise breakup is in note 2.1), ₹480 crore depreciation on ROU (details in note 2.3), and ₹35 crore amortization on Other Intangible Assets (details in note 2.2).

vii. Other Expenses

This is the placeholder for all expenses other than those reported as a separate line under Total Expenses on the income statement. Other expenses generally include expenses for manufacturing & providing service, selling & distribution, general & administration, research & development, as well as corporate social responsibility. It is useful to read the note for this item to understand the nature of various expenses incurred.

Table 2.11 Other Expenses

Amounts are in ₹ crore	Asian Paints		Avenue Supermarts		Infosys	
Year ended 31st March	2022	2021	2022	2021	2022	2021
Other Expenses	3,682	2,813	1,250	1,194	2,490	2,743
Travel Expenses					731	484
Communication Charges					433	464
Consultancy & Professional Charges					1,511	999
Sum above	3,682	2,813	1,250	1,194	5,175	4,690
As a % of Sales	14.73%	15.39%	4.13%	5.03%	4.98%	5.46%

For example, in 2021–22 Asian Paints reported Other Expenses aggregating ₹3,682 crore, comprising sixteen different expenses. The top 3 and bottom 3 expenses (in terms of amount) included were for Freight & handling charges (₹1,689 crore), Advertising expenses (₹805 crore), Miscellaneous expenses (₹524 crore), Commission to non-executive directors (₹5 crore), Directors' sitting fee (₹2 crore) and Auditor's remuneration (₹2 crore). Other Expenses also included travel expense (₹72 crore).

Avenue Supermarts reported other expenses of ₹1,250 crore in 2021–22, which was about 4.13% of sales. Compared to the previous year, the expense was higher in magnitude but lower as a percentage of Sales, suggesting a tight control over these expenses. We also see the same for Asian Paints and Infosys.

In 2021–22, Infosys had a total of ₹2,490 crore of Other Expenses, which included twelve items. The top three (in terms of amount) are Repairs & maintenance (₹824 crore), Brand & marketing (₹444 crore), and Contribution towards CSR (₹397 crore). The three lowest amounts are for Auditor's remuneration (₹5 crore), Commission to non-whole-time directors (₹11 crore), and Short-term leases (₹12 crore). Instead of including under Other Expenses,

Infosys reported Travel Expense (₹731 crore), Communication Charges (₹433 crore), and Consultancy & Professional Charges (₹1,511 crore) as a separate line item under total expense on its Income Statement.

Note that for some items we can clearly identify the function for which they were incurred, but not for others. For example, market research and advertising are clearly related to the marketing, selling & distribution functions. Again, there is no ambiguity that Auditors' remuneration and directors' fees are related to the general & administration function. By contrast, repairs & maintenance, miscellaneous expenses, and short-term leases could be for more than one function, and it is impossible to identify the amount incurred for each function without additional information. As a result, it is difficult to ascertain a company's conversion cost, selling & distribution cost, general & administrative cost, etc. for analytical purpose.

(c) Profit Before Exceptional Items and Taxes

This item is obtained by deducting total expenses from total income. It represents pre-tax profits ignoring any exceptional incomes, expenses, gains, and losses. Few companies report exceptional items and ,therefore, only these need to use the term "Profit Before Exceptional Items and Taxes". Companies that do not report exceptional items report Profit Before Taxes as the difference between total income and total expenses.

For example, Asian Paints reports exceptional items and ,therefore, reports Profit Before Exceptional Items and Taxes of ₹4,248 crore in 2021–22, whereas Infosys and Avenue Supermarts do not have exceptional items and, therefore, did not report Profit Before Exceptional Items and Taxes (instead, they report Profit Before Taxes).

(d) Exceptional Items

The term 'exceptional items' is defined neither in the Companies Act, 2013 nor in the Indian Accounting Standards. Therefore, there is ambiguity regarding what an 'exceptional item' is. Companies do provide a description of what they treat as exceptional items, but the description is often insufficient to explain what the term is. Financial analysts consider exceptional items as non-recurring items.

For example, Asian Paints provides the following description for exceptional items in its 2021–22 notes: "An ordinary item of income or expense, which by its size, nature, occurrence or incidence, requires a disclosure in order to improve understanding of the performance of the company is treated as an exceptional item in the Statement of Profit and Loss account."

Table 2.12 Exceptional Items

Amounts are in ₹ crore	Asian Paints		Avenue Supermarts		Infosys	
Year ended 31st March	2022	2021	2022	2021	2022	2021
Exceptional Items	–54	Nil	Nil	Nil	Nil	Nil

When a company reports exceptional items, it also provides some details. For example, Asian Paints reports Exceptional items of ₹54 crores (loss) in 2021–22. In note 43, the company mentions that this amount arises from recognizing (in accordance with Ind AS 109 – Financial Instruments) an expected credit loss on State government subsidies receivable for earlier years. Asian Paints also states in note 29 that "The Company is confident about the ultimate realization of the dues from the State governments. There is no credit risk attached to these receivables." However, it is not clear why this item is exceptional and why the amount (₹54 crores) is material, given it is too small compared to its total revenue of about ₹25,000 and net profit of ₹3,134 crore in 2021–22. Is it exceptional because government dues are supposed to have zero credit risk, or because of other reasons? Quite likely, credit loss on a sovereign bond is not normal and, therefore, it is disclosed as an exceptional item.

Note that exceptional items may be associated with operating or non-operating (investing or financing) activities. For example, if state government subsidies were received for capital expenditure, they are non-operating in nature and included in Other Income. If they are operating in nature, they are Other Operating Income.

(e) Profit Before Tax (PBT)

PBT is the pre-tax profits of a firm. It is obtained from Profit Before Exceptional Items and Taxes by adding all exceptional incomes & gains and deducting all exceptional expenses and losses. If a company does not have any exceptional item (whether income, gain, expense, or loss), then it reports the difference between total income and total expense as PBT.

Table 2.13 Profit Before Tax

Amounts are in ₹ crore	Asian Paints		Avenue Supermarts		Infosys	
Year ended 31st March	2022	2021	2022	2021	2022	2021
Profit Before Tax	4,194	4,090	2,182	1,545	28,495	24,477

The following PBT was reported in 2021–22, by Asian Paints ₹4,194 crore, Avenue Supermarts ₹2,182, and Infosys ₹28,495 crore. The positive amounts indicate that these companies generated pre-tax profits.

(f) Income Tax Expense

Income Tax Expense arises from direct taxes on corporate profits. There are two components of Income Tax Expense: Current Tax and Deferred Tax.

Tax Expense = Current Tax + Deferred Tax

Current Tax Expense is the amount of tax payable during a year computed as per income tax rules. Deferred Tax Expense is the difference between income tax expense and current tax expense. Deferred taxes arise due to *temporary* differences between PBT (obtained using accounting rules) and Taxable Income (obtained using tax rules), which arise from differences in accounting rules and tax rules. As temporary differences eventually reverse, so do deferred taxes. See Appendix: Calculation of income tax, current tax, and deferred tax expenses.

Table 2.14 Tax Expense

Amounts are in ₹ crore	Asian Paints		Avenue Supermarts		Infosys	
Year ended 31st March	2022	2021	2022	2021	2022	2021
Current Tax (a)	* 1,110	* 1,059	* 553	* 375	6,960	6,013
Deferred Tax (b)	-51	-21	13	4	300	416
Tax Expense (c) = (a)+(b)	*1,059*	*1,038*	*566*	*379*	*7,260*	*6,429*
Profit Before Tax (d)	4,194	4,090	2,182	1,545	28,495	24,477
Effective Tax Rate (c)÷(d)	*25.3%*	*25.4%*	*25.9%*	*24.5%*	*25.5%*	*26.3%*

* Current Tax includes short provisions for earlier years or adjustments of tax related to earlier years, although these are reported separately on Income Statement.

In 2021–22, Asian Paints incurred Income Tax Expense of ₹1,059 crore, which was 25.3% of PBT. The effective tax rate of 25.3% is quite close to the 25.168% statutory corporate tax rate. Total taxes consisted of Current Taxes of ₹1,107 crore, short tax provision for earlier years ₹3 crore, and negative Deferred Taxes of ₹–51 crore (indicating reversal).

In 2021–22, Avenue Supermarts had a tax expense of ₹566 crore, current taxes ₹540 crore, adjustment for tax related to earlier years ₹13 crore, and deferred taxes ₹13 crore. Given that its PBT was ₹2,182 crore, its effective tax rate turns out to be 25.9% (about 75 basis points higher than 25.168%, the statutory tax rate on corporate profits).

In 2021–22, Infosys reported PBT ₹28,495 crore and Taxes ₹7,260 crore. Thus, its effective tax rate was 25.48% of PBT (similar to the 25.168% statutory tax rate on corporate profits). Current Taxes were ₹6,960 crore and Deferred Taxes were ₹300 crore.

(g) Profit After Tax (PAT)

Profit After Tax is the profit available to shareholders. It is known by various names, including Net earnings, Net income, Net profit, Net profit after tax, Profit for the year, and simply, Profit. It is also informally referred to as the bottom line. It represents the aggregate performance of a firm from operating, investing, and financing activities. A company earns net income after meeting all expenses (including taxes) from total income. Thus, it is the total income net of total expenses. A company can pay dividends out of its net profit of the current and previous years (or retained earnings).

In 2021–22, the net profit reported by Asian Paints was ₹3,135 crore (a growth of 2.7% over 2020–21), Avenue Supermarts ₹1,616 crore (a growth of 38.7% year-on-year), and Infosys ₹21,235 crore (a growth of 17.7% over the previous year).

Table 2.15 Profit After Tax

Amounts are in ₹ crore	Asian Paints		Avenue Supermarts		Infosys	
Year ended 31st March	2022	2021	2022	2021	2022	2021
Profit After Tax	3,135	3,052	1,616	1,165	21,235	18,048
Growth in %	2.7%		38.7%		17.7%	

(h) Earnings per Share (EPS)

EPS is the earnings available to the equity shareholders on a per share basis. There are two measures of EPS: Basic EPS and Diluted EPS. When we just say EPS, we are generally referring to Basic EPS. For a detailed discussion on how to calculate Basic and Diluted EPS, See Appendix: Calculation of Basic and Diluted EPS.

$$\textit{(Basic) EPS} = \frac{\textit{Net Profit}}{\textit{Weighted average number of equity shares outstanding}}$$

The numerator is the same as Net Profit, whereas the denominator is obtained by taking the weighted average of the number of shares outstanding during the year. A company may have outstanding stock warrants, options, or restricted stocks (issued to employees and others) and convertible preference shares, debentures, or other debt securities. Such securities require issuing equity shares in the future. Diluted EPS helps us understand what would be the impact of these potential shares on Basic EPS. When these potential equity shares are issued in exchange for these securities, there would be an increase in the number of outstanding shares (the denominator), whereas the profit available to equity shareholders (the numerator) may either remain the same or increase. When the percentage change in the numerator (due to a change in profit available to equity shareholders) is not the same as the percentage change in the denominator (due to the issue of potential shares), Diluted EPS differs from Basic EPS.

Table 2.16 Earnings Per Share

Amounts are in ₹ crore	Asian Paints		Avenue Supermarts		Infosys	
Year ended 31st March	2022	2021	2022	2021	2022	2021
Basic EPS	₹32.68	₹31.82	₹24.95	₹17.99	₹50.27	₹42.37
Basic EPS Growth in %	2.7%		38.7%		18.6%	
Diluted EPS	₹32.68	₹31.82	₹24.75	₹17.86	₹50.21	₹42.33
Diluted minus Basic EPS	0	0	-0.20	-0.13	-0.06	-0.04

Asian Paints had (Basic) EPS of ₹32.68 in 2021–22, about 2.7% higher than the amount in 2020–21. The growth in EPS was entirely driven by the growth in Net Profit as there was no change in the number of equity shares outstanding during 2021–22. In 2021–22, Diluted EPS was the same as Basic EPS due to only 23,717 (an insignificant number compared to the total number of outstanding shares) potential shares due to stock options.

Avenue Supermarts (Basic) EPS is ₹24.95 in 2021–22, i.e., about 38.7% higher than ₹17.99 in 2020–21. The growth is entirely driven by a 38.7% rise in Net Profit. In 2020–21, its Diluted EPS was ₹24.75, about ₹0.20 less than Basic EPS, due to potential equity shares on account of employee stock option schemes. This employee stock option scheme is dilutive in nature as it causes Dilutive EPS to be lower than Basic EPS.

In 2021–22, Infosys had (Basic) EPS of ₹50.27 compared to ₹42.37 in the previous year. Thus, EPS grew by 18.6% due to not only the 17.7% growth in Net Profit but also a 1% decrease in the number of equity shares outstanding. In 2021–22, its Diluted EPS was ₹50.21, about ₹0.06 less than Basic EPS due to potential equity shares due to stock options outstanding. This employee stock option scheme is dilutive in nature.

III. Analysis of Multi-Step Income Statement

Multi-step Income Statement is the function-wise classification of a Statement of Profit & Loss. The format of this statement for a non-financial sector firm is given in Table 2.17.

Table 2.17 Multi-Step Income Statement Format

Sales	a
Cost of Sales or Cost of Goods Sold	b
Gross Profit	c = a – b
Operating Expense	d
Other Operating Income	e
Operating Profit	f = c – d + e
Non-Operating Income, Gains, & Losses	g
Profit Before Interest and Taxes (PBIT)	h = f + g
Interest Expenses & Finance Cost	i
Profit Before Taxes (PBT)	j = h – i
Tax Expenses	k
Profit or Net Profit or Profit After Taxes	l = j – k

A Multi-step Income Statement provides several measures of profit that can help us evaluate a company's production, service, purchase, marketing, administration, and finance functions. The multi-step income statement is mandatory in the U.S. but not in India. Therefore, it is available only for Indian companies listed on a U.S. stock exchange. These U.S.-listed Indian companies include a consolidated multi-step income statement in their Form 20-F filing with the SEC. They may or may not include it in their annual report sent to their shareholders. Various items appearing on a multi-step income statement were discussed earlier in this chapter. The remaining are explained in three appendices titled "Cost of Sales", "Operating Expenses", and "Non-Operating Incomes, Gains, & Losses".

(a) Infosys' Multi-Step Income Statement

Infosys reports the standalone multi-step income statement in its (see note 2.28, page 254) 2021–22 Annual Report, based on which the following multi-step income statement has been prepared (OCI section has been excluded). The multi-step income statement reveals that in 2021–22, the company generated a gross profit amount of ₹34,311 crore (versus ₹30,371 crore last year) on sales of ₹1,03,940 crore (versus ₹85,912 crore last year). Thus, the company achieved a gross profit ratio of 33.0%, which was 240 basis points lower than the last year's gross profit ratio of 35.4%. This indicates that the company had difficulty passing on increases in its cost of sale to its customers. However, the company could control its operating expenses causing operating expenses as a % of sales to decline by 100 basis points. As a result, its operating profit ratio declined by only 140 basis points to 24.4% in 2021–22 (from 25.8% in 2020–21). Its operating profit rose by 14.7% to reach ₹25,399 crore in 2021–22 (versus ₹22,136 crore in the previous year).

Table 2.18 Infosys Multi-Step Common-Size Income Statement

Infosys	2021–22		2020–21	
Multi-step Income Statement	₹ Crore	*% of Sales*	₹ Crore	*% of Sales*
Sales *(Sales Growth Rate 21%)*	1,03,940	*100.0%*	85,912	*100.0%*
Less Cost of Sales	–69,629	*–67.0%*	–55,541	*–64.6%*
Gross Profit	34,311	*33.0%*	30,371	*35.4%*
Less Operating Expenses	–8,912	*–8.6%*	–8,235	*–9.6%*
Add Other Operating Income	Nil		Nil	
Operating Profit (*Growth Rate 14.7%*)	25,399	*24.4%*	22,136	*25.8%*
Add Non-Operating Income, Gains, & Losses	3,224	*3.1%*	2,467	*2.9%*
Profit Before Interest & Taxes (PBIT)	28,623	*27.5%*	24,603	*28.6%*
Less Interest (Finance Cost)	–128	*–0.1%*	–126	*–0.1%*
Profit Before Taxes (PBT)	28,495	*27.4%*	24,477	*28.5%*
Less Tax Expense	–7,260	*–7.0%*	–6,429	*–7.5%*
Net Profit *(Growth Rate 17.7%)*	21,235	*20.4%*	18,048	*21.0%*

Prepared from the information disclosed by Infosys in Note 2.28 Function-wise Classification of Statement of Profit and Loss in 2021–22 Annual Report. Growth rate is the year-on-year change in sales, operating profit, or net profit divided by the 2020–21 amount.

The company's non-operating income was higher both in level and as a percentage of sales in 2021–22 than in the year before. The company curtailed taxes as a percentage of sales by 50 basis points in 2021–22. Overall, the company earned a net profit of ₹21,235 or about 20.4% of sales, which was 60 basis points lower than the year before. Infosys' net profit rose by 17.7%, somewhat lower than its sales growth rate of 21.0%. Although these numbers are quite good, they also indicate that the company is facing difficulty in controlling its overall cost and pricing its services during 2021–22 as compared to the previous year.

(b) Avenue Supermarts' Multi-Step Income Statement

Using the information on a company's reported income statement, we can prepare Avenue Supermarts' multi-step income statement. The multi-step income statement reveals that in 2021–22, the company generated a gross profit amount of ₹4,206 crore (versus ₹3,373 crore last year) on sales of ₹30,258 crore (versus ₹23,729 crore last year). This suggests that the company earned a gross profit ratio of 13.9%, which was 30 basis points lower than the last year's 14.2%. Thus, the gross margins suffered during the 2021–22 financial year relative to the prior year. However, the company controlled its operating expenses more effectively and increased its Operating Profit to ₹2,081 crore in 2021–22 (from ₹1,370 crore in the previous year) and the Operating profit ratio rose by 110 basis points (from 5.8% last year to 6.9% this year).

Table 2.19 Avenue Supermarts' Multi-Step Common-Size Income Statement

Avenue Supermarts	**2021–22**		**2020–21**	
Multi-step Income Statement	₹ Crore	*% of Sales*	₹ Crore	*% of Sales*
Sales Revenue *(Sales Growth Rate 27.5%)*	30,258	*100.0%*	23,729	*100.0%*
Less Cost of Sales **	–26,052	*–86.1%*	–20,356	*–85.8%*
Gross Profit	4,206	*13.9%*	3,373	*14.2%*
Less Operating Expenses ***	–2,219	*–7.3%*	–2,061	*–8.7%*
Add Other Operating Income	94	*0.3%*	58	*0.2%*
Operating Profit	2,081	*6.9%*	1,370	*5.8%*
Add Non-Operating Income, Gains, & Losses	141	*0.5%*	209	*0.9%*
Profit Before Interest & Taxes (PBIT)	2,222	*7.3%*	1,579	*6.7%*
Less Interest (Finance Cost)	–40	*–0.1%*	–34	*–0.1%*
Profit Before Taxes (PBT)	2,182	*7.2%*	1,545	*6.5%*
Less Tax Expense	–566	*–1.9%*	–379	*–1.6%*
Net Profit *(Profit Growth Rate 38.6%)*	1,616	*5.3%*	1,166	*4.9%*

Growth rate is the year-on-year change in sales, operating profit, or net profit divided by the 2020–21 amount. To prepare this statement: first, fill in the figures for Net Profit, Non-Operating Income, Gains & Losses (= Other Income), Taxes, PBT, and Finance Cost available on the reported income statement; next, from the notes, obtain and fill up Sales Revenue and Other Operating Income; after that, compute Cost of Sales and Operating Expenses from the income statement and notes, and finally, obtain the remaining figures for Gross Profit, Operating Profit, and EBIT. ** Cost of Sales (= Purchases + Freight Inward + Opening Stock – Closing Stock); freight inward has been taken as zero since it is not available on the income statement or notes. *** Operating Expenses (=Employee Benefits + Depreciation & Amortization + Other Expenses).

The company's PBIT, PBT, and PAT increased in amount and as a percentage of sales. Its net profit was ₹1,616 crore in the current year versus ₹1,166 crore last year. Its profit growth rate of 38.6% was higher than its sales growth rate of 27.5% in 2021–22. For every net sales of ₹100, the company earned a net profit of ₹5.30 in 2021–22 (versus ₹4.90 last year).

(c) Asian Paints' Multi-Step Income Statement

Asian Paints reported inventory turnover ratio and used Cost of Sales or Cost of Goods Sold to obtain the ratio. We could have back-calculated Cost of Sales from average inventory & inventory turnover (given on note 31) = 3.72 inventory turnover × (5278 + 3125) ÷ 2 average inventory = 3.72 × 4201.5 ≈ ₹15,630 crore for 2021–22; 3.39 × (3125 + 2827) ÷ 2 average inventory taken from 2020–21 annual report = 3.39 × 2976 ≈ ₹10,089 crore for 2020–21. Next, Operating Expenses could be obtained using the formula:

Operating Expenses = Gross Profit + Other Operating Income – Operating Profit.

However, we should *not* do so because Asian Paints appears to have defined Cost of Sales (or Cost of Goods Sold) as the sum of the cost of material consumed, purchase of stock-in-trade, and changes in inventory of work-in-progress, finished goods, and stock in trade; it has ignored conversion cost from Cost of Sales. Note that the Cost of Sales obtained above for 2021–22 ₹15,630 crore is very close to ₹15,609 crore: the sum of Cost of Materials Consumed ₹13,838.90, Purchases of Stock-in-Trade ₹2,978.69, and Changes in inventories of finished goods, stock-in-trade and work-in-progress –₹1,208.63. Similarly, for 2020–21, the Cost of Sales obtained above ₹10,089 is very close to ₹10,082.53 obtained from the income statement for 2020–21 (in the 2022 Annual Report). Thus, the conversion cost incurred to produce finished goods has not been considered in the Cost of Sales. For this reason, we should not use the back-calculated figure for the Cost of Sales (shown in the previous paragraph). Note that this issue is also seen in several other manufacturing and service firms. Without Cost of Sales, we can neither obtain Gross Profit, nor back-calculate Operating Expenses from Gross Profit, Other Operating Income, and Operating Profit. Therefore, we should drop the three lines for Cost of Sales, Gross Profit, and Operating Expenses and insert a single line for Cost of Sales & Operating Expenses on the multi-step income statement. We back-calculate a single value for the Cost of Sales & Operating Expenses:

Cost of Sales & Operating Expenses = Sales + Other Operating Income – Operating Profit

Table 2.20 Asian Paints' Multi-Step Common-Size Income Statement

Asian Paints	**2021–22**		**2020–21**	
Multi-Step Income Statement	₹ Crore	*% of Sales*	₹ Crore	*% of Sales*
Sales *(Sales Growth Rate 36.8%)*	25,003	*100.0%*	18,280	*100.0%*
Less Cost of Sales & Operating Expenses ***	–21,323	*–85.3%*	–14,721	*–80.5%*
Add Other Operating Income	186	*0.7%*	237	*1.3%*
Operating Profit	3,866	*15.5%*	3,796	*20.8%*
Add Non-Operating Income, Gain, & Loss (net **)	398	*1.6%*	366	*2.0%*
Earnings Before Interest & Taxes	4,264	*17.1%*	4,162	*22.8%*
Less Interest Expense (Finance Cost)	–70	*–0.3%*	–72	*–0.4%*
Profit Before Tax	4,194	*16.8%*	4,090	*22.4%*
Less Tax Expense	–1,059	*–4.2%*	–1,038	*–5.7%*
Profit After Tax *(Profit Growth Rate 2.7%)*	3,135	*12.5%*	3,052	*16.7%*

* To prepare this multi-step income statement, first fill in the figures for PAT, Taxes, PBT, Finance Cost, Other Operating Income, and Sales on the income statement. After that, obtain the remaining figures for EBIT, Non-Operating Income, Gains & Losses, and Operating Profit. ** Add Other Income and Exceptional Items to obtain Non-Operating Income, Gains, & Losses. *** It is not possible to obtain Cost of Sales, Gross Profit, and Operating Expenses due to lack of information needed to segregate various expenses (particularly, employee benefits expense, depreciation, amortization, as well as a few expenses among other expenses) into manufacturing and non-manufacturing portions; thus, we merge Cost of Sales and Operating Expenses into one item Cost of Sales & Operating Expenses. We back calculate this item as a balancing figure using the formula: Cost of Sales & Operating Expenses = Sales + Other Operating Income – Operating Profit.

Asian Paints' multi-step income statement reveals that in 2021–22, the company generated an operating profit of ₹3,866 crore, which is higher than the last year's ₹3,796 crore. Its operating profit ratio, at 15.5% of sales, was much lower than the last year's 20.8% of sales. Thus, the operating margins declined 530 basis points during the 2021–22 financial year relative to the prior year, which suggests that the company had difficulty controlling its cost of sales and operating expenses. The company's PBIT, PBT, and PAT increased, but as a percentage of sales these profit measures declined significantly. In 2021–22, the net profit is ₹3,135 crore, about 2.7% higher than ₹3,052 crore in the previous year. The net profit as a percentage of sales was 12.5% in the current year, or 420 basis points lower than 16.7% in 2020–21. The significant drop in the net profit ratio suggests that its profit after tax grew in 2021–22 (from 2020–21) at a lower rate 2.7% than the sales growth rate of 36.8% in 2021–22.

Appendix 2A: Cost of Sales of Retail, Manufacturing, and Service Firms

Cost of Sales is also known by various names such as Cost of Goods Sold, Cost of Services, and Cost of Revenues. It is useful for determining gross profit (= Sales – Cost of Sales). We separately discuss the cost for retailers, manufacturers, and service firms.

(a) Cost of Sales for a Retailer

Retailers, merchandisers, and traders sell stock-in-trade. To buy these stocks, they incur a *Cost of Purchase*. When these stocks are sold, the cost of purchase of the items sold is expensed as Cost of Sales. For these firms:

Cost of Sales = Opening Stock-in-Trade + Cost of Purchase – Closing Stock-in-Trade

Opening (Closing) Stock-in-Trade is the cost of stock-in-trade at the beginning (end) of the period. Cost of Purchase includes the amount for purchase of the stock-in-trade and freight inward and insurance costs (if incurred by the retailer) for bringing the stock-in-trade from the supplier's location to the place of sale.

We exclude any returns and allowances deducted from gross purchases. Furthermore, if the purchase price includes indirect tax (such as goods and services tax or export duty), such taxes must also be deducted. Similarly, if discounts and rebates are received but not reflected on the invoice (i.e., discounts and rebates are received after the invoice has been raised), such discounts and rebates must also be deducted from the total purchases.

For example, in its 2022 Income Statement, Avenue Supermarts reports Purchase of Stock-in-Trade ₹26,472 crore, Opening Stock ₹2,167 crore, and Closing Stock ₹2,586 crore. It did not report any freight inward and insurance cost for bringing purchased stock-in-trade (in its note 29 Other Expenses), so we take these costs as zero. From this, we find that Cost of Sales is ₹26,053 crore (= 2167 + 26472 + 0 – 2586). In the previous year, 2020–21, the company's Cost of Sales was ₹20,356 crore (= 1909 opening stock + 20614 purchases + 0 freight inward & insurance – 2167 closing stock). Thus, the Cost of Sales was 27.99% higher year-on-year in 2021–22, and this growth rate was about 44 basis points higher than the sales growth rate of 27.55%. Thus, the company purchased more than it could sell during the year.

Note that the cost of purchase is a product cost. Product costs are matched to revenue (i.e., expensed when goods are sold). To understand this idea, let us consider an example. Suppose, in 2022, a retailer purchased 2,500 bottles of shampoo at ₹240 each and sold 1,000 bottles at ₹300 each. There was no opening stock of shampoos. The retailer would recognize revenue of ₹3,00,000 (=1000 bottles sold × ₹300 per bottle) in 2022. Although the cost of purchases in 2022 was ₹600,000 (=2,500 bottles purchased × ₹240 per bottle), this entire amount would not be expensed in 2022. Since only 1,000 bottles were sold, ₹240,000 (=1,000 bottles sold × ₹240 per bottle) would be expensed as the Cost of Sales during 2022. The cost of the remaining 1,500 bottles, ₹360,000 (=1,500 bottles remaining × ₹240 per bottle) would be included in Closing Stock.

(b) Cost of Sales for a Manufacturer

Manufacturers sell finished goods, which they produce at their factories. They incur a *Cost of Goods Manufactured* to produce these goods. This cost is also a product cost and, thus, matched to revenue. Hence, when these finished goods are sold, the cost of goods manufactured for the items sold is expensed as the Cost of Sales for the period. The formula for Cost of Sales for manufacturers is as follows:

Cost of Sales = Opening Finished Goods + Cost of Goods Manufactured – Closing Finished Goods.

Opening [Closing] Finished Goods is the cost of finished goods (manufactured) in inventory at the beginning [end] of the period. Cost of Goods Manufactured is the cost incurred to manufacture finished goods, and these costs include direct material cost, direct labour cost, manufacturing overhead (i.e., all other costs incurred in manufacturing), and an adjustment for work-in-progress (WIP). The formula for the cost of goods manufactured is as follows:

Cost of Goods Manufactured = Direct Material Cost + Direct Labour Cost + Manufacturing Overhead Cost + Opening Work-in-Progress – Closing Work-in-Progress.

Let us understand how the cost of sales is computed for a manufacturer. We will do so in two steps: first, we obtain the cost of goods manufactured, and then we will obtain the cost of sales. For this, let us consider an example. Suppose, in 2022, a manufacturer produced 3 lakh bottles of shampoo, and incurred Direct Material Cost ₹60 lakh, Direct Labour Cost ₹30 lakh, and

Manufacturing Overhead ₹213 lakh. These costs include ₹5 lakhs for items still under production (i.e., work-in-progress, WIP) at the end of the year. The manufacturer had an opening WIP of ₹2 lakhs (at the beginning of the year). The opening and closing stocks of finished goods were ₹20 lakh and 8 lakh, respectively.

In this example, Cost of Goods Manufactured = ₹300 lakh = ₹2 lakh (Opening WIP) + 60 lakh (Direct Material) + 30 lakh (Direct Labour) + 213 lakh (Manufacturing Overhead) – 5 lakh (Closing WIP).

Furthermore, Cost of Sales = ₹312 lakh = ₹20 lakh (Opening Finished Goods) + 300 lakh (Cost of Goods Manufactured) – 8 lakh (Closing Finished Goods).

Notice that although the company spent ₹300 lakh to manufacture the finished goods, it will recognize only ₹312 lakh as the cost of sales since it sold more goods than it produced during the year.

Note that unless a manufacturing firm discloses what proportion of its employee benefit cost, depreciation & amortization, and other expenses are for manufacturing (or for everything else), we will not be able to know its Cost of Sales and Operating Expenses. In that case, we will not be able to compute its Gross Profit. Still, we can obtain Operating Profit [= Sales – Cost of Sales & Operating Expenses + Other Operating Income; OR = Profit Before Interest & Tax – Non-operating Income, Gains, & Losses]. The same is true for service firms as well.

(c) Cost of Sale for a Service Firm

Cost of Sale includes all direct and indirect costs incurred for providing services, including:

- any direct material consumed for rendering the service,
- direct labour cost of employees rendering the service,
- other direct costs incurred for providing service,
- service overheads, and
- an adjustment for incomplete service (work-in-progress).

Usually, direct labour costs are significantly large and direct material costs are a relatively small component of the Cost of Service. For example, in 2022, Infosys reports ₹2,985 crore as the cost of software packages and other third-party items bought for service delivery to clients (see note 2.20), whereas it reports ₹51,664 crore as the employee benefit expenses (on the income statement). According to Infosys' 20-F filings with SEC, about 90% of this employee benefit cost is included in the cost of sales.[9]

Cost of Service = Direct Material Cost + Direct Labour Cost + Other Direct Cost for Providing Service + Service Overhead + Opening WIP – Closing WIP.

In its Form 20-F filed with the SEC for fiscal 2022, Infosys reports the constituents of the Cost of Sales and their amount. Employee benefit cost $7,714 million (i.e., direct labour cost), Cost of technical sub-contractors $1,690 million (i.e., direct labour cost), third-party items bought for service delivery to clients $721 million (i.e., direct material cost), Depreciation & amortization $466 million (i.e., Service Overhead), and Cost of software packages for own use $179 million (i.e., other direct costs) were the five largest items. Cost of sales also included various other items (ranging from a low of $3 million to a high of $93 million): travelling costs, short-term leases, consultancy & professional charges, communication costs, provisions for post-sales client support, repairs & maintenance, and other expenses. There was no adjustment for work-in-progress.

Table 2A.1 Infosys Cost of Sales

Cost of Sales (Dollars in millions)	Fiscal 2022	Fiscal 2021	Change
Employee benefit costs	7,714	6,671	1,043
Depreciation and amortization	466	441	25
Travelling costs	93	65	28
Cost of technical sub-contractors	1,690	957	733
Cost of Software packages for own use	179	160	19
Third- party items bought for service delivery to clients	721	406	315
Short-term leases	3	4	(1)
Consultancy and professional charges	19	8	11
Communication costs	42	45	(3)
Provision for post-sales client support	10	5	5
Repairs and maintenance	51	65	(14)
Other expenses	8	1	7
Total cost of sales	10,996	8,828	2,168

Source: United States Securities And Exchange Commission, "Infosys Cost of Sales", www.sec.gov

[9] In its Form 20-F filed with the SEC for fiscal 2022, Infosys reports US $8,585 million employee benefit cost of which $7,714 is for the cost of sales. Therefore, 89.85% of its employee cost is included in its cost of sales. Please see https://www.sec.gov/Archives/edgar/data/0001067491/000156459022023521/infy-20f_20220331.htm

Infosys' Cost of Sales is useful for obtaining Gross Profit. The 2022 multi-step income statement reveals that Infosys earned a total revenue of ₹103,940 crore and incurred a cost of sales of ₹69,629 crore in 2022. Thus, it generated a gross profit of ₹34,311 crore (or 33.0% of revenue) in 2022. In 2021, Infosys' gross profit was ₹30,371 crore (or 35.4% of the revenue of ₹85,912 crore). Thus, although Infosys increased gross profit by 13% yearly, its ability to generate gross profit per rupee of sales diminished in 2022 compared to 2021.

Appendix 2B: Operating Expense

Operating Expenses are the period costs that are operating in nature and whose benefits have been consumed during the period (i.e., they have expired). Operating Expenses are comprised of marketing, selling & distribution expenses, general & administrative expenses, research & development expenses, and corporate social responsibility expenses.

Table 2B.1 Infosys' Selling & Marketing Expenses and Administrative Expenses

Selling & Marketing Expenses (Dollars in Millions)	Fiscal 2022	Fiscal 2021	Change
Employee benefit costs	572	548	24
Travelling costs	8	3	5
Branding and marketing	73	48	25
Short-term leases	1	1	—
Consultancy and professional charges	25	13	12
Communication costs	1	2	(1)
Other expenses	12	9	3
Total selling and marketing expenses	692	624	68

Administrative Expenses (Dollars in millions)	Fiscal 2022	Fiscal 2021	Change
Employee benefit costs	299	274	25
Consultancy and professional charges	209	150	59
Repairs and maintenance	110	125	(15)
Power and fuel	18	19	(1)
Communication costs	38	39	(1)
Travelling costs	9	7	2
Rates and taxes	35	35	—
Short-term leases	5	6	(1)
Insurance charges	22	18	4
Impairment loss recognized/(reversed) on financial assets	23	25	(2)
Commission to non-whole-time directors	2	1	1
Contribution towards Corporate Social Responsibility (CSR)	57	59	(2)
Other expenses	41	26	15
Total administrative expenses	868	784	84

Source: United States Securities And Exchange Commission, "Infosys' Selling & Marketing Expenses and Administrative Expenses", www.sec.gov

While product costs are expensed in the year in which goods are sold, period costs are expensed in the period in which their benefit is received (i.e., they are matched to a period in which they expire). For example, sales promotion expenditures are a period cost, and we expense them in the period in which the sales promotions were carried out. Similarly, legal fees are period costs and expensed in the period in which legal services were received.

The 2022 multi-step income statement reveals that Infosys incurred Operating Expenses of ₹8,912 crore, comprised of Selling & Marketing Expenses of ₹4,125 crore, and General & Administration Expenses of ₹4,787 crore. It also reported the breakup of these expenses in its SEC 20-F filings.

Appendix 2C: Non-Operating Income, Gains, & Losses

Non-operating income, gains, & losses could be found under Other Income, Other Expense, and Exceptional Items. Although Interest expense arises from a company's financing activity and is, therefore, a non-operating item, we exclude interest expense from here and put it as a separate line on a multi-step income statement to make it more insightful.

Here is a partial list of items (often reported under Other Income) that can be included under non-operating income, gains, and losses:

- Interest income
- Dividend income from subsidiaries, joint ventures, associates, and other companies
- Dividend income from mutual fund investments
- Gain/(Loss) on sale/revaluation of investments
- Gain/(Loss) on sale/disposal of PPE and investment properties
- Gain/(Loss) on modification/termination of leases
- Gain/(Loss) on foreign exchange
- Gain/(Loss) on foreign currency forward and options contracts
- Gain/(Loss) on the translation of foreign currency-denominated assets and liabilities
- Gain/(Loss) on insurance claims received
- Royalty received from subsidiaries, joint ventures, and associates
- Rent and amenities service income
- Others/Miscellaneous income reported under Other Income
- Impairment Losses and their reversals (often included under Other Expense)

Appendix 2D: Calculation of Depreciation and Amortization

Depreciation is an expense incurred for tangible fixed assets (Property, plant, & equipment other than Land, Right of Use, and Investment properties), whereas amortization is for Intangible fixed assets (other than Goodwill). Every year, a firm charges depreciation and amortization on these fixed assets (other than Land and Goodwill). As a result, there is a decrease in the carrying amount of fixed assets by the amount of depreciation & amortization charged during the year.

To obtain depreciation, we need three inputs: the historical cost, residual value, and useful life of the asset. In addition, we also need the depreciation method that will be used to compute depreciation. Let us understand these concepts next.

A company has several items of fixed assets that it intends to use over several years (*useful life*). For these assets, it has incurred *historical costs* (various costs to acquire/construct the assets and make them ready for use), which are capitalized. It may expect to receive some *residual value* (net proceeds from the disposal of these assets at the end of their useful life). The difference between the historical cost and the residual value is the *depreciable amount* that is systematically allocated over the useful life. Due to depreciation charged every year, the carrying amount of the asset reduces each year and reaches the residual value at the end of the useful life.

Let us understand these with an example. Suppose, a company buys a machine and installs it incurring a total cost of ₹20 lakh (historical cost). The management expects to use the machine for 3 years (useful life) and produce 8,000 units of output in year 1, 10,000 units in year 2, and 12,000 units in the last year. Furthermore, the management expects to sell the machine at the end of its useful life and expects to receive ₹5 lakh (residual value). The depreciable amount for the machine, ₹15 lakh (= 20 lakh historical cost – 5 lakh residual value), will be charged as depreciation over 3 years.

There are various methods for calculating depreciation. Companies can use the Straight Line Method (SLM), Written Down Value (WDV) method, and Unit of Production method, among others. For computing depreciation on a fixed asset, a company chooses a depreciation method that reflects the pattern of usage of the fixed asset. Continuing with the above example, let us compute depreciation under each of the three methods.

Annual Depreciation (SLM) = (Historical Cost – Residual Value) ÷ Useful Life

Under the SLM, the company will charge annual depreciation of ₹5 lakh (= 15 lakh ÷ 3 years) in each of the three years. As a result, the carrying amount, which was ₹20 crore at the start, decreases to ₹15 crore at year 1 end, ₹10 crore at year 2 end, and ₹5 crore at year 3 end. Note that at the end of the useful life (i.e., 3 years), the carrying amount of the asset is the same as the residual value.

Table 2D.1 Straight-Line Method Depreciation

Year	Gross Block	Beginning Carrying Amount	Depreciation Expense (Straight Line Method)	Accumulated Depreciation	Ending Carrying Amount
1	₹20 lakh	₹20 lakh	₹5 lakh	₹5 lakh	₹15 lakh
2	20 lakh	15 lakh	5 lakh	10 lakh	10 lakh
3	20 lakh	10 lakh	5 lakh	15 lakh	5 lakh

Under the Unit of Production method, the company will first obtain ₹50 as depreciation per unit of output {₹15 lakh ÷ (8,000 + 10,000 + 12,000 units)}. Using this rate, it will charge a depreciation of ₹4 lakh in year 1 (=50 × 8,000 units), ₹5 lakh in year 2 (=50 × 10,000 units), and ₹6 lakh in year 3 (=50 × 12,000 units). As a result, the carrying amount decreases from ₹20 crore at year 1 beginning to ₹16 crore at year 1 end, ₹11 crore at year 2 end, and ₹5 crore at year 3 end. Again, note that at the end of the useful life (i.e., 3 years), the carrying amount of the asset is the same as the residual value ₹5 crore.

Depreciation per unit of output = (Historical Cost – Residual Value) ÷ Total units of output expected over the useful life of the PPE

Annual Depreciation = Depreciation per unit of output × Actual Output during the year

Table 2D.2 Unit of Production Method Depreciation

Year	Gross Block	Beginning Carrying Amount	Depreciation Expense (Unit of Production Method)	Accumulated Depreciation	Ending Carrying Amount
1	₹20 lakh	₹20 lakh	8,000 units × ₹50 = ₹4 lakh	₹4 lakh	₹16 lakh
2	20 lakh	16 lakh	10,000 units × ₹50 = 5 lakh	9 lakh	11 lakh
3	20 lakh	11 lakh	12,000 units × ₹50 = 6 lakh	15 lakh	5 lakh

Under the WDV method, the company will first obtain the WDV rate of 37% = 1 – {(5÷20) ^ (1÷3)} = 1 – $\sqrt[3]{0.25}$ = 0.370039 ≈ 37% after rounding off to nearest percentage.

$$WDV\ Rate = 1 - \{(Residual\ Value \div Historical\ Cost) \wedge (1 \div Useful\ Life)\}$$ [10]

$$Annual\ Depreciation\ (WDV) = Beginning\ Carrying\ Value \times WDV\ Rate$$

Next, it obtains the amount of depreciation by multiplying the WDV rate and the carrying amount at the beginning of the year. As the carrying amount decreases from one year to another, so would the amount of depreciation. In year 1, WDV Depreciation is ₹7,40,000 (= ₹20 lakh × 37%). As a result, the machine's accumulated depreciation increases to ₹7,40,000 (= 0 + 7,40,000), and the carrying amount reduces to ₹12,60,000 (= 20 lakh – 7.4 lakh) at the end of year 1.

For year 2, WDV Depreciation is ₹466,200 (=12.6 lakh × 37%), which increases the accumulated depreciation to ₹12,06,200 (=7,40,000+4,66,200) and reduces the carrying amount to ₹793,800 (= 12,60,000 carrying amount – 4,66,200 annual depreciation = 20,00,000 gross block – 12,06,200 accumulated depreciation) at the end of year 2.

In Year 3, WDV depreciation would be ₹293,800 (= 793,800 – 500,000) and accumulated depreciation ₹15,00,000. Since the machine would be sold at the end of year 3 (useful life), the carrying amount of the machine should become ₹5 lakh (residual value). Thus, the difference of ₹293,800 between the carrying amount at the end of year 2 (₹793,800) and the residual value at the end of year 3 (₹5 lakh) will be the depreciation in year 3. This amount (293,800) is close to what we would get (293,706) by multiplying the WDV rate (37%) and the carrying amount at the end of year 2 (₹793,800). The difference in the two amounts (293,800 and 293,706) is because we had rounded off the WDV rate.

Table 2D.3 Written-Down-Value Method Depreciation

Year	Gross Block	Beginning Carrying Amount	Depreciation Expense (Written Down Value Method)	Accumulated Depreciation	Ending Carrying Amount
1	20 lakh	20,00,000	20,00,000 × 37% = 7,40,000	7,40,000	12,60,000
2	20 lakh	12,60,000	12,60,000 × 37% = 4,66,200	12,06,200	7,93,800
3	20 lakh	7,93,800	7,93,800 – 5,00,000 = 2,93,800	15,00,000	5,00,000

The above example illustrates several key takeaways. First, irrespective of the depreciation method, the carrying amount reaches the residual value at the

[10] *Historical Cost × {(1 – WDV Depreciation Rate) ^ Useful Life} = Residual Value,*

end of the useful life. Second, the depreciation amount is the same each year under SLM, which makes it easy to use. On the contrary, under WDV, the depreciation amount is maximum in the first year, keeps decreasing each year, and is the lowest in the last year of the useful life. Under the Unit of production method, the depreciation amount varies with the output produced by the fixed asset. Third, when there is no output, depreciation is zero under the unit of production method. That is not the case with the SLM and WDV, which always yields a non-zero amount for depreciation.

Most companies in India use SLM for estimating depreciation & amortization expense for income statement purposes. But they use WDV for obtaining depreciation & amortization for obtaining taxable income (for tax purposes), as the tax law does not give the option of charging depreciation calculated using any method other than the WDV method. Using WDV method allows higher depreciation deduction in the initial years of the useful life of an asset, lower taxable profits, and lower tax payment. This advantage goes away during the later years of the useful life.

Higher WDV depreciation (for tax purposes) and lower SLM depreciation (for income statement purpose) in the initial years results in the origination of Deferred Tax Expense and increases Deferred Tax Liabilities, as discussed in the appendix on taxes. Later years see a reversal of Deferred Tax Expense and a decrease in Deferred Tax Liabilities when WDV depreciation is lower than SLM depreciation as shown in the next graph.

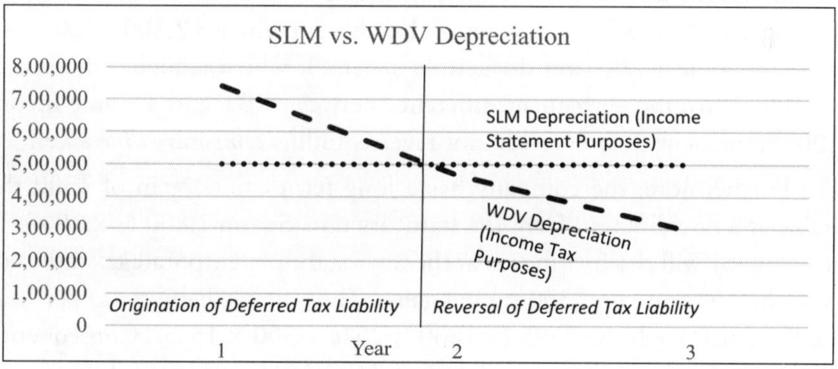

Note, we can apply the WDV method only if the residual value is a non-trivial percentage of the historical cost. If the percentage is too small, the WDV rate will be very high, and most of the historical cost would be charged as depreciation in the first few years. For example, if the residual value is 1% of the historical cost and the useful life is 6 years, the carrying amount would fall to 10% of the historical cost by the year 3 end, i.e., 90% of the historical cost is expensed in the first 3 years.

Appendix 2E: Calculation of Income Tax, Current Tax, and Deferred Tax Expense

Suppose S company has PBT and Taxable Income of ₹2,000 and the corporate tax rate is 25%. It would have a tax liability and Income Tax Expense of ₹500 = 2,000 × 25%.

- S Company: PBT = 2,000, Taxable Income = 2,000, Tax Expense = 500.

Current Tax Expense

Current Tax Expense is the amount of tax payable during a year computed as per income tax rules; therefore, this amount is the same as the tax liability as per the Income Tax Returns.

Suppose another company, P Company has a PBT of ₹2,000, and the corporate tax rate is 25%; both figures are the same as S Company. However, unlike S Company, P Company also has a tax-free income of ₹100, a non-deductible expense of ₹200 (i.e., the expense is not tax-deductible), and a gain from the sale of equity investment of ₹300 taxable at a 15% capital gains tax rate. The amount of tax P company would pay is not the same as ₹500 the tax liability of S Company.

Since tax-free income and non-deductible expense are not considered for computing Taxable Income (used for calculating tax liability as per tax rules), these items create a *Permanent Difference* between PBT and Taxable income. For P Company: PBT is ₹2,000, whereas Taxable Income is ₹2,100 (= 2000 – 100 tax-free income + 200 non-deductible expense), which is higher than its PBT by ₹100. Thus, the permanent difference between PBT and Taxable Income is ₹100. Permanent differences do not reverse, unlike *temporary differences.*

Furthermore, the company has a long-term capital gain of ₹300 that is taxable at a rate different from the statutory rate. So, on 1,800 (= 2,100 – 300), the company will pay income tax at the 25% statutory corporate tax rate and pay tax at the 15% rate on ₹300 capital gains. Thus, its tax liability (as per Income Tax Returns) would be ₹495 (= 1800 × 25% + 300 × 15%). Consequently, it will report Taxes and Current Taxes of ₹495 (and no Deferred Taxes) on its Income Statement.

- P Company: PBT = 2,000, Taxable Income = 2,100, Permanent Difference = –100, Temporary Difference = Nil, Income Tax Expense = 495, Current Tax Expense = 495, Deferred Tax Expense = Nil.

In the example given above, S Company and P Company had entire taxes arising from current taxes, and they did not have any deferred taxes.

Deferred Tax Expense

Deferred Tax Expense is the difference between total tax expense and current tax expense. Deferred taxes arise due to *temporary differences* between PBT and Taxable Income due to differences in accounting rules and tax rules. Suppose, like P Company, T Company also has PBT ₹2,000, tax-free income ₹100, non-deductible expense ₹200, and long-term capital gains from equity ₹300, statutory tax rate 25%, and long-term capital gains tax rate 15%. Therefore, its current taxes would be ₹495, the same as P Company. Let us assume these amounts will continue to be the same for T in the next year also.

Furthermore, suppose, unlike P Company, T Company's PBT includes an unpaid salary expense of ₹720 that will be paid next year, and this expense is tax-deductible on a cash basis. Since the company has not paid ₹720, this expense cannot be deducted when computing Taxable Income, causing Taxable Income to be ₹2,820 (= 2100 + 720) and income tax liability to be ₹675 (= 495 + 180; 180 = 25% × 720). Thus, T Company has a timing difference of ₹–720 and deferred taxes of ₹–180. These amounts are negative because current taxes (based on tax rules) are higher than tax expenses (based on accounting rules). The excess payment of ₹180 will reverse and will be recovered in the next year, so deferred taxes have created a Deferred Tax Asset.

- T Company, *Current Year*: PBT = 2,000, Taxable Income = 2,820, Total Difference = –820, Permanent Difference = –100, Timing Difference = –720, Income Tax = 495, Current Taxes = 675, Deferred Taxes = –180, Increase in Deferred Tax Asset = 180.

Reversal of Deferred Taxes

In the following year, although the company will pay ₹720 for the unpaid salary (an expense already recorded in the previous year), this amount cannot be deducted for computing PBT. As a result, Income Tax Expenses will continue to be ₹495. But ₹720 would be deducted for computing Taxable Income and consequently decrease current taxes. Thus, in the next year, taxable income would be ₹1,380 (= 2100 – 720), and current taxes would be ₹315 (=495 – 180; 180 = 25% × 720). Since tax expense is ₹495 and current tax expense is ₹315, deferred tax expense would be ₹180 (=495 – 315) in the next year. Also, note that deferred taxes of –180 has completely reversed in the next year.

- T Company, Next Year: PBT = 2,000, Taxable Income = 1,380, Total Difference = 620, Permanent Difference = –100, Timing Difference = 720, Income Tax = 495, Current Taxes = 315, Deferred Taxes = 180, Change in Deferred Tax Asset = –180.

Appendix 2F: Calculation of Basic and Diluted EPS

When we just say EPS, we are generally referring to Basic EPS.

$$\textit{Basic EPS} = \frac{\textit{Net Profit}}{\textit{Weighted average number of equity shares outstanding}}$$

The numerator is Net Profit, whereas the denominator is obtained by taking the weighted average of the number of equity shares outstanding during the year.[11]

Suppose Company B had 1,000 shares at the beginning of the year (April 1, 2022), issued 500 shares on October 1, 2022, and repurchased 180 shares on February 1, 2023. Thus, it had 1000 shares outstanding for 6 months (April 1 to September 30, 2022), 1500 shares outstanding for 4 months (October 1, 2022, to January 31, 2023), and 1320 shares outstanding for 2 months (February 1 to March 31, 2023). In that case, the denominator for Basic EPS, i.e., the weighted average number of shares outstanding is 1220 shares = 1000 × (6÷12) +1500 × (4÷12) + 1320 × (2÷12) = 1000 × (1/2) + 1500 × (1/3) + 1320 × (1/6). Thus, the weight assigned to a share is the proportion of time it was outstanding. If this company has a Net Profit of ₹6,100, then its Basic EPS is ₹5 (= 6,100 ÷ 1220).

A company may have issued stock warrants, options, or restricted stocks (to employees and others) and convertible debentures (or other convertible debt securities) that may require issuing equity shares in the future. When these potential equity shares are issued against these securities, EPS may either decrease or increase. Diluted EPS helps us understand what would be the EPS when these potential shares are issued. Thus, it helps us see the impact of these potential shares on Basic EPS.

Diluted EPS is computed as if all such securities have been converted into equity shares at the beginning of the current financial year. When stock options, warrants, or restricted stocks are converted into equity shares, there would be an increase in the number of outstanding shares (on the denominator), but there is no change in net profit (on the numerator). For this reason, Diluted EPS is lower than Basic EPS. For example, if Company X has 1,000 shares outstanding throughout the year, Basic EPS of ₹3, and 200 potential equity shares number will be issued against stock options, then its Diluted EPS would be ₹2.50 = 3000/1200 = (3 × 1000) ÷ (1000 + 200). Here Diluted EPS is less than Basic

[11] Under Ind AS, preference dividend is included in finance cost. Therefore, net profit is reported after deducting preference dividends. Hence, adjustment for preference dividends is no longer required to obtain earnings available to equity shareholders. Thus, a company's net profit is the earnings available to its equity shareholders.

EPS because the numerator did not change but the denominator increased by 20%. In this example, the stock option is considered a dilutive security as it causes Diluted EPS to be less than Basic EPS.

It is not always the case that Diluted EPS is lower than Basic EPS, particularly when a company has convertible debt or convertible preference shares. In that case, the conversion would increase not only the number of equity shares but also the profit available for equity shareholders. For example, when a company's convertible debentures are converted into equity shares, it would stop paying interest on those debentures (since these debentures no longer exist). However, it would also not get any tax shield on those interests (no tax deduction since it is no longer paying interest on those debentures). This would cause net profit to increase by the amount of interest saved minus the tax shield lost. Let us understand this with two examples.

First, suppose Company Y has 1,000 shares outstanding throughout the year, Basic EPS of ₹3, and 200 potential equity shares will be issued upon the conversion of convertible debentures (the company is paying ₹800 as interest on those debentures and its tax rate is 30%). Company Y's Diluted EPS would be ₹2.97 =3560/1200 = (3×1000 + 800 interest expense – 800× 30% tax shield on interest) ÷ (1000 + 200). In this example, Diluted EPS is lower than Basic EPS, as convertible debentures are *dilutive securities*. Dilutive securities are those that upon conversion cause basic EPS to decline (basic EPS then will be the same as the diluted EPS now, *ceteris paribus*).

Next, suppose Company Z has 1,000 shares outstanding throughout the year, Basic EPS of ₹3, and 200 potential equity shares will be issued upon the conversion of preference shares (the company pays ₹800 as total dividends on those preference shares, and preference dividends are not tax-deductible), then its Diluted EPS would be ₹3.17 =3800/1200 = (3×1000+800) ÷ (1000+200). Thus, Diluted EPS is higher than Basic EPS. In this example, convertible debentures are *anti-dilutive securities*. Anti-dilutive securities are those that upon conversion cause basic EPS to increase (basic EPS then will be the same as the diluted EPS now, *ceteris paribus*).

Diluted EPS would be higher [lower] than Basic EPS if upon the conversion/exercise the rate of increase in the numerator (i.e., change in earnings available for equity holders ÷ the numerator used for Basic EPS) is higher [lower] than the rate of increase in the denominator (i.e., potential equity shares issued ÷ the denominator used for Basic EPS).

Appendix 2G: Understanding Reported Income Statements of Banks

Banks prepare financial statements under the previous AS accounting standards as they are still exempted from adopting the newer Ind AS standards. The format of income statement is prescribed by the Government of India in its notification SO 240(E) dated 26-03-1992.[12] Their Total Income comprises Interest earned and Other income, and Total Expenses comprise Interest expenses, Operating expenses, and Provisions & contingencies. Net Profit is the excess of Total Income over Total Expenses.

Banks earn interest on advances and bills discounted, investments, balances with the central bank and other inter-bank funds, etc. They incur interest expenses on deposits received, borrowings taken from the central bank and inter-bank borrowings, and others. Net Interest Margin is the excess of interest earned over interest expense. Net Interest Margin is a bank's gross profit from its deposit and lending business.

Operating expenses largely consist of Employee benefits, Rent, rates, & lighting, Insurance, Depreciation, Repairs & maintenance, Printing & stationery, etc. Other Income has various incomes: some arise from operating activities, whereas others arise from investing activities. For example, Commission, exchange & brokerage, profit on exchange transactions (net), and Profit on sale/revaluation of investments (net) arise from a bank's operating activities, whereas Profit on sale of land, buildings, and other assets (net) arise from its investing activities.

Table 2G.1 SBI's Reported Income Statement

State Bank of India's Income Statement for the year ended (amount in ₹ crore)	Schedule No.	March 31, 2022	March 31, 2021
Income:			
Interest Earned	13	275,457	265,151
Other Income	14	40,564	43,496
Total Income		316,021	308,647
Expenses:			
Interest Expense	15	154,750	154,401
Operating Expense	16	93,398	82,652
Provisions & Contingencies		36,198	51,144
		284,345	288,237
Profit:			
Net Profit for the year		31,676	20,410

[12] See https://rbidocs.rbi.org.in/rdocs/content/pdfs/83MD01092021_A1.pdf for the required Balance Sheet & Income Statement format. See https://rbidocs.rbi.org.in/rdocs/Publications/PDFs/78904.pdf for the details of balance sheet items, income statement items, and notes of accounts to be reported by banks.

For the year ended March 31, 2022, the State Bank of India (SBI) reported a Total Income of ₹316,021 crore, Total Expenses of ₹284,345 crore, and a Net Profit of ₹31,676 crore. SBI recorded an annual profit growth rate of 55%, largely driven by a reduction in provisions and contingencies (greater in magnitude than the increase in operating expense) and an increase in interest earnings without a corresponding increase in interest expenses.

Its Interest earnings were ₹275,457 crore (3.9% higher than the previous year amount) and Interest expenses were ₹154,750 crore (about the same as the previous year). Thus, Net Interest Margin (Interest Income less Interest Expense) was ₹120,707 crore, 43.8% of Interest earned (up from 41.8% in 2020–21).

Note 14 reveals that Other Income ₹40,564 crore (6.7% lower than the previous year) was made up of the following seven items (only the fifth and sixth items are from investing activities, the rest are from its operating activities):

i. Commission, exchange, and brokerage income of ₹24,565 crore,
ii. Miscellaneous income ₹8,596 crore (including ₹7,782 crore for recoveries made from accounts previously written-off),
iii. Profit on sale of investment (net) ₹3,485 crore,
iv. Profit on exchange transactions (net) ₹3,479 crore,
v. Dividend Income from its subsidiaries, associate companies, joint ventures ₹718 crore,
vi. Profit/(Loss) on sale of land, buildings, & other assets ₹(17) crore, and
vii. Profit/(Loss) on revaluation of investment (net) ₹(263) crore.

SBI reported Operating Expenses of ₹93,398 crore (a 13% increase from last year). Note 16 shows twelve items constituting operating expenses. The five biggest items are:

i. Employee cost ₹57,562 crore,
ii. Other expenditure ₹18,996 crore,
iii. Rent, taxes, and lighting ₹5,362 crore,
iv. Insurance expense ₹5,240 crore, and
v. Depreciation ₹3,249 crore.

Total Expense also includes Provisions & Contingencies ₹36,198 crore (29% decrease from last year). SBI did not provide any breakup of this expense.

CHAPTER THREE

Balance Sheet

Balance Sheet is a very important source of financial information. A balance sheet and notes provide information on assets, liabilities, and equity. We must scrutinize them to understand a firm's financial position and assess whether it can thrive in the future. Here are 10 relevant questions about the financial position that can be answered from its balance sheet and notes:

1. What is the size of the company?
2. How much equity does the company have? Does it have enough assets to pay its liabilities? Is the company solvent?
3. How much capital is employed in the company? What is the source of funds for capital employed? How much has each source contributed to the total capital employed?
4. How much working capital does the company have? Is the working capital negative?
5. How much does the company owe that needs to be paid in the short term? Does the company have sufficient assets that can be quickly liquidated to pay short-term dues?
6. How much funds are tied to fixed assets, investments, inventory, trade receivables, and cash? Which assets are the most significant for the company?
7. How much does the company owe for borrowings, leases, purchases, expenses, and taxes? Which liabilities are the most significant for the company?
8. What is the aging schedule of its trade receivables and trade payables? Is the company stretching collections from customers and payments to suppliers?
9. Is the company able to convert capital work-in-progress to fixed assets speedily?
10. Does the company have unusually high levels of some asset or liability?

Balance Sheets are prepared on a specific date, which is often the end of a financial year (or quarter). To understand balance sheets, it is important to broadly understand various key terms, such as asset, liability, equity, financial asset & liability, and current asset & liability. We do so in the next section. For a deeper insight, it is also necessary to understand various assets, liabilities, and equity items on the balance sheet. The discussions on these assets, liabilities, and equity of a non-financial company are in subsequent sections. Finally, we will also understand how to calculate capital employed and working capital in the last section of this chapter.

I. Key Terms

(a) Asset, Liability, and Equity

An asset is a resource that an enterprise owns or controls and from which it expects to receive economic benefits in the future. For example, property, plant, & equipment (PPE), patents, investments, inventory, trade receivables, bank balances, cash, prepaid expenses, etc. are some assets. A company expects to produce goods from its factory, gain a business advantage or earn income from investments, consume the benefits of prepaid expenses, and receive cash from its trade receivable. Assets may arise from either operating or investing activities. For example, PPE, patents, and investments result from investing activities, whereas inventory, trade receivables, and prepaid expenses arise from operating activities. On the Balance Sheet, assets are grouped into current and non-current and further into financial assets and non-financial assets.

By contrast, a liability is a present obligation that must be settled in the future by paying cash or another asset or by conversion into equity shares. For example, borrowings, lease liability, provisions, trade payable, taxes payable, dividend payable, advance from customers, bank overdraft, etc. are some liabilities. An enterprise expects to pay cash to settle taxes due, pay off trade payables, provide goods/services to customers who have paid in advance, and pay off bank overdrafts. Some liabilities can also be settled by conversion into equity shares. For example, a company settles its convertible bonds by issuing its equity shares. Liabilities may arise from either operating, investing, or financing activities. For example, trade payables, expenses payable, and advances from customers arise from operating activities, payables for machinery and software stem from investing activities, whereas borrowings and lease liabilities arise from financing activities. On the Balance Sheet, liabilities are grouped into current and non-current and further into financial and non-financial liabilities.

Equity is the residual interest in the assets of an enterprise after deducting all its liabilities. Thus, equity is the excess of total assets over total liabilities. It is also known by other names, such as net assets, net worth, shareholders' funds, etc. It belongs to the owners of the enterprise. For example, equity share capital, share premium, retained earnings, general reserves, capital reserve, etc. are some equity items.

Table 3.1 Assets, Liabilities, & Equity

Amounts are in ₹ crore	Asian Paints		Avenue Supermarts		Infosys	
Balance as at 31st March	2022	2021	2022	2021	2022	2021
Total Assets	19,908	17,581	15,404	13,646	99,387	93,939
Growth in Assets %	13%		13%		6%	
Total Liabilities	6,559	5,492	1,480	1,341	30,081	22,408
Growth in Liabilities %	19%		10%		34%	
Total Equity	13,349	12,089	13,924	12,305	69,306	71,531
Growth in Equity %	10%		13%		–3%	

From its March 31, 2022, Balance Sheet, we learn that Asian Paints had Total Assets of ₹19,908 crore (13% higher than the year before), Total Liabilities of ₹ 6,559 crore (19% higher than the previous year), and Equity of ₹13,349 crore (10% higher than the last year).[1] Assets are funded two-thirds by equity and one-third by liabilities. Thus, Equity is twice the liabilities. A large amount of equity relative to total liabilities suggests high solvency of Asian Paints.

Avenue Supermarts had ₹15,404 crore in Total Assets and owed ₹1,480 crore, which resulted in shareholder's equity of ₹13,924 crore at the end of the current financial year 2021–22. Compared to the previous year, in the current year, assets grew by 13%, which was funded by a 13% increase in equity and a 10% increase in liability. Assets are funded largely by equity (nine-tenths) and only partially by liabilities (one-tenth). Total Assets being ten times total liabilities indicate that the solvency of Avenue Supermarts is very high.

On 31-3-2022, Infosys had Total Assets of ₹99,387 crore, which was funded by Total Liabilities of ₹30,081 crore and Equity of ₹69,306 crore. The 34% increase in liabilities supported the 6% increase in assets and the 3% decrease in equity. Assets are funded largely by equity (seven-tenths) and partially by liabilities (three-tenths). Thus, the company has enough assets to pay its obligations suggesting high solvency.

[1] Reported amounts (in this and other chapters) have been rounded off to ₹ crore, unless mentioned otherwise. Due to rounding off, the sum of the amounts given in a table/list in this book may differ from those reported by ₹1 crore.

(b) Current and Non-Current Assets

Current assets are assets that are (i) expected to be realized within 12 months after the reporting period, (ii) expected to be consumed, sold, or realized within its operating cycle if it is longer than 12 months, (iii) held primarily for trading, or (iv) cash and cash equivalent unless restricted from being used to pay off liability for at least 12 months after the reporting period.[2] All other assets must be classified as non-current assets. For the purpose of current and non-current classification in 2021–22, Asian Paints and Avenue Supermarts have used twelve months as their normal operating cycle. Infosys did not provide any information about its normal operating cycle in 2021–22 in its notes.

In simple terms, an item of current asset (on a Balance Sheet) is expected to no longer exist within one year from the Balance Sheet date. It will get converted into cash (for example, trade receivable and investments) or another asset (for example, raw material becomes work-in-progress, work-in-progress becomes finished goods, and finished goods are sold on credit, creating trade receivable), exchanged to settle a liability (for example, cash is paid to trade payable), or used up (for example, supplies and prepaid expenses are consumed).

By contrast, non-current assets are expected to remain with the enterprise beyond 12 months after the reporting date. For example, PPE, CWIP, intangible assets, and investments in subsidiaries and joint ventures are some non-current assets.

Table 3.2 Non-Current & Current Assets

Amounts are in ₹ crore	Asian Paints		Avenue Supermarts		Infosys	
Balance as at 31st March	2022	2021	2022	2021	2022	2021
Total Assets	19,908	17,581	15,404	13,646	99,387	93,939
Non-Current	7,160	7,634	12,053	9,686	46,950	45,657
Growth %	–6%		24%		3%	
% of Total Assets	36%	43%	78%	71%	47%	49%
Current	12,748	9,947	3,351	3,961	52,437	48,282
Growth %	28%		–15%		9%	
% of Total Assets	64%	57%	22%	29%	53%	51%

[2] Operating Cycle is the time between obtaining raw material for the production of finished goods and collecting cash from customers. Thus, a manufacturer's operating cycle includes the time the raw material is in inventory until issued to production, the time taken to convert raw material to finished goods, the time between production is complete and sale is made, and the time between the sale and the collection of cash from trade receivables. A retailer's operating cycle is the time between obtaining stock-in-trade and collecting cash from customers; therefore, operating cycle is usually shorter for a retailer than for a manufacturer.

As at 31-3-2022, Asian paints had ₹7,160 crore of non-current assets and ₹12,748 crore of current assets. Current assets increased by 28% compared to the previous year and accounted for about two-thirds of total assets in the current year. Non-current assets declined 6% and represented about one-third of all assets.

Avenue Supermarts had ₹12,053 crore of non-current assets at the end of the current financial year (31-3-2022), which was 24% higher than the previous year. Current assets were ₹3,351 crore, about 15% lower than last year. Non-current and current assets, respectively, accounted for 78% and 22% of total assets as at 31-3-2022.

For Infosys, non-current assets were ₹46,950 crore (47% of total assets) on 31-3-2022, or 3% higher compared to 31-3-2021. Current assets ₹52,437 crore (53% of total assets) were 9% higher compared to the previous year.

(c) Current and Non-Current Liabilities

Current Liabilities are liabilities that are (i) due to be settled within 12 months after the reporting period, (ii) expected to be settled within an operating cycle, if the operating cycle is longer than 12 months (iii) held primarily for trading, or (iv) not deferable beyond 12 months after the reporting date. All other liabilities are classified as non-current liabilities.

In simple terms, an item of current liability (on a Balance Sheet) ceases to exist by the next Balance Sheet date. It will either be settled or become another liability. For example, companies must pay off a trade payable (a liability) within the due date (often a few days or weeks after the invoice date); when they do, the trade payable is no longer a liability. Similarly, for a company that has received an advance (a liability) from a customer for the supply of goods, when it provides the goods to the customer, the company no longer has any obligation to that customer and the liability is no more.

By contrast, non-current liability will be settled by the enterprise beyond 12 months after the reporting date (i.e., it will be after the next Balance Sheet date). For example, debenture, term loans, lease liabilities, and deferred tax liabilities are some non-current liabilities.

Table 3.3 Non-Current & Current Liabilities

Amounts are in ₹ crore	Asian Paints		Avenue Supermarts		Infosys	
Balance as at 31st March	2022	2021	2022	2021	2022	2021
Total Liabilities	6,559	5,492	1,480	1,341	30,081	22,408
Non-Current	912	916	386	269	5,105	4,786
Growth %	0%		43%		7%	
% of Total Liabilities	14%	17%	26%	20%	17%	21%
Current	5,647	4,575	1,094	1,072	24,976	17,622
Growth %	23%		2%		42%	
% of Total Liabilities	86%	83%	74%	80%	83%	79%

For Asian Paints, current liabilities of ₹5,647 crore account for the lion's share (86%) of total liabilities on 31-3-2022. Current liabilities grew 23% from 31-3-2021 to 31-3-2022. Non-current liabilities were ₹912 crore on 31-3-2022, about ₹4 crore lower than on 31-3-2021.

For Avenue Supermarts, too, current liabilities accounted for a large share of total liabilities. On 31-3-2022, current liabilities were ₹1,094 crore (up 2%) and non-current liabilities ₹386 crore (up 43% from a year before).

Infosys also had current liabilities close to four-fifths of total liabilities. On 31-3-2022, the company had ₹24,976 crore of current liabilities (up 42% from the previous year) and ₹5,105 crore of non-current liabilities (up 7% from the year before).

(d) Financial and Non-Financial Assets

Assets are classified into either financial assets or non-financial assets. Financial assets are contractual claims to receive cash or another financial asset. Examples of financial assets are trade receivables, investments, bank balances, cash, etc. Note that these assets get converted into cash: for example, trade receivables pay cash, investments fetch cash, and cash can be withdrawn from or deposited into a bank account.

All other assets (i.e., assets not classified as financial assets) are non-financial assets. Examples of non-financial assets are inventory, PPE, intangible assets (such as software), prepaid expenses, Capital Work-in-Progress (CWIP), capital advances, etc. A non-financial asset is either held for use by the enterprise or expected to yield another non-financial asset. For example, capital advances (advances to procure a PPE) and CWIP will result in PPE. PPE is held for the running of the enterprise or for use in the production of goods. Raw material and work-in-progress (WIP) inventory will be used to produce finished goods. Prepaid expenses are expected to be consumed.

Table 3.4 Summary of Financial and Non-Financial Assets

Amounts are in ₹ crore	Asian Paints		Avenue Supermarts		Infosys	
Balance as at 31st March	2022	2021	2022	2021	2022	2021
Total Assets	19,908	17,581	15,404	13,646	99,387	93,939
- Financial	*8,056*	*7,940*	*2,413*	*3,183*	*67,132*	*64,259*
- Non-Financial	*11,852*	*9,641*	*12,991*	*10463*	*32,255*	*29,680*
Non-Current Assets	7,160	7,634	12,053	9,686	46,950	45,657
- Financial	*1,022*	*1,564*	*1,791*	*1,511*	*23,630*	*22,761*
- Non-Financial	*6,138*	*6,070*	*10,262*	*8,175*	*23,320*	*22,896*
Current Assets	12,748	9,947	3,351	3,961	52,437	48,282
- Financial	*7,034*	*6,376*	*622*	*1,672*	*43,502*	*41,498*
- Non-Financial	*5,714*	*3,571*	*2,729*	*2,289*	*8,935*	*6,784*

* The amounts of Financial and Non-Financial assets are computed from the information on the balance sheet. See the next two tables for the assets that are included under Financial and Non-Financial Assets.

Table 3.5 List of Financial Assets (discussed later in the chapter)

Amounts are in ₹ crore	Asian Paints		Avenue Supermarts		Infosys	
Balance as at 31st March	2022	2021	2022	2021	2022	2021
Financial Assets (Non-Current):						
Investments	551	985	532	402	22,869	22,118
Loans	Nil	Nil	Nil	Nil	34	30
Other Financial Assets	471	579	1,259	1,109	727	613
Total Fin. Assets (Non-Current)	1,022	1,564	1,791	1,511	23,630	22,761
Financial Assets (Current):						
Trade Receivables	2,916	1,810	231	72	18,966	16,394
Investments	2,164	3,179	Nil	Nil	5,467	2,037
Cash & Cash Equivalents	276	113	83	181	12,270	17,612
Other Bank Balance	33	22	200	1,251	*	*
Loans	Nil	Nil	Nil	Nil	219	229
Other Financial Assets	1,645	1,252	107	168	6,580	5,226
Total Financial Assets (Current)	*7,034*	*6,376*	*622*	*1,672*	*43,502*	*41,498*
Total Financial Assets	*8,056*	*7,940*	2,413	3,183	67,132	64,259
% of Total Assets	*40%*	*45%*	*16%*	*23%*	*68%*	*68%*

Totals may differ due to rounding off. * Infosys include Other Bank Balance in Cash & Cash Equivalents.

Table 3.6 List of Non-Financial Assets (discussed later in the chapter)

Amounts are in ₹ crore	**Asian Paints**		**Avenue Supermarts**		**Infosys**	
Balance as at 31st March	2022	2021	2022	2021	2022	2021
Non-Fin. Assets (Non-Current):						
Property, Plant, & Equipment	3,690	3,972	7,577	5,773	11,384	10,930
Capital Work-in-Progress	225	119	1,073	1,006	411	906
Right-Of-Use Assets	786	715	1,146	847	3,311	3,435
Investment Properties	Nil	Nil	96	91	Nil	Nil
Goodwill	35	35	Nil	Nil	211	167
Other Intangible Assets	43	42	10	9	32	67
Investment in Subsidiaries	1,096	1,016	*	*	*	*
Deferred Tax Assets (net)	Nil	Nil	Nil	Nil	970	955
Income Tax Assets (net)	145	133	1	1	5,585	5,287
Other Non-Current Assets	120	38	359	447	1,416	1,149
Total Non-Financial Assets (Non-Current)	*6,138*	*6,070*	*10,262*	*8,175*	*23,320*	*22,896*
Non-Financial Assets (Current):						
Inventories	5,278	3,125	2,587	2,167	Nil	Nil
Other Current Assets	436	446	142	122	8,935	6,784
Total Non-Financial Assets (Current)	*5,714*	*3,571*	*2,729*	*2,289*	*8,935*	*6,784*
Total Non-Financial Assets	*11,852*	*9,641*	*12,991*	*10463*	*32,255*	*29,680*
% of Total Assets	*60%*	*55%*	*84%*	*77%*	*32%*	*32%*

Totals may differ due to rounding off. * Avenue Supermarts and Infosys included Investment in Subsidiaries as Financial Assets under the head Investments under Non-Current Assets.

As at 31-3-2022, Asian Paints had total financial assets worth ₹8,056 crore (non-current ₹1,022 crore and current ₹7,034 crore), representing about 40% of total assets, and non-financial assets ₹11,852 crore (non-current ₹6,138 crore, current ₹5,714 crore), representing 60% of total asset. While financial assets were the same compared to a year before, non-financial assets were about 23% higher than that at the end of the previous year.

As at 31-3-2022, Avenue Supermarts had ₹2,413 crore of total financial assets (down about 25% from the last year) and ₹10,262 crore of non-financial assets (up about 25% from the last year).

By contrast, Infosys had ₹67,132 crore of total financial assets, more than twice of ₹32,255 crore of non-financial assets as at 31-3-2022. Two-thirds of financial assets are current assets, whereas three-fourths of non-financial assets are non-current assets.

(e) Financial and Non-Financial Liabilities

Liabilities are classified into either financial or non-financial liabilities. Financial liabilities must be settled in cash or by transferring a financial instrument (such as bank cheques). For example, trade payable, expense payable, taxes payable, borrowings, lease liabilities, etc. are financial liabilities. By contrast, non-financial liabilities must be settled either by transferring an asset other than cash (for example, by delivering goods or services) or will be converted into a financial liability before being settled in cash. For example, advances received from customers are settled by delivering goods or services. Provisions must get converted into a financial liability and then settled in cash (for example, a provision for gratuity becomes gratuity payable after an employee has retired/ resigned, and only then will the amount be paid in cash).

Table 3.7 Summary of Financial & Non-Financial Liabilities

Amounts are in ₹ crore	Asian Paints		Avenue Supermarts		Infosys	
Balance as at 31st March	2022	2021	2022	2021	2022	2021
Total Liabilities	6,559	5,492	1,480	1,341	30,081	22,408
- Financial	*5,737*	*4,739*	*1,218*	*1,117*	*18,400*	*14,034*
- Non-Financial	*822*	*752*	*262*	*224*	*11,681*	*8,374*
Non-Current	912	916	386	269	5,105	4,786
- Financial	*536*	*484*	*321*	*217*	*3,904*	*3,626*
- Non-Financial	*376*	*432*	*65*	*52*	*1,201*	*1,160*
Current Liabilities	5,647	4,575	1,094	1,072	24,976	17,622
- Financial	*5,201*	*4,255*	*897*	*900*	*14,496*	*10,408*
- Non-Financial	*446*	*320*	*197*	*172*	*10,480*	*7,214*

* The amounts of Financial & Non-Financial liabilities are computed from the information on the balance sheet. See the next two tables for the liabilities that are included under Financial and Non-Financial Liabilities.

Table 3.8 List of Financial Liabilities (discussed later in the chapter)

Amounts are in ₹ crore	**Asian Paints**		**Avenue Supermarts**		**Infosys**	
Balance as at 31st March	2022	2021	2022	2021	2022	2021
Fin. Liabilities (Non-Current):						
Borrowings	16	14	Nil	Nil	Nil	Nil
Lease Liabilities	519	469	320	217	3,228	3,367
Other Financial Liabilities	1	1	*	*	676	259
Total Financial Liabilities (Non-Current)	*536*	*484*	*321*	*217*	*3,904*	*3,626*
Financial Liabilities (Current):						
Borrowings	Nil	8	Nil	Nil	Nil	Nil
Lease Liabilities	179	157	96	79	558	487
Trade Payable	3,497	2,814	531	566	2,669	1,562
Other Financial Liabilities	1,525	1,277	270	255	11,269	8,359
Total Financial Liabilities (Current)	*5,201*	*4,255*	*897*	*900*	*14,496*	*10,408*
Total Financial Liabilities	*5,737*	*4,739*	*1,218*	*1,117*	*18,400*	*14,034*
% of Total Liabilities	*87%*	*86%*	*82%*	*83%*	*61%*	*63%*

Totals may differ due to rounding off. * When rounded off, the amount is 0.

Table 3.9 List of Non-Financial Liabilities (discussed later in the chapter)

Amounts are in ₹ crore	**Asian Paints**		**Avenue Supermarts**		**Infosys**	
Balance as at 31st March	2022	2021	2022	2021	2022	2021
Non-Fin. Liabilities (Non-Current):						
Provisions	168	164	Nil	Nil	Nil	Nil
Deferred Tax Liabilities (net)	205	265	65	52	841	511
Other Non-Current Liabilities	2	3	Nil	Nil	360	649
Total Non-Financial Liabilities (Non-Current)	*376*	*432*	*65*	*52*	*1,201*	*1,160*
Non-Financial Liabilities (Current):						
Provisions	38	58	33	22	920	661
Income Tax Liabilities (net)	101	88	111	113	2,179	1,737
Other Current Liabilities	307	174	52	38	7,381	4,816
Total Non-Financial Liabilities (Current)	*446*	*320*	*197*	*172*	*10,480*	*7,214*
Total Non-Financial Liabilities	*822*	*752*	*262*	*224*	*11,681*	*8,374*
% of Total Liabilities	*13%*	*14%*	*18%*	*17%*	*39%*	*37%*

Totals may differ due to rounding off.

As at 31-3-2022, Asian Paints had total financial liabilities worth ₹5,737 crore (non-current ₹536 crore and current ₹5,201 crore), representing about 85% of total liabilities, and non-financial liabilities ₹822 crore (non-current ₹376, current ₹446 crore), representing about 15% of total liabilities. While financial liabilities increased 21% compared to a year before, non-financial liabilities were 9% higher.

As of 31-3-2022, Avenue Supermarts had ₹1,218 crore of financial liabilities (up about 9% from last year) and ₹262 crore of non-financial ones (up about 20% from the year before).

By contrast, Infosys had a much higher amount of total financial liabilities ₹18,400 crore (40% year-on-year increase) and ₹11,681 crore in non-financial liabilities (39% increase) on 31-3-2022. Four-fifths of financial liabilities and nine-tenths of non-financial liabilities are current liabilities.

II. Assets

In this section, we will discuss several types of assets found on balance sheets: property, plant, & equipment, capital work-in-progress, right-of-use assets, investment properties, goodwill, other intangible assets, intangible assets under development, deferred tax assets, current tax assets, investments, inventories, trade receivables, loans, cash & cash equivalents, other bank balances, other financial assets, and other assets. While the discussion is for non-finance companies, this would also apply to financial firms since most of these assets are also possessed by banks and other financial firms.

(a) Property, Plant, & Equipment (PPE)

PPEs are tangible fixed assets.[3] They are expected to be used during more than one financial period either in the production or supply of goods or services, in the selling and distribution of goods or services, in the administration of the enterprise, or for rentals to others. PPE also includes bearer plants (see Appendix for a brief discussion).

On the balance sheet, PPE is reported at its net carrying amount (or net block). Net Block is the gross carrying amount (or gross block) less Accumulated

[3] Fixed assets are assets held for long-term use in the business or for rentals to others. They cannot be converted quickly into cash. For example, land, building, machinery, software, patents, etc. The term 'fixed asset' is no longer found on the balance sheet. However, PPE, Capital Work-In-Progress (CWIP), Right-Of-Use (ROU) assets, Investment Properties, Intangible Assets (including goodwill), and Intangible assets under development, are fixed assets that appear on reported Balance Sheets.

Depreciation and Accumulated Impairment.[4] As per Ind AS 16 (Property, Plant, and Equipment), the Gross Block is the historical cost when an enterprise elects to use the cost model for the reporting of PPE, which most companies do. The historical cost includes (i) the construction cost (for self-constructed PPE) or purchase price (for acquired PPE) excluding discounts, rebates, and refundable duties and taxes, (ii) the directly attributable cost of making the PPE ready for the intended use, (iii) borrowing cost if the PPE takes a substantial amount of time to get ready for its intended use, and (iv) the initial estimate of retirement obligation (including the cost of decommissioning and safe disposal of the PPE, restoration of the site, and similar liabilities). Subsequently, if a company incurs an expenditure that increases the capacity or useful life of the PPE beyond the initially assessed level, then the expenditure is also capitalized (i.e., included in the historical cost of the PPE).

When an item of PPE is retired for disposal, we remove its gross block, accumulated depreciation, and any accumulated impairment. This causes the total PPE to decrease by the net block of the item retired. Some net proceeds from the disposal may be generated. If the net proceeds are more than the netblock, the difference is the gain on disposal (a non-operating income); otherwise, there is a loss on disposal (a non-operating loss).

Table 3.10 Property, Plant, & Equipment

Amounts are in ₹ crore	**Asian Paints**		**Avenue Supermarts**		**Infosys**	
Balance as at 31st March	2022	2021	2022	2021	2022	2021
Gross PPE	6,249	6,043	8,932	6,826	26,018	24,593
Less Accumulated Depreciation	–2,559	–2,071	–1,355	–1,054	–14,634	–13,663
Net PPE	*3,690*	*3,972*	*7,577*	*5,773*	*11,384*	*10,930*

In its 2022 Balance Sheet, Asian Paints reported PPE of ₹3,690 crore and provided the breakup in note 2A. This note reveals gross block of PPE of ₹6,249 crore and accumulated depreciation of ₹2,559 crore at the end of the financial year. During the year 2021–22, the company invested ₹220 crores in PPE, which was much lower than ₹500 crore depreciation charged, causing a decline in the net carrying amount of PPE. The note also shows the details of various types of PPE: land, building, plant & machinery, furniture and fittings, vehicles, office equipment, information technology hardware, and leasehold improvements. Of these, Plant & Equipment had the highest net carrying amount ₹2,076 crore,

[4] For Impairment Loss, see the Appendix at the end of this chapter. For Depreciation & Amortization, see the appendix at the end of the previous chapter.

Building was the second highest at ₹1,095 crore and, together, they account for 86% of the net block of PPE.

Avenue Supermarts reported net PPE of ₹7,577 crore on its Balance Sheet as at 31-3-2022. On this date, the company had a gross block of ₹8,932 crore, which was about 30% higher compared to a year before. The company invested ₹2,072 crore in new PPE, particularly ₹801 crore in land and ₹910 crore in buildings during the financial year 2021–22.

Infosys had gross PPE of ₹26,018 crore, accumulated depreciation of ₹14,634 crore, and net PPE ₹11,384 crore on 31-3-2022. During the year, the company added ₹2,381 crore of new PPE, including ₹1,281 crore of new computer equipment and ₹569 crore of new buildings. It also discarded ₹956 crore of PPE (including ₹572 crore of computer equipment and ₹331 crore of plant and machinery) during 2021–22. As per note 2.1, the net block of ₹11,384 crore comprises Freehold Land ₹1,429 crore, Buildings ₹6,281 crore, Plant & Machinery ₹560 crore, Office Equipment ₹257 crore, Computer Equipment ₹2,076 crore, Furniture & Fixtures ₹456 crore, Leasehold Improvements ₹318 crore, and Vehicles ₹7 crore.

(b) Capital Work-in-Progress

Companies must replace their PPE. Some PPEs are ready for its intended use when purchased (for example, a car or a laptop), whereas others need time for construction or installation. CWIP represents the cost of a PPE that is not yet ready for its intended use (as on the Balance Sheet date). Once the PPE becomes ready, the cost is deducted from CWIP and added to PPE.

Table 3.11 Capital Work-in-Progress

Amounts are in ₹ crore	Asian Paints		Avenue Supermarts		Infosys	
Balance as at 31st March	2022	2021	2022	2021	2022	2021
Capital Work-in-Progress	*225*	*119*	*1,073*	*1,006*	*411*	*906*

Asian Paints discloses ₹225 crore as CWIP on its 2022 Balance Sheet. In note 3, it discloses that ₹215 crore is for a period of less than 1 year. In its 2022 balance sheet, Avenue Supermarts reported CWIP of ₹1073 crore. The company also provides an aging schedule in note 2, which shows that ₹744 crore is for projects started within 1 year and ₹297 crore for projects started between 1 and 2 years back. On March 31, 2022, Infosys had CWIP of ₹411 crore, which includes ₹267 crore for a period of less than 1 year.

(c) Right of Use (ROU) Assets

ROU assets are assets taken on lease. Therefore, an entity does not own ROU assets but has control over their use. If a lease duration is more than 12 months and the leased asset is not of low value, the leased asset must be reported as an ROU asset.[5] At the commencement of such leases, the entity must record an ROU asset and a Lease Liability. The amount capitalized for an ROU asset includes (i) the initial direct cost incurred for taking up the lease, (ii) the down payment made on the lease, (iii) the present value of the lease rentals for the non-cancellable period plus any additional period over which the lease is expected to be extended, and (iv) asset retirement obligation (if any). Any lease incentives are deducted from the amount capitalized. ROU assets are depreciated and reported on the balance sheet at their net carrying amount. When a lease is terminated, its net carrying amount is removed and deducted from ROU assets.

Table 3.12 Right of Use Assets

Amounts are in ₹ crore	Asian Paints		Avenue Supermarts		Infosys	
Balance as at 31st March	2022	2021	2022	2021	2022	2021
Right of Use Assets (ROU)	*786*	*715*	*1,146*	*847*	*3,311*	*3,435*

Asian Paints had ROU assets of ₹786 crore as on March 31, 2022. In note 2B, during the year, the company reported total additions of ₹305 crore to ROU assets, deletions of ₹(34) crore, and depreciation of ₹(200) crore. Its ROU assets were categorized into leasehold land, buildings, and vehicles, and the building category accounted for 81% of ROU assets at the 2021–22 year-end.

Avenue Supermarts had ROU assets of ₹1,146 crore on its 2022 Balance Sheet. During the year, additions to ROU assets were ₹454 crore and depreciation ₹(93) crore, as note 3 discloses. Its ROU assets included land, buildings, and plant & equipment. Land accounted for 68% of ROU assets.

Infosys' 2022 Balance Sheet had ROU assets of ₹3,311 crore. In note 2.13, Infosys reports that the additions to ROU assets were ₹374 crore, deletions ₹(18) crore, and depreciation ₹(480) crore during 2021–22. It also reported that these figures are for three categories of ROU assets: land, buildings, and computers. Buildings accounted for 79% of the ROU assets on March 31, 2022.

[5] Short-term leases (12 months or less) and low-value leases are *not* included under ROU assets. Unlike long-term leases of high-valued assets that appear on the balance sheet as ROU assets, short-term leases and low-value leases are off-balance sheet.

(d) Investment Properties

Investment properties are land and building that are currently not in use by a company for the production or supply of goods and services or for administrative purposes. These are held for earning rental income from operating leases, for capital appreciation, or for future use. Investment properties also include buildings under construction for use as an investment property. These properties may be owned by the company or taken on a long-term lease.

As on March 31, 2022, Asian Paints and Infosys did not report Investment Properties on their balance sheet, whereas Avenue Supermarts did. In note 4, Avenue Supermarts reports that its investment properties have a historical cost of ₹111 crore, accumulated depreciation of ₹15 crore, net carrying amount of ₹96 crore, and fair value of ₹425 crore. The company also disclosed that during the year 2021–22, these properties earned a gross rental income of ₹16.5 crore; the company incurred direct operating expenses ₹0.9 crore and depreciation ₹3.7 crore on these properties. Thus, the company generated an income (net of expenses) of ₹11.9 crore on these properties, an amount less than 3% (= 11.9 ÷ 425) of their fair value.

Table 3.13 Investment Properties

Amounts are in ₹ crore	Asian Paints		Avenue Supermarts		Infosys	
Balance as at 31st March	2022	2021	2022	2021	2022	2021
Investment Properties Gross	Nil	Nil	111	103	Nil	Nil
Less Accumulated Depreciation	Nil	Nil	−15	−11	Nil	Nil
Investment Properties, *Net*	*Nil*	*Nil*	*96*	*91*	*Nil*	*Nil*

(e) Goodwill

Goodwill arises from business combinations, i.e., mergers and acquisitions. When a company acquires another entity (or its division), the acquirer pays a consideration for all assets taken over (less all liabilities taken over). While most assets are individually identified and separately recognized and valued, a few assets may not be identifiable individually and, hence, not separately recognized. For example, an efficient supply chain network, loyal customers, productive employees, and conducive organizational culture. These assets are expected to fetch future economic benefits to the company. Goodwill represents the total value of those assets.

Goodwill = Acquisition Price – (Value assigned to all assets separately recognized – Value of all liabilities taken over)

Goodwill is an intangible asset as it does not have a physical existence. Unlike other intangible assets, goodwill is not amortized. However, like other intangible assets, it is tested for impairment. Goodwill can decrease only due to recognition of impairment loss. In a separate note, companies report various assumptions used for testing of impairment of goodwill. An increase in goodwill signals a business combination event, whereas a decline signals an impairment of goodwill. For most companies in India, goodwill is either not there on the Balance Sheet or has a very small amount relative to other assets. This is because business combinations are not as common or as large in India as they are in the developed countries.

Table 3.14 Goodwill

Amounts are in ₹ crore	Asian Paints		Avenue Supermarts		Infosys	
Balance as at 31st March	2022	2021	2022	2021	2022	2021
Goodwill	*35*	*35*	*Nil*	*Nil*	*211*	*167*

Avenue Supermarts did not have any goodwill on its 2022 and 2021 Balance Sheets, indicating no business combination wherein the amount paid was over the value of all assets & liabilities individually identified and separately recognized.

Asian Paints had Goodwill of ₹35 crore as on March 31, 2022, as well as on March 31, 2021. Thus, there was no change in the amount of goodwill on its balance sheet – neither any addition nor any impairment. This goodwill pertained to the acquisition of its Bath Fittings Business.

Infosys had Goodwill of ₹211 crore on March 31, 2022, and ₹167 crore on March 31, 2021. The increase in goodwill ₹44 crore was on account of taking over the business of its subsidiary Brilliant Basics during the financial year 2021–22 (see page 212, note 2.5.1 in 2022 Annual Report of Infosys). The amount of goodwill on the Balance Sheet is less than 1% of the total assets of Infosys (₹99,387 crore), as it is for Asian Paints (₹19,908 crore).

(f) Other Intangible Assets

Other Intangible Assets (OIA) are intangible assets other than goodwill. Computer software, trademark, patents, customer list, mining rights, carbon emission rights, etc. are some examples of OIA, which can be found in a separate note. For most companies in India (including Asian Paints, Avenue Supermarts, and Infosys), computer software is usually the biggest item of other intangible assets. However, often, the amounts are too small to be material.

Table 3.15 Other Intangible Assets

Amounts are in ₹ crore	Asian Paints		Avenue Supermarts		Infosys	
Balance as at 31st March	2022	2021	2022	2021	2022	2021
Gross Other Intangible Assets	219	196	29	25	219	219
Less Accumulated Amortization	–176	–154	–19	–16	–187	–152
Other Intangible Assets, Net	*43*	*42*	*10*	*9*	*32*	*67*

Asian Paints had a net OIA of ₹43 crore (= ₹219 crore less ₹176 crore), whereas Avenue Supermarts reported a net OIA of ₹10 crore (=cost ₹29 crore less accumulated amortization ₹19 crore). These amounts are too small to be material, given the total assets of these companies. As at March 31, 2022, Infosys reported ₹32 crore as the net carrying amount of OIA, which was obtained as gross carrying amount (or historical cost) ₹219 crore less ₹187 crore accumulated amortization.

(g) Intangibles under Development

Intangibles under Development (IUD) are the amounts incurred during the development phase of a product or process, after the completion of the research phase. They remain classified as intangible assets under development until the development is complete. None of the three companies, Asian Paints, Avenue Supermarts, and Infosys reported any IUD on their Balance Sheet. Hindalco reported IUD of ₹8 crore on 31-3-2022 (₹122 crore on 31-3-2021), a small amount relative to its total assets.

(h) Investments

Investments are financial assets and are found under non-current and current assets on the Balance Sheet and their details are provided in notes. Any interest, dividend, and rental incomes and capital gains from investments are non-operating income and are included in Other Income on the Income Statement.

Companies make investments in subsidiaries, associates, and joint ventures primarily for strategic and business advantage. These investments are usually non-current assets as they are held for a long period. Such investments can be in equity or debt instruments. Investments in equity instruments of subsidiaries and associates are accounted at cost following Ind AS 27 (Separate Financial Statements) and carried at their cost less impairment loss (if any).

Investments in debt instruments of subsidiaries and associates are carried at amortized cost (so that the carrying amount on the maturity date of these instruments converges to the amount receivable on these instruments). Amortized cost is obtained using the effective interest method wherein future cash receipts are discounted using the effective interest rate (not the stated interest rate on those securities).[6]

Companies may make other investments (i.e., investment in instruments of entities other than subsidiaries, associates, and joint ventures) to earn an income on surplus funds or for capital gains.[7] These investments are either non-current or current, depending upon the duration over which they are expected to be held. Accordingly, such investments can be (i) held to maturity, (ii) available for sale, or (iii) held for trading.

Held-to-maturity investments are those on which a company expects to collect contractual cash flows on all specific dates when these cash flows become receivable. These investments are carried at amortized cost (explained above).

Held-for-trading investments are those a company expects to sell. Such investments are carried at their fair value, and any increase/decrease in their value is included in Other Income on the income statement, i.e., such change in value is a non-operating gain or loss for the year. For this reason, we say these investments are measured at FVTPL (Fair Value Through Profit & Loss).

Available-for-sale investments are those a company expects to not only collect contractual cash flows on some or all specific dates but also sell the investments, i.e., the company could do either. Investments classified as available for sale are also carried at their fair value, but any increase/decrease in their value is included in Other Comprehensive Income without affecting the net profit of the year. Thus, these investments are measured at FVTOCI (Fair Value Through Other Comprehensive Income).

---

[6] For example, a 10-year zero coupon bond, having a nominal value of ₹1,000, was issued at a price of ₹386 six years ago (and therefore will mature in four years). Suppose, today, it has an effective interest rate (or yield to maturity) of 10%. Discounting ₹1000 cash inflow four years from now yields an amortized cost of ₹683. This investment in debt instrument will appear at ₹683 on the balance sheet.

[7] The return on these investments is usually much lower than what a company earns from the funds deployed in its own business. Therefore, these investments usually lower the overall rate of return generated by a company.

Table 3.16 Investments

Amounts are in ₹ crore	Asian Paints		Avenue Supermarts		Infosys	
Balance as at 31st March	2022	2021	2022	2021	2022	2021
Investment In Subsidiaries, ...*	1,096	1,016	*	*	*	*
Non-Current Investments	551	985	532	402	22,869	22,118
Current Investments	2,164	3,179	Nil	Nil	5,467	2,037
Total	*3,821*	*5,180*	*532*	*402*	*28,336*	*24,155*

* Asian Paints reported Investment in Subsidiaries and Associates as a separate line item under Non-Current Assets (but not under Financial Assets) on its balance sheet. By contrast, Avenue Supermarts and Infosys included the amount in Investments within Financial Non-Current Assets; thus, for these two companies, Investments (within Financial Non-Current Assets) include investments in subsidiaries, associates, and joint ventures. Avenue Supermarts' entire non-current investment is in its subsidiaries, whereas Infosys' ₹10,379 crore were investments in its subsidiaries.

Asian Paints reported investments in subsidiaries and associates ₹1,096 crore (included under non-current assets but *not* under financial assets), non-current investments (included under financial assets) ₹551 crore, and current investments (included under financial assets) ₹2,164 crore. Thus, Asian Paints had total investments of ₹3,811 crore as at 31-03-2022. By contrast, Avenue Supermarts had ₹532 crore investments (at cost) in subsidiaries (under non-current financial assets) and did not have any other investments as at March 31, 2022.

As per note 2.5, on March 31, 2022, Infosys held investments of ₹28,336 crore, of which non-current investments are ₹22,869 crore and current investments are ₹5,467 crore. ₹10,379 crore were investments in subsidiaries (₹9,061 crore in equity shares and ₹1,318 crore in redeemable preference shares) carried at cost. It did not have any investment in debt securities of subsidiaries (carried at amortized cost) at the end of this period, but it did have those at the end of the previous financial year. Investments in tax-free bonds and government bonds were carried at amortized cost (totalling ₹2,114 crore: non-current ₹1,901 crore, current ₹213 crore). Investments in equity and preference shares, non-convertible debentures, government securities, and certificates of deposit were measured at FVTOCI (totalling ₹14,423 crore), whereas investments in liquid mutual funds, convertible debentures, and others were measured at FVTPL (totalling ₹1,420 crore).

(i) Inventories

Inventories comprise raw materials, components, packing materials, work-in-progress (WIP), finished goods (FG), stocks-in-trade (SIT), stores, supplies, fuels, etc. A manufacturer uses raw materials, components, and packing materials to produce finished goods for sale. Work-in-progress is the intermediate stage between raw materials and finished goods. A retailer/trader buys stock-in-trade for resale. A service provider may not have any inventory. Inventories are expected to be consumed or sold within an operating cycle; they are included under current assets on a Balance Sheet.

Inventories are carried at cost or net realizable value, whichever is lower. Valuing inventory at cost or net realizable value, whichever is lower, is an example of the application of the conservatism principle (discussed in Chapter 1). However, if finished goods are expected to be sold at a profit, raw materials, components, and other items held to produce finished goods are always carried at cost. Net realizable value is the estimated selling price less the estimated cost to complete (in case of work-in-progress) and the estimated cost to sell. For raw materials, components, and other items used in production, the net realizable value is their replacement cost.

Table 3.17 Inventories

Amounts are in ₹ crore	**Asian Paints**		**Avenue Supermarts**		**Infosys**	
Balance as at 31st March	2022	2021	2022	2021	2022	2021
Finished Goods	2,262	1,407	Nil	Nil	Nil	Nil
Stock-in-Trade	658	360	2,587	2,167	Nil	Nil
Raw Materials	1,944	1,038	Nil	Nil	Nil	Nil
Packing Materials	85	69	Nil	Nil	Nil	Nil
Work-in-Progress	177	121	Nil	Nil	Nil	Nil
Stores, Spares, ...	151	130	Nil	Nil	Nil	Nil
Total Inventories	*5,278*	*3,125*	*2,587*	*2,167*	*Nil*	*Nil*

Inventories represented the biggest item among assets on Asian Paints' balance sheet as at March 31, 2022. Total Inventories of ₹5,278 crore is comprised of Finished Goods ₹2,262 crore, Raw materials ₹1,944 crore, Stock-in-trade ₹658 crore, Work-in-Progress ₹177 crore, Stores, Spares, & Consumables ₹151 crore, and Packing Material ₹85 crore. Being a retailer, Avenue Supermarts had only stock-in-trade inventories of ₹2,587 crore as on 31-3-2022. Infosys did not have any inventories on its 2022 balance sheet.

(j) Trade Receivables

Trade receivables are the amount due (from customers) arising from credit sales in the ordinary course of business. On the balance sheet, trade receivables are reported net of allowances for expected credit loss (ECL). They are usually reported under current assets. Within financial assets, they could also be reported under non-current financial assets when some amount is expected to be received after the next balance sheet date.

On the balance sheet date, gross trade receivables are divided into considered good and considered doubtful. An allowance for doubtful debt (expected credit loss) is created out of profits for receivables considered doubtful. This allowance has the same amount as that of doubtful receivables. An increase in this allowance is included under Other Expense; any decrease is also included but with a negative sign, thereby decreasing Other Expense. When we deduct allowance for doubtful debt from gross trade receivables, we are left with good receivables.

Receivables that are now considered good may turn doubtful in the future. For these receivables, a company assesses lifetime ECL based on its experience (i.e., historically observed default rates over the expected life of trade receivables) and future expectations. Lifetime ECL is the credit loss that may arise from all possible default events over the expected life of a financial asset such as trade receivable. Allowance for ECL (provision for doubtful debts) is included as Other Expense. By contrast, reversal of ECL is an income and is included with a negative sign under Other Expense (thus, it decreases Other Expense).

Table 3.18 Trade Receivables

Amounts are in ₹ crore	Asian Paints		Avenue Supermarts		Infosys	
Balance as at 31st March	2022	2021	2022	2021	2022	2021
Gross Trade Receivable	3,010	1,868	231	72	19,539	16,937
Allowance for Doubtful Debt	–94	–58	Nil	Nil	–85	–120
Allowance for ECL	Nil	Nil	Nil	Nil	–488	–423
Trade Receivable, Net	*2,916*	*1,810*	*231*	*72*	*18,966*	*16,394*

On its 2022 Balance Sheet, Asian Paints reported trade receivables of ₹2,916 crore (about 12% of its Sales of ₹25,003 crore). Trade receivables are the third largest asset on its balance sheet. In note 10, Asian Paints also reveals that from its gross receivables of ₹3,010 crore (considered good ₹2,916 crore and considered doubtful ₹94 crore), it deducted allowance for doubtful debt ₹94 crore. Note 10 also provides an aging schedule for trade receivables. The note shows that for trade receivables considered good, ₹2,739 crore amount is not due (i.e., the due date is after March 31, 2022), ₹148 crore is overdue for less than 6 months (from the due date), and ₹30 crore is overdue for 6 to 12 months. It also shows the age-wise amounts for doubtful receivables.

Avenue Supermarts, being a retailer, has a modest amount of ₹231 crore trade receivables on 31-03-2022. From note 10, we learn that the entire trade receivables are good and due for less than 6 months. Of these, ₹164 crore (₹29 crore last year) is due from its subsidiary, Avenue E-Commerce Ltd., in which it holds 99.85% ownership interest (as per note 31).

Infosys reported trade receivables of ₹18,966 crore as on 31-3-2022 (about 18% of its Sales of about ₹105,00 crore). Note 2.8 reveals that gross receivable is ₹19,539 crore: considered good ₹19,454 crore and considered doubtful ₹85 crore. Infosys has deducted ₹85 crore as allowance for impaired receivables and ₹488 crore as allowance for ECL. It has not written off the impaired receivables, as it still wants to follow up with customers. Write-off would remove the receivables from the books of accounts. Of the receivables considered good, ₹14,555 crore is not due, ₹4,703 crore is overdue for less than 6 months, ₹133 crore overdue for 6 to 12 months, and the rest is overdue for more than 1 year.

(k) Loans

Loans are financial assets. A loan represents an amount that an entity (lender) has advanced to another (borrower) for a specific duration. On a lender's balance sheet, a loan is an asset. Lenders earn interest income on loans given. Companies may give loans and advances to employees, associates, subsidiaries, joint ventures, associates, and other entities for a long or short duration. Thus, loans may be either non-current or current, and they may appear as a separate line item on the balance sheet or may be included under Other Financial Assets.

Table 3.19 Loans

Amounts are in ₹ crore	Asian Paints		Avenue Supermarts		Infosys	
Balance as at 31st March	2022	2021	2022	2021	2022	2021
Loans - Non-Current	Nil	Nil	Nil	Nil	34	30
Loans - Current	Nil	Nil	Nil	Nil	219	229

Asian Paints and Avenue Supermarts did not have any loan (assets) on their 2022 balance sheets. By contrast, Infosys reported loans to employees, ₹34 crore (non-current) and ₹219 crore (current), on its 2022 balance sheet.

(l) Cash, Cash Equivalents, and Other Bank Balances

Cash is the most liquid asset. Eventually, profits must be realized in cash. It is cash that a company must use to replace PPE, build factories/stores/service centres, repay debt, and pay dividends. Adequate cash provides liquidity, solvency, and financial flexibility to a company.

Cash comprises currency notes, coins, cheques, and demand drafts with the company and amounts in current, overdraft, and cash credit accounts with banks. While overdraft account balances are generally negative, cash credit account balances can be either positive or negative. A negative balance implies the company owes the amount and, therefore, the item is not an asset but a liability even though it is included with assets. The amounts owed for overdraft and cash credit are repayable on demand (i.e., not for a fixed tenure) and hence deducted from C&CE. The balance in these two types of accounts may fluctuate from negative to positive and vice versa.

Cash equivalents are short-term, highly liquid investments that are subject to an insignificant risk of changes in value and can be easily converted into known amounts of cash. Here, short-term refers to initial maturity of 3 months or less. Examples of cash equivalents are deposits (having initial maturity of 3 months) with banks and financial institutions. A company keeps cash equivalents as part of its cash management system to meet short-term cash requirements, and not for investment or any other purpose.

Other Bank Balances (OBB) refers to amounts lying in a bank but has been excluded from cash and cash equivalents. The three most common items included in OBB are (i) fixed deposits having initial maturity of more than 3 months (thus they are not cash equivalents), (ii) balances earmarked for specific purposes (for example, unclaimed dividends and corporate social responsibility), and (iii) margin money deposited in a bank account and held as a lien by the bank against bank guarantees given on behalf of the company (thus, this amount is blocked from use).

Often, companies report Cash and Cash Equivalents (C&CE) as a single item on the balance sheet (under current assets, financial assets). This is also useful for the Cash Flow Statement that reports inflows and outflows of C&CE. OBB is usually reported under current assets, but its constituents can also be found under non-current assets.

Table 3.20 Cash & Cash Equivalents and Other Bank Balances

Amounts are in ₹ crore	Asian Paints		Avenue Supermarts		Infosys	
Balance as at 31st March	2022	2021	2022	2021	2022	2021
Cash and Cash Equivalent	276	113	83	181	12,270	17,612
Other Balances with Bank	33	22	201	1,251	*	*

* Infosys included OBB within C&CE.

As of 31-3-2022, Asian Paints reported on its Balance Sheet ₹276 crore of C&CE and ₹33 crore of OBB. From note 11(A), we find that C&CE is comprised of cash on hand ₹0.03 crore, cheques & drafts on hand ₹47 crore, current account balances with banks ₹221 crore, and cash credit account balance with a bank ₹8 crore. These items are components of cash. Thus, there are no cash equivalents in its C&CE. From note 11(B), we learn that OBB includes earmarked amounts for unclaimed dividends, fractional bonus shares, and corporate social responsibility.

On its 31-03-2022 balance sheet, Avenue Supermarts disclosed C&CE of ₹83 crore (made up of cash on hand and current account bank balances as per note 11) and OBB of ₹201 crore (made up of fixed deposits and margin money for bank guarantees as per note 12).

By contrast, Infosys appears to have included an item of OBB with C&CE on its 2022 balance sheet, with adequate disclosure. From note 2.9, we learn that Infosys' C&CE of ₹12,270 crore comprised ₹9,375 crore in balances with banks in current and time deposit accounts and ₹2,895 crore in time deposits with financial institutions. The restricted cash and bank balances included under C&CE included restricted balances of ₹60 crore for margin money deposits against guarantees. The total C&CE amount is quite large and represents about 12% of total assets (₹99,387 crore). Thus, Infosys is highly liquid, giving its creditors great comfort.

At the same time, such a high level of C&CE ₹12,270 crore and current investments ₹5,467 crore depresses return on assets of Infosys. This is because a company usually earns a rate of return on these amounts, which is much lower than the return on assets deployed in the company's own business and also compared to the company's cost of capital. For example, in 2021–22, Infosys generated 5.9% return on quoted and 8.7% on unquoted investment as per note 2.27, which are much lower than its Operating Profit Ratio of 24% (operating profit ratio is not affected by investment income and investments & C&CE) and ROA of 22% (ROA is affected by, among other investment income, investments, & C&CE).[8] Thus, a company makes a trade-off between liquidity and profitability.

(m) Deferred Tax Assets, Current Tax Assets, and Income Tax Assets

Deferred tax assets (DTA) are the amounts of income taxes paid in the current year or previous year for which credit will be allowed in future years while computing the taxable income. It arises due to deductible temporary differences. Deferred tax asset also results from carryforward of unused tax losses, and carryforward of unused tax credits, as deductions are available for those items in computing taxable income. To the extent sufficient taxable profits will probably be available, an entity recognizes DTA for all deferred tax benefits (i.e., all deductible temporary differences). At the end of each financial year, a company must review the carrying amount of DTA and reduce the amount if it is no longer probable that sufficient taxable profits will be available to benefit from the reversal. The carrying amount of DTA also depends on the management's judgment of the future recoverability of deferred tax benefits from taxable profits.

Current Tax Assets (CTA), also known as Income Tax Assets (ITA), represent current taxes paid in excess of the amount due for the current and previous periods. For example, if the current taxes are 40 and a company has paid 42, then a company recognizes a CTA of 2; either it will get a refund of this amount in the foreseeable future, or it can adjust the amount against next year's tax payments. Note that CTA arises from current taxes, whereas DTA arises from deferred taxes on the income statement.

Companies net the amounts of DTA and Deferred Tax Liabilities (DTL) arising from the same tax jurisdiction and report the net amount (instead of reporting DTA and DTL separately). For example, if DTA is more than DTL, they deduct DTL from DTA and report the net amount as DTA (net). They may, similarly, net the amounts of CTA and CTL and report CTA (net) when CTA exceeds CTL.

Table 3.21 Tax Assets

Amounts are in ₹ crore	Asian Paints		Avenue Supermarts		Infosys	
Balance as at 31st March	2022	2021	2022	2021	2022	2021
Deferred Tax Assets	Nil	Nil	Nil	Nil	970	955
Income Tax Assets (net), Non-current	145	133	1	1	5,585	5,287
Current Tax Assets (net)	Nil	Nil	Nil	Nil	Nil	Nil

[8] Chapter 5 discusses these and other financial ratios.

Asian Paints' 2022 Balance Sheet has ₹145 crore of Income Tax Assets (net) under non-current assets. This amount represented advance payment of income taxes net of income taxes payable. There was no line item for DTA (net) on Asian Paints' 2022 balance sheet. However, from note 18C, we can ascertain that DTA ₹89 crore was deducted from DTL. This amount of DTA arose from expenses that are tax-deductible when paid ₹35 crore, expected credit loss ₹21 crore, difference in right-of-use assets and lease liabilities ₹26 crore, and defined benefit plans ₹7 crore.

Avenue Supermarts also reported Income Tax Assets (net) of ₹1 crore under non-current assets on its 2022 Balance Sheet. Although it did not report any DTA (net) on the balance sheet, note 18 for DTL (net) suggests that it had netted DTA of ₹18 crore. DTA of ₹7 crore arose from Employee Benefits (expense already recorded on income statement but will be tax deductible when the employee benefits are paid in the future) and ₹11 crore from the difference in Right-of-use assets and lease liabilities.

On its 2022 balance sheet, Infosys reported DTA (net) ₹970 crore and ITA (net) ₹5,585 crore under non-current assets. It also reported DTL (net) under non-current liabilities and Income Tax Liabilities or ITL (net) under current liabilities. This is because the company has two major tax jurisdictions – India and the USA – and set-offs are permitted only within a tax jurisdiction. For this reason, a company may have DTA (net), DTL (net), ITA (net), and ITL (net) on its balance sheet.

(n) Other Financial Assets under Non-Current and under Current Assets

These two groups are for those financial assets that did not appear as a separate line item on a balance sheet. It is important to review the notes for different items that are aggregated under the Other Financial Assets category.

These include security deposits given, advances given, all receivables other than trade receivables, fixed deposits (maturity greater than 12 months for non-current), investment income accrued (i.e., earned but not due, therefore not a receivable), forward exchange contracts, etc.

Table 3.22 Other Financial Assets

Amounts are in ₹ crore	Asian Paints		Avenue Supermarts		Infosys	
Balance as at 31st March	2022	2021	2022	2021	2022	2021
Non-Current Other Fin. Assets	471	579	1,259	1,109	727	613
Current Other Financial Assets	1,645	1,252	107	168	6,580	5,226

Asian Paints reported Other Financial Assets of ₹471 crore under non-current assets and ₹1,645 crore under current assets. From its notes, we find that the largest amount was ₹366 crore for Subsidy receivable from state government less expected credit loss (non-current) and ₹1,030 crore for Term deposits with more than 12 months of original maturity (under current assets as the amount will mature next year).

Avenue Supermarts reported Other Financial Assets of ₹1,259 crore under non-current assets and ₹107 crore under current assets. From its notes, we can see that the largest amount was ₹1,035 crore for Term deposits with more than 12 months of original maturity (non-current assets, note 7) and ₹98 crore for advances given to related parties (current assets, note 13).

The 2022 Balance Sheet of Infosys reveals Non-Current and Current Other Financial Assets of ₹727 crore and ₹6,580 crore, respectively. Its note 2.7 shows that the largest item was ₹320 crore for net investment in sublease of right-of-use asset (under non-current) and ₹3,543 crore for unbilled revenues (under current).

(o) Other Non-Current Assets and Other Current Assets

These two groups are for those non-financial assets that did not appear as a separate line item on a balance sheet. To know the items that were aggregated under these categories, we should review the notes. Other Assets generally include prepaid expenses, advances to suppliers (for supply of goods and services), capital advances (advances for the purchase of fixed assets), balance with government authorities, taxes & duty recoverable from governments, advances to employees, etc.

Table 3.23 Other Assets

Amounts are in ₹ crore	Asian Paints		Avenue Supermarts		Infosys	
Balance as at 31st March	2022	2021	2022	2021	2022	2021
Non-Current Other Assets	120	39	359	447	1,416	1,149
Current Other Assets	436	446	142	122	8,935	6,784

Asian Paints reported Other Non-Current Assets of ₹120 crore and Other Current Assets of ₹436 crore. In note 8, we find that the largest item is for balances with government authorities of ₹277 crore under other current assets.

Avenue Supermarts had ₹349 crore of Other Non-current Assets and ₹142 crore of Other Current Assets on its 2022 balance sheet. The largest item was Capital Advances ₹357 crore under other non-current assets.

Infosys had ₹1,416 crore of other non-current assets and ₹8,935 crore of other current assts on its 2022 balance sheet. Its note 2.10 reveals that the largest item was under ₹5,365 crore for unbilled revenues, which was classified as non-financial asset and included under other current assets because the contractual rights to consideration (for revenue recognition) is not yet clearly established and depends upon the completion of contractual milestones. Once the contractual rights are established, the amount will be reclassified as Trade Receivables.

III. Liabilities

In this section, we will discuss eight types of liabilities found on balance sheets: Borrowings, Lease Liabilities, Deferred Tax Liabilities, Current Tax Liabilities, Provisions, Trade Payables, Other Financial Liabilities, and Other Liabilities. While the discussion is for non-finance companies, this would also apply to financial firms since several of these liabilities also exist on the balance sheet of banks and other financial firms.

(a) Borrowings

Borrowings are financial liabilities. A borrowing represents an amount that a borrower has taken from a lender for a specific duration. Borrowers incur interest cost on borrowings. Borrowings may be taken from banks, other financial institutions, governments, other entities, and the public. Borrowings from governments could be in the form of Deferred Payment Liability, wherein a company keeps the taxes collected and repays the amount after a few years (with or without interest). Borrowings may be long-term or short-term. Long-term borrowings may be payable over several years, and the amount due in the next period is called the current maturities of long-term borrowing. Borrowings may be either non-current or current liabilities, and they may appear as a separate line item on the balance sheet or may be included under Other Financial Liabilities.

Table 3.24 Borrowings

Amounts are in ₹ crore	Asian Paints		Avenue Supermarts		Infosys	
Balance as at 31st March	2022	2021	2022	2021	2022	2021
Borrowings: Non-Current	16	14	Nil	Nil	Nil	Nil
Borrowings: Current	Nil	8	Nil	Nil	Nil	Nil

There were no borrowings on the 2022 balance sheets of both Avenue Supermarts and Infosys. Asian Paints reported borrowings of only ₹16 crore (non-current). Thus, all three companies do not have material amounts of loans and borrowings on their balance sheets. Low levels of borrowing reflect a conservative financing strategy adopted by these firms. By contrast, on its 2022 balance sheet, Hindalco reported total borrowings of ₹19,079 crore: ₹11,668 crore of non-current, ₹6,007 crore of current-maturities of long-term borrowings, and ₹1,404 crore of short-term borrowings. In notes 18A & 18B, Hindalco reported various types of borrowings, namely, secured non-convertible debentures, secured loans from banks (Rupee loans and Foreign currency loans), and other borrowings.

(b) Lease Liabilities

Lease liabilities represent the present value of amounts payable in the future for right-of-use (ROU) assets. The amount payable during the next twelve months after the balance sheet date is reported under current financial liabilities and the remaining amounts are disclosed under non-current financial liabilities.

Under Ind AS 116 (Leases), when an entity takes a short-term or a low-value lease, the leased asset and liability remain off-balance sheet, and lease rentals are expensed. For all other types of leases, the lessee must record an ROU asset and a Lease Liability at the inception of the lease. Subsequently, each year, lease liability increases by finance cost (or interest expense) and decreases by the amount paid (i.e., lease rentals paid). Finance cost is expensed each year. The carrying amount of lease liability decreases in years when payments exceed the interest on lease liability, and vice versa. At the end of the lease term, the carrying amount of lease liability is expected to become zero.

The value at which lease liability is recognized is the present value of lease payments that will be paid in the future. Obtaining present value requires three inputs: discount rate, amount to be paid, and when payments will be made. The discount rate used for obtaining present value is the interest rate implicit in the lease (if known to the lessee) or else the incremental borrowing rate of the lessee. A lease may allow the lessee to extend the duration of the lease (also known as extension option) or to buy the leased asset at the end of the lease period (also known as purchase option). The lease payments include not only fixed payments and variable lease payments (linked to an index or a rate known at the commencement of the lease) but also any extension option payments and any purchase options payments if it is reasonably certain that the options will be exercised. A lessee is expected to make lease payments, as per a payment schedule, over a period the lease is expected to be continued. This period includes the non-cancellable period of the lease. The period is adjusted for any option to extend or terminate the lease if it is reasonably certain that such an option will be exercised.

Prior to Ind AS 116 (Leases) becoming effective, a lease was classified into either an operating lease or a finance lease. Like low-value or short-term leases, operating leases were off-balance sheet, and rentals paid were expensed. By contrast, finance leases were brought on the balance sheet by recognizing both a lease-hold asset and a lease obligation. Lease-hold assets were depreciated. Lease obligations were increased by interest expense and reduced by the amount paid.

Table 3.25 Lease Liabilities

Amounts are in ₹ crore	Asian Paints		Avenue Supermarts		Infosys	
Balance as at 31st March	2022	2021	2022	2021	2022	2021
Lease Liabilities: Non-Current	519	469	320	217	3,228	3,367
Lease Liabilities: Current	179	157	96	79	558	487
Total	698	626	416	296	3,786	3,854

On its 2022 balance sheet, Asian Paints reported Lease liability of ₹519 crore under non-current financial liabilities and ₹179 crore under current financial liabilities. The company discloses an analysis of the maturity of lease liabilities in note 29(C)(3). Against the total lease liabilities of ₹698 crore, the company will pay ₹828 crore: ₹224 crore within one year, ₹508 crore from one to five years, and ₹96 crore after five years. The total amount paid is higher than lease liability due to finance cost (interest expense). Thus, ₹130 crore (=828 – 698) is the finance cost payable on the lease liabilities.

As of 31-3-2022, Avenue Supermarts had total lease liabilities of ₹416 crore consisting of ₹320 crore non-current and ₹96 crore current. From the additional details provided for the lease liabilities in note 3, we learn that during the year 2021–22, the company recognized ₹240 crore for new leases and repaid ₹120 crore of lease liabilities and recorded an interest expense (or finance cost) of ₹38 crore on lease liabilities. Avenue Supermarts also paid ₹0.78 crore as rentals on short-term leases, and this amount was included under Other Expense on the income statement.

On the Balance Sheet as at March 31, 2022, Infosys reported lease liability of ₹3,228 crore under non-current financial liabilities and ₹558 crore under current financial liabilities. From note 2.3, we learn that during the year, additions to lease liabilities were ₹394 crore, deletions were ₹18 crore, an addition due to translation difference was ₹58 crore, finance cost added were ₹126 crore, and total lease payments (including interest) were ₹628 crore. We also learn that against ₹3,786 crore lease liabilities as of 31-3-2022, the company will pay ₹4,256 crore: ₹637 crore within one year, ₹2,100 crore from one to five years, and ₹1,519 crore beyond five years. Thus, on the lease liabilities, the company will recognize ₹520 crore (= 4256 – 3786) as the finance cost over the remaining lease term.

(c) Trade Payables

Trade payables are the amount payable to operational creditors for goods purchased and services consumed related to operating activities and may also include any acceptances. Acceptances are arrangements where the suppliers are initially paid by banks, and the buyer recognizes the amount as payable until it pays the amount to the banks. Note that for manufacturing and trading companies, Trade payables include only amount due for purchase of goods that are needed for production or sale (for example, raw material, component, packing material, stock in trade, etc.). These companies include the dues for services consumed under other liabilities (such as expense payable). By contrast, some companies, especially service firms, also include amount due for services consumed in Trade Payable. Therefore, it is important to know what all are included under Trade Payable.

The amount due to operational suppliers depends upon not only the credit purchases of goods and services but also the credit period availed. If the credit period availed is significantly longer than what is the normal practice in the industry, the purchase price will reflect a financing cost, which is deducted when recognizing credit purchases and trade payable. Trade Payable is a current liability and is usually found on almost all balance sheets since all companies buy goods and services on credit, and some amount is still outstanding on the reporting date.

Table 3.26 Trade Payables

Amounts are in ₹ crore	Asian Paints		Avenue Supermarts		Infosys	
Balance as at 31st March	2022	2021	2022	2021	2022	2021
Trade Payables: Current	3,497	2,814	531	566	2,669	1,562

Asian Paints reported Trade Payable (including acceptances) of ₹3,497 crore under current liabilities on its 2022 Balance Sheet. From note 20, we learn that acceptances amounted to ₹318 crore. We also see an aging schedule for trade payable, which reveals that of ₹3,497 crore trade payable, ₹3,154 crore is not yet due and ₹342 crore has been due for less than 1 year. The remaining ₹1 crore is overdue for more than 1 year.

Avenue Supermarts owed ₹531 crore to trade payable as of 31-3-2022. From note 19, we find that ₹129 crore is not due yet, ₹381 crore is due for less than 1 year, and the remaining amount is due for more than 1 year.

Infosys has Trade Payable of ₹2,669 crore as of March 31, 2022. Note 2.14 tells us that ₹2,134 crore is not yet due and ₹535 crore is due for less than 1 year. No amount is due for more than 1 year, which suggests that the company is timely in its payment to its suppliers.

(d) Other Financial Liabilities under Non-current and under Current Liabilities

These two groups are for those financial liabilities that did not appear as a separate line item on a balance sheet. These liabilities include Unpaid dividends, Salaries and wages payable, Expenses payable, Payable towards stores, spares, & consumables, Payable towards services received, Capital creditors (i.e., payable towards capital expenditure), Interest accrued but not due, Escrow deposits received, Retention monies received, Security & other deposits taken, Forward exchange contract, Foreign currency forward and option contracts, etc.

Table 3.27 Other Financial Liabilities

Amounts are in ₹ crore	Asian Paints		Avenue Supermarts		Infosys	
Balance as at 31st March	2022	2021	2022	2021	2022	2021
Other Financial Liabilities: Non-Current	1	1	0	0	676	259
Other Financial Liabilities: Current	1,525	1,277	270	255	11,269	8,359

Asian Paints reported Other Financial Liabilities of ₹1 crore under non-current assets and ₹1,525 crore under current liabilities. From its note 16, we find that the large amounts included under Other current financial liabilities are ₹585 crore for payable towards services received, ₹207 crore for payable to employees, and ₹635 crore for payable towards other expenses. The note also reveals that the entire amount of Other non-current financial liabilities ₹1 crore is for retention monies relating to capital expenditure.

Avenue Supermarts had ₹0.41[9] crore of non-current other financial liabilities (for rent deposits taken) and ₹270 crore of current other financial liabilities on its 2022 balance sheet. The latter consisted of escrow deposits received ₹55 crore, salary & wages payable ₹50 crore, and capital creditors (payable for fixed assets) ₹165 crore.

The 2022 Balance Sheet of Infosys reveals Non-Current and Current Other Financial Liabilities of ₹676 crore and ₹11,269 crore, respectively. Its

[9]When 0.41 crore is rounded off to nearest crore, we get 0 crore as can be seen in 2022 for Avenue Supermarts in Table 3.27.

note 2.13 shows that most of these amounts were for accrued expenses and payables to employees.

(e) Deferred Tax Liability, Income Tax Liability, and Current Tax Liability

Deferred tax liabilities (DTL) are the amounts of income taxes arising due to taxable temporary differences. DTL is a non-current liability. It must reverse and become a current tax liability, and after that, a company will pay the amount as taxes. However, it is uncertain when the reversal would happen. Until then, DTL is a source of long-term funds from the taxman, representing an amount not taken by the taxman and thus indirectly provided at no interest to the company. Depreciation is an important source of DTL, and most manufacturing companies report DTL.

Current Tax Liability (CTL), also referred to as Income Tax Liability (ITL), represents the amount of taxes – for the current and previous years – that are still payable. For example, if the current taxes are 40 and taxes paid 33, CTL is 7, and the company must pay this amount in a foreseeable future. Note that CTL arises from current taxes (not deferred taxes).

As discussed in the previous section, companies net the amounts of DTL and DTA arising from the same tax jurisdiction and report the net amount instead of reporting DTL and DTA separately on the balance sheet. For example, if DTL is more than DTA, a company reports DTL (net). ITL (net) is reported when ITL exceeds ITA.

Table 3.28 Tax Liabilities

Amounts are in ₹ crore	Asian Paints		Avenue Supermarts		Infosys	
Balance as at 31st March	2022	2021	2022	2021	2022	2021
Deferred Tax Liabilities (net): Non-Current Liabilities	205	265	65	52	841	511
Current Tax Liabilities (net) or Income Tax Liabilities (net): Current Liabilities	101	88	111	113	2,179	1,737

Asian Paints' 2022 Balance Sheet reports ₹205 crore of DTL (net) under non-current liabilities and ₹101 crore of ITL (net) under current liabilities. From note 18C, we can ascertain that the amount of DTL (net) was obtained after deducting total DTA ₹89 crore. Thus, total DTL is ₹294 crore. The biggest source of DTL (as on 31-3-2022) was the ₹269 crore of difference in accumulated depreciation as per the books of accounts and Income Tax Act.

Note that this item is lower than ₹297 crore amount on 31-3-2021, and ₹316 crore amount on 31-3-2020, which indicates reversal of the DTL amount attributed to depreciation in 2021–22 and 2020–21.

Avenue Supermarts reported ₹65 crore as DTL (net) under non-current liabilities on the 2022 balance sheet. Note 18 suggests that DTL (net) amount was obtained after deducting DTA of ₹18 crore. Thus, DTL gross amount was ₹83 crore, which was entirely due to depreciation. DTL due to depreciation has increased in 2021–22 as well as in 2020–21. The company also reported Current Tax Liabilities of ₹111 crore under Current Liabilities, for which it did not provide any additional disclosures.

On its 2022 balance sheet, Infosys reported DTL (net) ₹841 crore under non-current liabilities and ITL (net) ₹2,179 crore under current liabilities. From note 2.17, we find that DTL was ₹1,692 crore and arose from four sources: Derivative financial instruments ₹24 crore, Intangible assets through business transfer ₹4 crore, Branch profit tax ₹834 crore, and SEZ Re-investment Reserve ₹830 crore.

(f) Provisions

A provision is either a liability (or an amount set aside for potential losses) that can be measured only by using a substantial degree of estimation. Examples are provision for pension, provision for gratuity, provision for compensated absences (or leave entitlement), provision for post-retirement medical benefits, provision for post-sales client support, asset retirement obligations, provision for environmental liability, provision for enterprise social commitment, etc. Provisions appear under non-current liabilities as well as under current liabilities on a balance sheet.

Provisions are created out of profit. Thus, increases in provisions are expensed (often included under Other Expenses on the Income Statement), and decreases are deducted from expenses. The amount for provision (on the reporting date) cannot be accurately ascertained and requires judgment. For example, employees are entitled to receive gratuity when they leave an organization after completing a minimum of five years of service, and the amount they receive depends upon not only the number of years served but also the salary at the time of leaving. It is uncertain when employees will leave and what will be their salary at the time of leaving. Thus, the amount for provision for gratuity (on the balance sheet date) would have to be based on experience, past data, actuarial model, and assumptions. Companies provide a separate note to disclose the assumptions used for employee benefits-related provisions. For example, Asian Paints provides note 37 and Avenue Supermarts note 43 for the inputs used for provisions related to employee benefits (such as provision for pension, provision for gratuity, for compensated absences, for post-retirement medical benefits, etc.).

Table 3.29 Provisions

Amounts are in ₹ crore	Asian Paints		Avenue Supermarts		Infosys	
Balance as at 31st March	2022	2021	2022	2021	2022	2021
Provisions: Non-Current	168	164	Nil	Nil	Nil	Nil
Provisions: Current	38	58	33	22	920	661
Total	206	222	33	22	920	661

Asian Paints had non-current provisions of ₹168 crore and current provisions of ₹38 crore as of March 31, 2022. Non-current provisions were entirely related to employee benefits: for compensated absences ₹166 crore, for pension ₹1 crore, and for post-retirement medical benefits ₹1 crore. Current Provisions were made up of the above-mentioned employee benefits totalling ₹25 crore, provisions for excise duty ₹2 crore, and provisions for central sales tax and value-added tax ₹11 crore.

Avenue Supermarts reported only current provisions of ₹33 crore on its 2022 Balance Sheet. In note 22, the company discloses that it had provision for gratuity ₹7 crore and provision for leave entitlement ₹26 crore.

Infosys reported provisions of ₹920 crore under current liabilities on its 2022 Balance Sheet. Further, in note 2.16, the company discloses that this amount is for post-sales client support. During the 2021–22 financial year, the provision decreased by ₹152 crore due to utilization, and ₹343 crore was added out of profits (i.e., expensed). It is interesting to note that Provision did not have any employee benefits related provision. It appears that the company has netted employee benefit provisions with assets created to fund the provisions, and it has reported the net amount of the liability as Accrued defined benefit plan liability under Other non-current liability.

(g) Other Non-Current Liabilities and Other Current Liabilities

These two groups are for those non-financial liabilities that did not appear as a separate line item on a balance sheet. To know the items that were aggregated under these categories, we should review the notes. Other Liabilities include advances received from customers, statutory dues payable, deferred income arising from government grants, unearned revenue or deferred revenue arising from the sale of services, liability towards corporate social responsibility, etc.

Table 3.30 Other Liabilities

Amounts are in ₹ crore	Asian Paints		Avenue Supermarts		Infosys	
Balance as at 31st March	2022	2021	2022	2021	2022	2021
Other Liabilities: Non-Current	2	3	Nil	Nil	360	649
Other Liabilities: Current	307	174	52	38	7,381	4,816

The 2022 Balance Sheet of Asian Paints had Other non-current liabilities of only ₹2 crore and Other current liabilities of ₹307 crore. As per note 19, Statutory dues payable ₹255 crore was the largest item included in Other current liabilities.

As of 31-3-2022, Avenue Supermarts had Other current liabilities of ₹52 crore, mostly comprising statutory dues of ₹41 crore as can be seen in note 21.

Infosys reported Other non-current liabilities of ₹360 crore and Other current liabilities of ₹7,381 crore on its 2022 Balance Sheet. From note 2.15, we learn that of Unearned revenue (i.e., service revenue collected but not earned) ₹5,179 crore and Withholding taxes & others ₹2,190 crore accounted for the bulk of Other current liabilities. Accrued defined benefit plan liability ₹332 crore was the largest item included in Other non-current liabilities. Accrued defined benefit plan liability of ₹ crore was also included under other current liabilities.

IV. Equity

Shareholders and lenders are two sources of capital. Lenders provide borrowings and shareholders provide funds as equity and preference capital. Although few companies may choose not to have any borrowings and most Indian companies no longer have preference capital issued, all companies limited by shares have equity shares outstanding, and thus, they have equity on their balance sheets. This makes equity an important item to study.

In this section, we will discuss first equity shares and, thereafter, the two components of equity, namely, Equity Share Capital and Other Equity. Note that for analysis, we simply use the amount of total equity and ignore its breakup into equity share capital and other equity. Although we discuss equity in the context of non-finance companies, the discussion is also relevant for banks and other financial firms since both components also exist on the balance sheet of financial firms.

(a) Equity Shares

Companies limited by shares (or simply, companies) must have share capital. A company raises share capital by issuing equity shares (or ordinary shares) and/or preference shares. Equity shares have no contractual obligation for payment of dividends and return of capital. By contrast, preference shares must be redeemed no later than 20 years from their date of issue, as per section 55 of the Companies Act, 2013, and dividends on preference shares must be paid before paying any dividends on equity shares. Although preference shares were issued by many companies in the past, they were subsequently redeemed and are now uncommon. None, Asian Paints, Avenue Supermarts, and Infosys, has any preference shares outstanding.

Every share has a nominal value (or par value, face value), which may vary across companies. For example, the face value is ₹1 for Asian Paints' , ₹10 for Avenue Supermarts', and ₹5 for Infosys' equity shares. Face values can be altered. Companies may decrease par value by splitting shares or increase face value by doing a reverse stock-split. A stock split reduces the par value, increases the number of shares available for trading, and decreases the market price of shares, making the shares more affordable to buy. By contrast, a reverse stock split increases the par value, decreases the number of shares, and raises the market price of shares. A stock split or reverse stock split only changes the face value and the number of shares. It does not change the amounts of equity share capital and other equity and, therefore, the equity on the balance sheet remains unchanged.

Every company has an authorized share capital and thus an authorized number of shares that can be issued. For example, Avenue Supermarts had an authorized share capital of ₹750 crore comprising 75 crore equity shares of ₹10 each. A company cannot raise more than authorized share capital by issuing shares in excess of the authorized number. However, the number of authorized shares can be increased by shareholders.

A company has issued, subscribed, and fully paid-up capital. Issued shares are the shares the company has transferred to shareholders, irrespective of whether the shares are still subscribed/outstanding or not. Subscribed shares are the shares that are still outstanding, i.e., currently owned by the shareholders. Fully paid-up shares are the shares on which the entire issue price has been received from the shareholders. Shares may be issued at par value or at a premium. When a share is issued at a premium, a company receives an amount in excess of the par value. This amount is added to the Share Premium account that is included in Other Equity.

In the early phases of their lifecycle, companies raise capital from a limited number of investors. To raise cash from the primary market, they make an Initial Public Offering (IPO), and subsequently they come out with Follow on Public Offering (FPO). Companies may list their shares on a stock exchange to facilitate their trading on the secondary market and for easier entry and exit for investors.

A company may also issue shares to obtain another asset or in mergers and acquisition transactions. A company may offer bonus shares to its existing shareholders, against which it does not receive anything cash or another asset. A bonus issue increases the number of shares. Furthermore, it increases Equity share capital and reduces Other equity by the same amount (equal to the number of bonus shares issued multiplied by the face value of the shares). As a result, there is no change in the total equity on the balance sheet. Theoretically, a bonus issue should not change the market value of the company (since the number of shares increases while the equity remains the same), the market price of shares should decrease proportionately, and the product of the two remains unchanged. However, the share price does go up when a bonus issue is announced.

The number of subscribed shares may be less than the number of issued shares when a company has cancelled shares after buyback or upon forfeiture. Companies forfeit shares when shareholders fail to pay any amount due on the shares (such as amounts payable on allotment). This would happen in the past when shareholders would pay the amount in part. It no longer happens and, therefore, it is uncommon to see companies forfeiting shares nowadays.

Companies buy back their own shares to reduce the number of shares outstanding (thereby increasing the earnings per share) and shareholders' equity (thereby increasing financial leverage and return on equity). A company may also buyback its own shares to issue them to its employees against the exercise of employee stock options. Until the repurchased shares are cancelled, they are referred to as *treasury shares*. Their face value is deducted from Equity Share Capital and the net amount is reported on the Balance Sheet. Similarly, Other Equity is reported after deducting any amount paid in excess of the par value. As a result, when the repurchased shares are extinguished, both equity share capital and other equity are reduced. Equity share capital decreases by an amount equal to the number of shares cancelled multiplied by the face value of shares. Other equity decreases by the amount paid for buyback minus the equity share capital reduced by the cancellation.

(b) Equity Share Capital

Equity Share Capital amount is the product of the nominal value of equity shares and the number of equity shares outstanding adjusted for treasury shares.

Table 3.31 Equity Shares & Capital

	Asian Paints		Avenue Supermarts		Infosys	
Balance as at 31st March	2022	2021	2022	2021	2022	2021
Nominal Value per share	₹1	₹1	₹10	₹10	₹5	₹5
Number of Shares Outstanding	95.92 crore	95.92 crore	64.78 crore	64.78 crore	420.67 crore	426.07 crore
Equity Share Capital	₹96 crore	₹96 crore	₹648 crore	₹648 crore	₹2,103 crore	₹2,130 crore

On Asian Paints' 2022 Balance Sheet, equity share capital is ₹96 crore, a small amount relative to its total equity of ₹13,349 crore. In note 12, the company discloses that it has about 95.92 crore equity shares outstanding, each ₹1 nominal value, as of 31-3-2022. No shares were issued during the 2021–22 financial year. In this note, the company also discloses that one of its trusts purchased 2,23,240 equity shares from the secondary market, and these shares remained as treasury shares at the end of the year.

Avenue Supermarts' 2022 Balance Sheet discloses equity share capital of ₹648 crore, which is a small amount relative to its total equity of ₹13,924 crore. In note 15, the company reports that, as of 31-3-2022, 64.78 crore equity shares are outstanding each having ₹10 nominal value. No shares were issued during the 2021–22 financial year. The last time it had issued shares was on February 11, 2020, when it allotted 2 crore shares through Qualified Institutional Placement (QIP) to eligible Qualified Institutional Buyers (QIB) at an issue price of ₹2,049 per share (at a premium of ₹2,039 = 2,049 – 10) and raised ₹4,098 crore.

Infosys has an equity share capital of ₹2,103 crore, again a small amount relative to its total equity of ₹69,306 crore. In note 2.12, the company reports that, as of 31-3-2022, 420.67 crore equity shares are outstanding each having a ₹5 nominal value. During 2021–22, the company granted 18.85 lakh shares under its employee stock option plans, which caused Equity Share Capital to increase by about ₹1 crore. Furthermore, in 2021–22, Equity Share Capital decreased by ₹28 crore (as per Statement of Changes in Equity) due to buyback of 5.58 crore shares that were subsequently extinguished (as per note 2.12). For this buyback, the company has spent ₹11,125 crore (as per the cash flow statement), which included ₹9,200 crore for the shares repurchased at an average price of ₹1,648.53 and ₹1,925 crore in transaction cost and taxes on buyback. In the past, the company had allotted bonus shares in a 1:1 ratio (1 bonus share for every share held) in 2018–19.

(c) Other Equity

Other Equity is often the largest item on the balance sheet for many companies, particularly those that are large and mature. This item consists of various reserves and surpluses, such as Retained Earnings, General Reserves, Share Premium, Capital Reserve, Capital Redemption Reserve, Share-based Payment Reserve, Other Comprehensive Income, etc. A company may not provide a separate note for Other Equity because the Statement of Changes in Equity discloses the constituents of Other Equity and reports their beginning balance, changes in balance, and ending balance.

For many financial analyses, the breakup of other equity is of less importance and so is the breakup of equity into equity share capital and other equity as was pointed out at the start of this section. However, what is important is the change in other equity during the year and what has caused the change. Generally, Other Equity increases due to comprehensive income (i.e., net profit and other comprehensive income) and decreases due to dividends declared and price paid in excess of par value of shares repurchased during the year. Other equity may also increase due to the issue of shares at a premium, acquisition of a business at a price lower than the fair value assigned to net assets, and gain on redemption of debentures.

Table 3.32 Other Equity

Amounts are in ₹ crore	Asian Paints		Avenue Supermarts		Infosys	
Balance as at 31st March	2022	2021	2022	2021	2022	2021
Other Equity	13,253	11,993	13,276	11,658	67,203	69,401

Asian Paint reported on its 2022 balance sheet that its Other Equity is ₹13,253 crore. Other equity increased by ₹1,261 crore during the 2021–22 year. The change was affected largely by four items: Net Profit ₹3,135 crore, negative Other Comprehensive Income ₹(73) crore, Dividends declared ₹(1,741) crore, and Purchase of treasury shares ₹(75) crore, as per the Statement of Changes in Equity.

The 2022 Balance Sheet of Avenue Supermarts discloses Other Equity of ₹13,276 crore as at 31-3-2022. Other equity increased by ₹1,618 crore during the year. Note 16 reveals that the change was largely due to Net Profit of ₹1,616 crore. From Cash Flow Statement, we learn that the company did not pay any dividends during the year.

Infosys reported Other Equity of ₹67,203 crore as at 31-3-2022. The amount was ₹2,198 crore lower despite a net profit of ₹21,235 crore. The major drivers for the decline were Dividends declared ₹12,700 crore and buyback of its own shares ₹11,065 crore (=11093–28) as per the Statement of Changes in Equity.

V. Analysis of Balance Sheet

Here we discuss working capital and capital employed, which are useful for analysis.

(a) Working Capital

Working capital is the fund needed to carry out day-to-day operations. An entity needs to have current assets (for example, inventories, account receivables, prepaid expenses, and cash) to carry out its operating activities on a day-to-day basis. Some of these current assets are funded from current liabilities arising from operating activities (such as trade payables and expense payables) and financing activities (such as short-term borrowings). Working Capital is the excess of current assets over current liabilities. Although working capital is not reported on the Balance Sheet, we can easily obtain it as follows:

Working Capital = Current Assets – Current Liabilities

The amount of working capital of the three companies are computed below.

Table 3.33 Calculation of Working Capital

Amounts are in ₹ crore	Asian Paints		Avenue Supermarts		Infosys	
Balance as at 31st March	2022	2021	2022	2021	2022	2021
Current Assets	12,748	9,947	3,351	3,961	52,437	48,282
Less Current Liabilities	5,647	4,575	1,094	1,072	24,976	17,622
Working Capital	*7,101*	*5,372*	*2,257*	*2,889*	*27,461*	*30,660*

All three companies have a positive working capital, which indicates the use of long-term funds (equity and long-term liabilities) for working capital to support day-to-day operations of the business. Asian Paints has a working capital of ₹7,101 crore, Avenue Supermarts ₹2,257 crore, and Infosys ₹27,461 crores as of 31-3-2022.

(b) Capital Employed

Capital is a long-term source of funds for an enterprise. Firms need capital to acquire fixed assets, invest in subsidiaries, associates, and joint ventures, and provide working capital to sustain operations. Equity and debt are the two principal sources of capital funded by shareholders and debtholders, respectively. Firms issue equity shares to raise equity capital (external sources of funds), and they retain profits made during the year (internal sources of funds). They may also borrow money from banks, other lenders, and the public (external sources of funds). Capital employed is not reported on balance sheets, but we can easily compute it as follows:[10]

$$Capital\ Employed = Equity + Debt$$

Equity and debt are on balance sheets. Equity comprises equity share capital and other equity. Debt includes all borrowings (whether non-current or current), all lease liabilities (both non-current and current), and preference capital. As per Section 55(2) of the Companies Act 2013, preference shares carry a contractual obligation for return of capital within 20 years from the date of issue and for payment of dividends. Equity shares have no such contractual obligations to pay dividends or return capital. Therefore, preference share capital should also be included in total debt. Furthermore, although short-term borrowings are not usually a source of capital, many companies continue to have large amounts of short-term borrowings throughout the year, year after year. Thus, these borrowings are contracted as short-term, although, in spirit, they are long-term and a source of capital and should be included in total debt for capital employed.

Table 3.34 Calculation of Capital Employed

Amounts are in ₹ crore	Asian Paints		Avenue Supermarts		Infosys	
Balance as at 31st March	2022	2021	2022	2021	2022	2021
Borrowings (NC)	16	14	Nil	Nil	Nil	Nil
+ Borrowings (Current)	Nil	8	Nil	Nil	Nil	Nil
+ Lease Liabilities (NC)	519	469	320	217	3,228	3,367
+ Lease Liabilities (C)	179	157	96	79	558	487
Total Debt	=714	=646	=416	=296	=3,786	=3,854
Add Total Equity	13,349	12,089	13,924	12,305	69,306	71,531
Capital Employed	14,063	12,735	14,340	12,601	73,092	75,385

[10] Capital Employed is computed in many ways, apart from the one used in this textbook. An alternate way is to use equity plus non-current liabilities. One may also compute capital employed as tangible net worth plus total debt, where tangible net worth is equity less intangible assets. Another way is to consider tangible net worth, total debt, plus DTL (net). Each formula has its pros and cons.

As on 31-3-2022, Asian Paints had equity ₹13,349 crore and debt ₹714 crore. Therefore, their sum ₹14,063 crore is Asian Paints' capital employed as of 31-3-2022. Avenue Supermarts' capital employed is ₹14,340 crore made up of equity ₹13,924 crore and debt ₹416 crore. Infosys employed capital of ₹73,092 crore consisting of equity ₹69,306 crore and debt ₹3,786 crore.

Appendix 3A: Biological Assets and Bearer Plants

Biological assets are living animals and plants. Biological assets are classified into bearer plants (included under PPE) and biological assets other than bearer plants (included under current assets).

According to Ind AS 16 (Property, Plant, and Equipment), bearer plants are living plants that are (i) used in the production or supply of agricultural produce, (ii) expected to bear produce for more than one period, and (iii) are remotely likely to be sold as agricultural produce except for incidental scrap sales. Thus, bearer plants are *not*: (i) annual crops (such as rice or wheat), (ii) plants cultivated to be harvested as agricultural produce (such as trees grown as lumber), and (iii) plants, although cultivated primarily for agricultural produce, may also be harvested and sold (for example, trees cultivated for their fruits and lumber). Although they are biological assets, Bearer Plants related to agriculture activities are classified as PPE following Ind AS 16 (Property, Plant, and Equipment). Therefore, these assets are accounted for as self-constructed PPE and reported at their net block.

As on 31-3-2022, Dhunseri Tea & Industries Ltd. had Bearer Plants (Gross Block ₹126 crore, Accumulated Depreciation ₹14 crore, Net Block ₹113 crore) included in PPE as per note 3a. Note that Asian Paints, Avenue Supermarts, and Infosys are not from the agriculture industry, and their PPE does not include any bearer plants.

Biological Assets other than Bearer Plants include (i) produce from orchards and plantations such as fruits, seeds, leaves, latex, and lumber, (ii) annual crops such as rice, wheat, lentils, and vegetables, (iii) floriculture such as flowers, (iv) aquaculture such as fish and shrimps, (v) livestock such as dairy, wool, and meat, (vi) poultry such as eggs and meat, etc. These assets are accounted for following Ind AS 41 (Agriculture) and are reported similar to inventory under current assets at fair value less any cost to sell.

As on 31-3-2022, Dhunseri Tea & Industries Ltd. had Biological Assets other than Bearer Plants of ₹72 lakh (2.49 lakh kg) reported under Current Assets. Another company, Kaveri Seed reported Biological Assets (comprising standing crops) of ₹82 crore under Current Assets on its Balance Sheet as at March 31, 2022. Again, Asian Paints, Avenue Supermarts, and Infosys did not have any biological assets other than bearer plants.

Appendix 3B: Impairment Loss and Reversal of Impairment Loss

Impairment loss represents a write-down of the carrying amount of an item of PPE due to a significant drop in the amount that can be recovered from that item. Impairment loss is the excess of the carrying amount of a PPE over the amount that can be recovered from the PPE. Recognition of impairment loss is an example of the application of the conservatism principle.

Companies must test the impairment of their fixed assets on the balance sheet date. A trigger event must have happened for the impairment test. A trigger event is a substantial and sustained adverse economic event that severely affects a firm and causes a significant and long-lasting decline in revenues or earnings from its fixed assets. For example, the COVID-19 pandemic, the Russia-Ukraine war, and a sharp rise in interest rates could be trigger events.

If there is a trigger event, a company must check whether there is a significant drop in the amount that can be recovered from a PPE. To do this, they need to ascertain the PPE's recoverable amount, which requires two inputs: value-in-use and net fair value. The first input, value-in-use is the present value of incremental cash flows generated by the PPE if the PPE were to continue being used. This requires forecasting the PPE's incremental cash flows each year over its useful life, converting these future values into their present value equivalents using a discount rate, and summing the present values.[11] The second input, net fair value is the net amount that would be received if the PPE were sold immediately. Net fair value is equal to fair value of the PPE less cost to sell. A PPE's recoverable amount is the value-in-use or the net fair value, whichever is higher.

If the carrying amount of a PPE is more than the PPE's recoverable amount, the PPE is said to be impaired and an impairment loss needs to be recognized. Impairment loss is the difference between the carrying amount and the recoverable amount of a PPE. Impairment loss is added to Accumulated Impairment, a contra-asset paired with PPE. Like Accumulated Depreciation, Accumulated Impairment is deducted from Gross Block of a PPE. Hence

[11] How to obtain present value? Suppose, we expect to receive ₹1,000 five years from now. As this amount will become available in the future, it is a future value. We obtain the present value of a future cash flow value by discounting the cash flow using an appropriate discount rate (or interest rate). Suppose, the appropriate discount rate is 12%. Present Value of ₹1,000 to be received five years from now = $1000 \div (1 + 12\%)^5 = 567.43$. If ₹567.43 were invested now in a 5-year fixed deposit yielding 12% interest per annum, we will receive 1,000 upon maturity of the fixed deposit five years from now.

impairment causes the carrying amount of PPE to reduce by the impairment loss recognized and to become equal to the recoverable amount.

Let us take an example to understand the concept. Suppose PPE's net block is 200, accumulated impairment is zero, and a trigger event has occurred. The management must now do an impairment test, and it takes help from a certified valuer to estimate net fair value and value-in-use. Suppose the valuer has estimated that this PPE has a net fair value of 60 (estimated fair value 62 – estimated cost to sell 2) and a value-in-use of 90 (the sum of the present value of annual cash flows generated from the PPE). In that case, the recoverable amount is 90 (= 60 or 90, whichever is higher). As the recoverable amount 90 is less than the net block 200, an impairment loss of 110 (=200 – 90) must be recognized. The impairment loss is expensed, which reduces profit for the year.

Furthermore, just as depreciation is added to accumulated depreciation, impairment loss is added to accumulated impairment, which reduces the carrying amount of the PPE. Accumulated Impairment is the total impairment loss for the PPE over the years. The entity will recalculate depreciation based on the revised carrying amount (after recognizing impairment loss), residual value, and remaining useful life. In this example, Accumulated Impairment will increase to 110.

If the economic environment becomes favourable again and the entity enjoys a substantial and sustained rise in revenue or earnings, the previously recognized impairment loss may be reversed. For that to happen, the recoverable amount must become higher than the carrying amount. However, due to a reversal of impairment loss, the net carrying amount must not exceed the hypothetical carrying amount that would have been today if impairment loss was not recognized previously.[12] Thus, we can raise the carrying amount to the recoverable amount or the hypothetical carrying amount, whichever is lower. Let us illustrate this.

Suppose, after a few years, today, the net block is 50 and the economic environment has become highly favourable causing the recoverable amount to be 70. Since the recoverable amount is higher than the carrying amount of the PPE and previously an impairment was recognized for this PPE, we can proceed to recognizing a reversal of impairment loss and increasing the carrying amount of the PPE. Can we recognize a reversal of 20 (=70 – 50)? Suppose, if no impairment loss were recognized previously, the carrying amount would

[12] As per Ind AS 16 (Property, Plant, & Equipment), upon a reversal of impairment loss, the net carrying amount of an asset must not exceed the net block if there was no impairment loss in the first place.

have been 68 today. In that case, we can increase the carrying amount from 50 to 68 (=lower of 70 or 68). Thus, the reversal of impairment loss would be 18 and included either in the income for the year or as a negative amount under Operating Expense. In either case, reversal has an income-increasing effect. Furthermore, this reversal amount reduces Accumulated Impairment to 92 (=110 – 18) and increases the carrying amount of the PPE to 68 (=50 + 18).

It is important to note that the occurrence of a trigger event is usually beyond the control of the management and, therefore, impairment loss and impairment loss reversals should be treated as non-operating in nature.

Appendix 3C: Understanding Reported Balance Sheet of Banks

Banks prepare balance sheet as per the format prescribed by the Government of India in its notification SO 240(E) dated 26-03-1992.[13] In this format, assets and liabilities are neither bifurcated into current and non-current nor separated into financial and non-financial. Instead, this format has five categories of Capital and Liabilities and six categories of Assets:

Assets

1. Cash and Balances with the Reserve Bank of India (RBI), which includes cash in hand and balances with the RBI in current account and other accounts.
2. Balances with Banks and money at call and short notice, which are similar to cash equivalents. Banks earn interest income on these amounts.
3. Investments, which includes investments made in government and other approved securities, shares, bonds, debentures, mutual funds, and investments in subsidiaries, associates, and joint-ventures. Banks earn interest and dividend income on investments.
4. Advances, which includes long-term loans, short-term loans, cash credits, overdrafts, and bills purchased and discounted. Banks earn interest income on advances.
5. Fixed Assets, which is similar in nature to Property, Plant, and Equipment, Capital Work-in-Progress, and Intangible Assets.
6. Other Assets, which includes all other assets not included in the first five categories.

Capital and Liabilities

1. Capital, which is similar to Equity Share Capital.
2. Reserves and Surplus, which is similar in nature to Other Equity.
3. Deposits, which comprises demand, savings, and term deposits received.
4. Borrowings, which includes those taken from the Reserve Bank of India (RBI), other banks, other institutions and agencies, and capital

[13] See https://rbidocs.rbi.org.in/rdocs/content/pdfs/83MD01092021_A1.pdf for the required Balance Sheet & Income Statement format. See https://rbidocs.rbi.org.in/rdocs/Publications/PDFs/78904.pdf for the details of balance sheet items, income statement items, and notes of accounts to be reported by banks.

instruments such as Innovative Perpetual Debt Instruments (IPDI, qualifying as Tier I capital) and subordinated debt (qualifying as Tier II capital).

5. Other Liabilities and Provisions, which includes all liabilities (including provisions) other than deposits and borrowings.

In addition to the eleven items mentioned above, a bank is also required to report two additional items on its balance sheet: Contingent Liabilities and Bills for Collection. Contingent liabilities are obligations that are either unlikely to be paid (as the management estimates that the likelihood of settlement is less than 50%) or whose value cannot be estimated reliably. Banks are required to include in their contingent liabilities: Claims against the bank not acknowledged as debts; Liability for partly paid investments; Liability on account of outstanding forward exchange contracts; Guarantee

Table 3C.1 SBI's Reported Balance Sheet

State Bank of India's Balance Sheet as at (amounts are rounded off to ₹ crore)	Schedule No.	March 31, 2022	March 31, 2021
Capital and Liabilities:			
Capital	1	892	892
Reserves & Surplus	2	2,79,196	2,52,983
Deposits	3	40,51,534	36,81,277
Borrowings	4	4,26,043	4,17,298
Other Liabilities and Provisions	5	2,29,932	1,81,980
Total		**49,87,597**	**45,34,430**
Assets:			
Cash and Balances with the RBI	6	2,57,859	2,13,202
Balances with Banks and money at call and short notice	7	1,36,693	1,29,837
Investments	8	14,81,445	13,51,705
Advances	9	27,33,967	24,49,498
Fixed Assets	10	37,708	38,419
Other Assets	11	3,39,925	3,51,769
Total		**49,87,597**	**45,34,430**
Contingent Liabilities	12	20,07,083	17,06,950
Bills for Collection		77,730	56,516
Significant Accounting Policies	17		
Notes to Accounts	18		

Source: State Bank of India,"SBI's Reported Balance Sheet", www.sbi.co.in

given on behalf of constituents (letters of credit and bills accepted on behalf of customers); Acceptances, endorsements and other obligations; and Other items for which the bank is contingently liable. Bills for Collection are the domestic sales and export documents presented by sellers to their bank to collect the payment from the buyer through the buyer's bank. Furthermore, banks provide their significant accounting policies and additional disclosures in a Notes to Accounts.

As at 31-3-2022, SBI had total assets of ₹49.88 lakh crore, liabilities of ₹47.08 lakh crore, and equity of ₹2.80 lakh crore. Its equity comprises Capital of ₹892 crore and Reserves & Surplus of ₹2.79 lakh crore. Its liabilities are made up of Deposits ₹40.52 lakh crore, Borrowings ₹4.26 lakh crore, and Other Liabilities and Provisions ₹2.30 lakh crore. Not surprising is that deposits are the biggest liabilities on its balance sheet. The largest assets are Advances ₹27.34 lakh crore followed by Investments ₹14.81 lakh crore. SBI has Cash and Cash Equivalents of ₹3.95 lakh crore consisting of Cash and Balances with the RBI of ₹2.58 lakh crore and Balances with Banks and money at call and short notice of ₹1.37 lakh crore.

CHAPTER FOUR

Statement of Cash Flows

Cash is the most liquid of assets, which a company uses to pay operational creditors, replace PPE and build productive capacity, repay debt, and pay dividends. Cash-rich companies can make cash purchases at a discount enjoying some cost advantages. Adequate cash also provides liquidity, solvency, and financial flexibility to a company. Although we can derive only some of the useful cash flows from income statements and comparative balance sheets, Cash Flow Statements provide a comprehensive picture of cash flows from operating, investing, and financing activities. Here are 10 relevant questions that can be answered using the information on a cash flow statement:

1. Is the company generating cash or using cash in operations? How much? Is it sustainable?
2. Why are operating cash flows (before taxes) higher/lower than operating profit?
3. What non-operating expenditures are funded with operating cash flows? How much?
4. How much capital expenditure did the company make during the year? Does the expenditure maintain productive capacity or augment capacity?
5. How much did the company invest in subsidiaries, associates, and joint ventures? Do these investments provide business/strategic advantage to the company?
6. How much cash did the company raise from equity and debt? How much cash did it use to buy back shares, repay debt, and pay interest and dividends? Where did the company deploy cash received (if any) from the issue of shares and raising debt?
7. What is the free cash flow generated by the company? Are free cash flows growing?

8. How did it use the free cash flows? How much cash did it use for debt repayments/prepayments, share buybacks, regular dividends, and special dividends?
9. What did the company do with the surplus cash generated during the year? Did it deploy them in non-current or current investments or retain them as cash & cash equivalents?
10. Which stage of its lifecycle is a company currently in?

I. Key concepts

Statement of Cash Flows (or simply Cash Flow Statement) is an integral part of the financial statements for each period. It must be prepared according to applicable accounting standards (for example, the newer Ind AS 17 for listed non-banking companies and the older AS 3 for other companies). This section provides an overview of various important concepts that are necessary for understanding cash flow statements.

(a) Cash & Cash Equivalents (C&CE)

On a Cash Flow Statement, *cash flows* are inflows to and outflows from C&CE. Therefore, it is important to revisit the concept of cash and cash equivalent, which we had discussed in the Balance Sheet chapter. As discussed in the previous chapter, *Cash* comprises currency notes and coins with the company, cheques and demand drafts in hand or in transit, amounts in current, overdraft, and cash credit accounts with banks, etc. The amounts owed for overdraft and cash credit are repayable on demand and hence deducted from C&CE. The balance in these two types of accounts may fluctuate from negative to positive.

Cash equivalents are short-term, highly liquid investments that are subject to an insignificant risk of changes in value and can be easily converted into known amounts of cash. Here, short-term refers to initial maturity of three months or less. Examples of CE are deposits having initial maturity of 3 months or less with banks and financial institutions, investments in liquid mutual funds, etc. A company keeps cash equivalents as part of its cash management system to meet short-term cash requirements, and not for investment or any other purpose.

(b) Cash Flows

Cash flows are either cash inflows or cash outflows. Cash inflows are receipts and they increase total C&CE. Examples of cash inflows are cash sales, cash received from trade receivable, cash proceeds from sales of fixed assets, cash proceeds from sales of investments, interest received, borrowings received, cash proceeds from the issue of equity shares, etc. By contrast, cash outflows are cash payments, and they reduce total C&CE. Examples of cash outflows are cash purchases, amounts paid to trade payable, capital expenditure, purchase of investments, borrowings repaid, interest paid, dividends paid, share buyback, etc.

On cash flow statements, cash inflows are written as positive numbers, whereas cash outflows are written as negative numbers (within parentheses). Thus, a cash inflow of ₹99 will be shown as 99, whereas an outflow of ₹100 will be written as (100) on cash flow statements. Accordingly, when we see an amount in parentheses, such as (250), we should treat it as a cash payment/outflow of ₹250. When we see an amount not in parentheses, such as 123, we treat it as a cash inflow of ₹123.

It is important to remember that cash flows exclude all movements from one item of C&CE to another, and such movements are not reported on a cash flow statement (they may be disclosed separately). Some examples of such intra-C&CE movements (not considered as cash flows) are paying someone a ₹500 note and receiving five notes of ₹100, a cash withdrawal from a bank account, a deposit of proceeds from a fixed deposit (having initial maturity of one month) into a bank account, a purchase of units in a liquid mutual fund, etc.

(c) Operating, Investing, and Financing Activities

Everything that a company does can be classified into operating, investing, or financing activities. Cash Flow Statements present cash flow information for each of these three activities separately in three sections: Operating, Investing, and Financing.

Financing activities are related to equity capital, preference capital, borrowings, and lease liabilities. Transactions such as issuing shares, buying back shares, paying dividends, taking on borrowings & lease liabilities, repaying borrowings & lease liabilities, and paying interest are examples of financing activities. Investing activities are related to fixed assets and investments. Transactions such as capital expenditure, sale of fixed assets, loans given, return of loan given, purchase of investments, sale of investments, and receiving interest, dividend, & any other income from investments are examples of investing activities. Note that financing activities and investing activities together are referred to as non-operating activities.

Operating Activities include the principal revenue-producing activity of an entity and all related things and anything that is not classified as non-operating (i.e., investing or financing activity). Some examples of operating activities are sales & services rendered, other operating income, purchase of materials & stock-in-trade, incurring overheads, production of finished goods, employing workers and managers, paying suppliers of goods & services, engaging auditors, paying taxes, etc.

The above description is appropriate for entities that are not banks or financial institutions. For financial firms, interest paid, interest received, and dividends received are generally classified as cash flows arising from operating activities because earning interest on loans advanced, interest and dividends on investments made, and paying interest on deposits is their business.

(d) Direct & Indirect Method

Cash flow statements may be prepared by direct method or indirect method or a mix of both. Under the direct method, a company reveals the sources of cash inflows and the uses for cash outflows during the period. Indian companies use the direct method to report cash flows from investing and financing activities. For example, they would show interest received, proceeds from the sale of investments, capital expenditures, interest paid, dividends paid, borrowings repaid, etc.

Companies are free to use either the direct method or the indirect method to report operating cash flows. If they use the direct method for operating activities, they would report cash collected from customers, other operating income collected, cash paid to suppliers, cash paid to or on behalf of employees, cash paid for various expenses, taxes paid, etc. This information is useful in forecasting future cash flows.

However, companies use the indirect method for reporting operating cash flows as per Ind AS 7 (Statement of Cash Flow). Instead of disclosing the sources of cash inflows and the uses of outflows, they reconcile profit before taxes to operating cash flows. In the process, they provide information that, in aggregate, yields the amount of operating cash flows before taxes, and they next deduct taxes paid to obtain net cash generated from (or used in) operating activities. This method is explained in detail in the context of operating cash flows in the next section. Although this may seem odd, there can be interesting benefits of this type of disclosure. All non-cash items and non-operating income, gains, expenses, and losses affecting profits can be found in one place, and we do not need to search for them in various notes for various analyses, including an assessment of the quality of earnings and the reasons for the difference between operating profit and operating cash flows.

(e) Obtaining Cash Flows

We can obtain the total amount paid (cash outflow) or received (cash inflow) for any asset, liability, or equity item on a balance sheet. To do so, we need to know what caused the item to increase and decrease. The following identity is useful for this:

$$Beginning + Additions = Deductions + Ending$$

From this identity, we can obtain the following three useful equations:

$$Change = Ending - Beginning = Additions - Deductions$$

$$Additions = Deductions + Change = Deductions + Ending - Beginning$$

$$Deductions = Additions - Change = Additions + Beginning - Ending$$

Let us consider three examples to understand these concepts and ascertain cash flows. First, consider trade payable (a liability), which increases due to purchases from suppliers but decreases due to cash paid to suppliers. Let us say, Trade Payable at the beginning of the period is 95, at the end of the period is 105, and Credit Purchases are 400 during the period. In this example, change in trade payable is 10 (= 105 – 95). So, Cash paid to Suppliers (deduction) = Purchases (addition) 400 – Change in the Balance of Trade Payables 10 = 390. Thus, during the period, ₹(390) was the cash outflow, i.e., paid to trade payables.

Next, consider gross Trade Receivable (an asset), which increases when goods are sold but decreases when not only cash is collected but also bad & doubtful debt is written off. Suppose the Beginning gross Trade Receivable is 209, the Ending gross Trade Receivable is 179, Credit Sales are 2000, all trade receivables are considered good, and there was no Bad & Doubtful Debt. Here, the change in gross trade receivables is negative, –30 =179 – 209. Cash Received (deduction) = Sales (addition) 2000 – Bad & Doubtful Debt Expense (deduction) 0 – Change in the Balance of Trade Receivables (–30) = 2000 + 30 = 2,030. Thus, during the period, the company collected 2,030 from customers, i.e., cash inflows from trade receivables amounted to ₹2,030.

Finally, consider Advance from Customers (a liability), which increases when cash is collected from customers and decreases when goods or services are delivered (i.e., sales are recognized for these goods or services). Suppose, Change in Advance from Customers is 60, Sales to these customers is 500. So, Cash Received (addition) = Sales (deduction) 500 + Change 60 = 560. Therefore, ₹560 was the cash inflow during the year from advance from customers.

These three examples illustrate that knowing what causes a balance sheet item to go up (additions) and down (deductions) is the key to deriving cash flows for an individual item of asset, liability, equity, or at an aggregate level, such as operating cash flows under the indirect method.

II. Cash Flows from Operating Activities (CFOA)

Operating cash flows are the cash flows from principal revenue-producing and related activities. To obtain operating cash flows under the direct method, a company needs to report/use gross cash inflows or cash outflows. According to Ind AS 17 (Statement of Cash Flow), these include:

i. cash received from the sale of goods and the rendering of services;
ii. cash received from royalties, fees, commissions, and other revenue;
iii. cash paid to suppliers for goods and services;
iv. cash paid to and on behalf of employees;
v. cash paid of income taxes or cash refunds received unless they can be specifically identified with financing and investing activities;
vi. for an insurance entity only: cash received and cash paid for premiums and claims, annuities, and other policy benefits;
vii. for banks and other financial institutions only: cash received for interest and dividend income and cash paid for interest;
viii. for entities holding securities, loans, and contracts (such as forwards, futures, and options) for dealing or trading purposes: cash received and cash paid on those items, which are like their inventory for resale; and
ix. cash paid to make or buy assets held for rental to others and subsequently held for sale and cash received from rental income and subsequent sales of such assets are also included under operating cash flows (see the last para under point 14 on page 703 of Ind AS 7).

For the 2021–22 financial year, Asian Paints, Avenue Supermarts, and Infosys reported Operating Cash Flows under the indirect method. Since operating cash flows are due to transactions that determine operating profit or loss, companies obtain operating cash flows under the indirect method as follows:

i. Start with PBT (profit before taxes) to obtain operating cash flows before taxes.
ii. Next, all *Non-operating expenses & losses* (including interest expenses) are added back to PBT, and all *Non-operating income & gains* are

deducted. This step yields Operating profit (not reported on cash flow statements).[1]

iii. After that, all *Non-cash operating expenses* are added back (for example, depreciation and amortization expense, impairment loss, bad debt written off, expenses arising out of increases in provisions related to employee benefits, etc.), and all *Non-cash operating incomes & gains* are deducted (for example, reversal of impairment loss, income arising out of decreases in provisions related to employee benefits) since these incomes and expenses do not affect cash flows. These adjustments to operating profit are made to obtain cash-operating profit (or the portion of operating profit that would affect cash flows), which is reported as "*Operating Profit Before Working Capital Change*" (OPBWCC) on cash flow statements.

iv. Next, changes in *operating liabilities* are added, whereas changes in *operating assets* are deducted, except for income tax-related assets & liabilities. The result is reported as "*Operating Cash Flows Before Taxes*".

v. Finally, *Taxes Paid* are deducted to obtain the *Net Cash Generated from (used in) Operating Activities* (i.e., Cash flow from Operating Activities).

From the above step (ii), we can infer that the difference between PBT and Operating Profit arises due to the presence of non-operating incomes, gains, expenses, and losses. Furthermore, the difference between operating profit (before taxes) and operating cash flow (before taxes) arises due to the presence of not only non-cash operating income and expense (step iii) but also changes in operating assets and liabilities (step iv). Among the non-cash operating items, the biggest is often depreciation & amortization, and together the rest of the items are often smaller than depreciation & amortization.

Another insight to draw (from the above steps), is from changes in operating assets and liabilities. Increases in operating liabilities and decreases in operating assets cause operating cash flows to be higher than operating profit, and vice versa. Therefore, it is important to scrutinize changes in trade receivable, inventories, and trade payable during the year, and see how they affected operating cash flows. Trade payable increases when payment to suppliers is less than purchases. This could imply that payments are being delayed, i.e., why are payments being stretched? Is the company suffering from liquidity shock? Is the

---

[1] Note: Operating Profit + Non-operating Income & Gains – Non-operating Expenses & Losses (excluding Interest Expense) = EBIT; EBIT – Interest Expense = PBT; Thus, PBT + Non-operating Expense & Losses (including Interest Expense) – Non-operating Income & Gains = Operating profit.

company using short-term funds for long-term assets? Similarly, a rise in trade receivables could imply cash collected from customers was less than sales, i.e., are collections slowing down? Are too many sales orders booked towards the end of the year? An increase in inventories could be when a company could not sell as much as it produced or procured, i.e., are sales slowing down? Are the sales forecasting process poor?

We must also note that income taxes are affected by operating, investing, and financing activities. For example, interest and dividends received are taxed, and interest and other finance cost paid are tax deductible. Still, the entire tax payment is deducted from operating cash flows before taxes to obtain the net cash flow from operating activities. Therefore, the reported operating cash flows may be either overstated or understated due to the effects of these non-operating income and expenses.

Let us now discuss the operating cash flows of Asian Paints, Avenue Supermarts, and Infosys.

Table 4.1 Summary of Operating Cash Flows (Indirect Method)

CFOA (summarized)	Asian Paints		Avenue Supermarts		Infosys	
₹ crore 31-3-	2022	2021	2022	2021	2022	2021
Profit Before Tax	4,194	4,090	2,182	1,545	28,495	24,477
OPBWCC	4,868	4,699	2,516	1,762	29,083	25,782
Cash Generated from Operations **(before taxes)**	2,369	4,474	1,868	1,642	28,832	25,963
Taxes Paid (net of refunds)	(1,109)	(1,015)	(553)	(256)	(6,736)	(6,061)
Net CFOA	*1,260*	*3,459*	*1,315*	*1,385*	*22,096*	*19,902*

Asian Paints reported much lower operating cash flows ₹1,260 crore in 2021–22 than ₹3,459 crore in 2020–21, although its OPBWCC were somewhat similar in the two years. This ₹2,199 crore decline can be attributed largely to a ₹2,153 crore increase in inventories in 2021–22 (the amount was ₹297 crore in the previous year) and a ₹1,142 crore increase in trade receivables (₹724 crore increase last year). Thus, it appears that the company could not fully utilize its raw materials purchased to produce finished goods and could not fully sell the finished goods produced and stock-in-trade purchased during the year (that is why inventories increased). The company also appears to have stretched the collection of amounts due from customers (the aging schedule reported in note 10 shows that the amount overdue for 6–12 months, 2–3 years, and more than 3 years are much higher in 2021–22 than in 2020–21) and booked disproportionately higher sales towards the end of the year compared to the last year, for example, the amount *not due* at the end of the current year is 65% more than the amount last year (₹2,739 crore versus ₹1,655 crore last year), and this rate of increase is much higher than the sales growth rate of 37%.

Avenue Supermarts reported an operating cash flow of ₹1,315 crores after paying ₹553 crore in taxes during 2021–22. The operating cash flows are about ₹70 crore or 5% lower (although OPBWCC is ₹754 crore higher) in 2021–22 compared to the previous year. Upon further examination of the changes in working capital components and taxes paid, we find that inventory and trade receivables increased by ₹579 crore, and taxes paid were ₹297 crore higher in 2021–22 compared to the previous year. These were the three major factors causing lower operating cash flows in 2021–22 than the year before. Thus, the company sold less inventory than it bought, and its collections from customers were much less than its sales (these two factors could reverse next year), and it paid much higher taxes during the year 2021–22 than the year before. However, taxes paid are unlikely to reverse next year given that taxes paid and current tax expense are similar.

Infosys reported higher operating cash flows of ₹22,096 crore in 2021–22 compared to ₹19,902 crore in 2020–21. This ₹2,194 crore increase is supported by an increase of ₹3,301 crore in OPBWCC in 2021–22 over the year before (₹29,083 crore vs. ₹25,782 crore obtained by summing the numbers reported), which suggests that the operating cash flow is sustainable. Although trade receivables and unbilled revenue increased significantly (₹5,725 crore increase in 2021–22 compared to ₹1,414 crore increase in 2020–21), this increase has been funded by a similar increase in operating liabilities (₹6,599 crore this year versus ₹2,279 crore last year). If the year 2021–22 were an aberration for trade receivables and unbilled revenue, we could expect that next year, the increase will be much lower (or perhaps there could be a decrease in these two assets) as these amounts will be collected, resulting in higher operating cash flows next year.

III. Cash Flows from Investing Activities (CFIA)

Investing activities are related to fixed assets (PPE, CWIP, intangible assets, ROU assets, and investment properties) and investments (investment in subsidiaries, associates, & joint ventures, other non-current investments, and current investments). For classifying as investment activities, an item of expenditure towards fixed assets must be of the nature of capital expenditure (i.e., expenditure for acquiring or constructing fixed assets). Hence, repairs and maintenance, which are revenue expenditures in nature, are not included in investment activities but within operating activities. Furthermore, the fixed assets may be either acquired or self-constructed, and investments could be in equity instruments or debt of another entity or mutual funds (other than those mutual funds treated as cash equivalents). Companies make investments in subsidiaries, joint ventures, and associates generally for business advantage. Investments in other entities, whether in their equity or debt instruments, are generally made for earning investment income and capital gains, i.e., purely for financial advantage, not a business one.

Investing activities include the acquisition and sale of fixed assets and investments and the earning of dividends, interest, or other income on investments. Some examples of cash payments and receipts classified as investing activities are cash paid towards capital expenditure, cash proceeds from the sale of fixed assets, cash given out as a loan to another entity, cash received when the loan is repaid by the other entity, cash payment for the purchase of investments, cash proceeds from the sale of investments, cash received for dividends, interest, and any other income from investments, etc.

Irrespective of the amount, the net capital expenditure made during the year is an important use of cash as it is an important signal of future operating capacity and the origination/reversal of deferred tax liabilities. Companies will be unable to maintain sales if they do not replace their worn-out fixed assets, nor will they be able to increase sales if they do not augment capacity, particularly when they are operating closer to 100% capacity. Therefore, we must pay attention to the amount they are spending on capital expenditure. We must also check whether the expenditure exceeds depreciation and amortization, which would increase fixed assets, thereby increasing DTL and reducing tax payments; otherwise, a decrease in fixed assets would cause a reversal of DTL and an increase in tax payments.

Asian Paints reported net cash used in investing activities, or net investing cash outflows, of ₹(340) crore for the current year ended 31-3-2022, which was lower in magnitude than ₹(436) crore in the previous year. In the current year, it paid ₹(403) crore for the purchase of PPE and other intangible assets and ₹(12) crore for acquiring ROU assets (i.e., both are capital expenditures) and received ₹27 crore from the sale of PPE. Thus, its capital expenditure (net) amount was ₹(388) crore in the current year, much higher in magnitude than ₹(193) crore in the previous year. However, capital expenditure (net) is much lower than the amount of depreciation & amortization expense of ₹722 crore for the current year, which appears to suggest that the capital expenditure may not be enough to maintain the capacity of fixed assets. The company received ₹71 crore in interest and dividend income during the year. It also invested ₹(80) crore in a subsidiary and generated ₹57 crore as proceeds from the sale of other investments (net of any purchases).

Table 4.2 Summary of Investing Cash Flows (Direct Method)

CFIA (summarized)		Asian Paints		Avenue Supermarts		Infosys	
₹ crore	31-3-22	2022	2021	2022	2021	2022	2021
Capex (net) Paid *		(388)	(193)	(2,282)	(1,968)	(1,787)	(1,720)
Investment Income Received		71	63	67	142	2,876	1,661
Investments in Subsidiaries, JVs, Associates, & M&A		(80)	0	(130)	(115)	(163)	(1,467)
Others including those related to Other Investments **		57	(306)	1,053	786	(4,076)	(4,783)
Net CFIA		*(340)*	*(436)*	*(1,292)*	*(1,155)*	*(3,150)*	*(6,309)*

* Capex (net) includes payment for acquiring property, plant, and equipment, other intangible assets, and right-of-use assets, net of any receipt from their disposal. ** Others primarily include receipts net of payments from investments in entities other than subsidiaries, joint ventures, and associates; these investments include fixed deposits, mutual funds, loans, debentures, equity shares, etc.

By contrast, Avenue Supermarts reported net investing cash outflows, i.e., net cash used in investing activities, of ₹(1,292) crore in the current year ending on 31-3-2022, which was similar to ₹(1,155) crore in the previous year. In both years, the company made a substantial net capital expenditure of ₹(2,282) crore in the current year and ₹(1,968) crore in the previous year, and the expenditure exceeded depreciation and amortization in those years. The capital expenditure appears to be funded partly from the net proceeds from the sale of other investments (fixed deposits) and partly from operating cash flows. The company also paid ₹(130) crore for investment in a subsidiary. Its interest and rent receipts were ₹67 crore, which was significantly lower than the last year's ₹142 crore.

In 2021–22 financial year, Infosys reported a negative amount ₹(3,150) crore for net cash outflow from investing activities, which is about half in magnitude compared to the year before. It made capital expenditure of ₹(1,787) crore, about the same as last year, but significantly less than ₹2,429 crore amount of depreciation & amortization in the current year. The company received ₹2,876 crore in income from investment (dividends and interest). During the year, it invested ₹163 crore in subsidiaries (vs. ₹1,467 crore last year). Thus, investments in subsidiaries have slowed down. Infosys also acquired and sold – for a net amount ₹(4,076) crore – investments in equity & preference securities, tax-free bonds, government securities, certificates of deposits, non-convertible debentures, liquid mutual funds, and fixed maturity plan securities.

Note that companies may acquire and sell large amounts of investments, although their net amount may be small. For example, in 2021–22, Infosys bought mutual fund units paying ₹(48,139) crore and sold mutual fund units receiving ₹48,219 crore, among several other such transactions. These suggest that Infosys has an active treasury management team. Similarly, in 2021–22, Asian Paints purchased term deposits paying ₹(1,048) crore and received ₹897 crore as proceeds from the maturity of term deposits. We don't find anything similar in the case of Avenue Supermarts.

IV. Cash Flows from Financing Activities (CFFA)

Financing activities are related to the capital structure of a company, i.e., equity and debt. Note that debt may take the form of preference capital, borrowings, notes, bonds, mortgages, leases, and other short-term or long-term borrowings, as discussed in Chapter 3 (Balance Sheet). Financing cash flows arise from the issuance and repayment/repurchase of equity capital, preference capital, and borrowings, besides paying lease liabilities, interest, and dividends. Some examples of cash receipts and payments classified as financing activities are cash proceeds from issuing shares, cash paid for buying back shares, cash paid as dividends, cash received from borrowings, cash paid for repaying borrowings, cash paid for prepaying borrowings, cash paid for the principal portion of lease liabilities, and interest and dividend paid, etc.[2] [3]

[2] Repayment happens on or after the date the amount is due. Prepayment occurs before the amount is due.

[3] A lease rental comprises the interest portion and the principal portion of lease liabilities. Interest is computed on the balance of lease liability. Companies generally report the payment of interest on lease liabilities and the payment of the principal portion of lease liabilities separately.

Table 4.3 Summary of Financing Cash Flows (Direct Method)

CFFA (summarized)	Asian Paints		Avenue Supermarts		Infosys	
₹ crore 31-3-22	2022	2021	2022	2021	2022	2021
Dividends Paid	(1,741)	(466)	–	–	(12,697)	(9,155)
Finance Cost Paid *	(68)	(69)	(39)	(36)	(126)	(125)
Principal portion of Lease Liabilities *	(183)	(159)	(81)	(66)	(472)	(295)
Borrowings (net)	78	111	0	(38)	–	–
Issue of Shares	–	–	–	–	11	9
Buyback of Shares	(75)	0	–	–	(11,125)	–
Others	–	–	–	–	134	–
Net CFFA	*(1,989)*	*(583)*	*(121)*	*(140)*	*(24,275)*	*(9,566)*

* Unlike Asian Paints and Avenue Supermarts, Infosys did not bifurcate the lease rentals paid into the interest portion and the principal portion of lease liabilities. In note 2.3, Infosys reported finance cost accrued (i.e., interest expense) of ₹126 crore in 2021–22 and ₹125 crore in 2020–21. Thus, the principal portion of lease liabilities paid is ₹472 (= 598 – 126) during the current year and ₹295 = (420 – 125) during the previous year.

Asian Paints reported ₹(1,989) crore of net cash used in financing activities for the year ended 31-3-2022, which was more than thrice the amount ₹(583) crore reported in the year before. In both these years, the net financing cash flows were driven by the amount of dividend paid, ₹(1,741) crore this year versus ₹(466) crore last year. The company also reported cash outflows for repayment of non-current borrowings ₹(8) crore, repayment of lease liabilities ₹(183) crore, interest paid ₹(68) crore, treasury shares purchased by its ESOP trust ₹(75) crore, and net cash inflow from acceptances ₹86 crore in the current year. Thus, the company neither raised any equity nor received a significant amount from borrowings during the financial year.

Avenue Supermarts reported a much smaller amount ₹(121) crore of net financing cash outflow in the current year 2021–22, versus ₹(140) crore previous year 2020–21. During the current year, the company received ₹248 crore and repaid ₹(248) crore of short-term borrowings. It paid ₹(81) crore towards the principal portion of the lease liability and ₹(38) crore towards interest on lease liability. It also paid a small amount of ₹(1) crore towards interest on borrowings. The company did not pay any dividends in the current year as well as in the past year. Furthermore, the company did not raise any amount from equity and borrowings during the financial year.

Infosys' Cash Flow Statement shows a negative amount for cash flow from financing activities, ₹(24,275) crore, which was largely driven by dividend paid ₹(12,697) crore and share buyback ₹(11,125) crore. It also paid ₹(598) crore towards lease liabilities. The company also reported two cash inflow items ₹11 crore from the issue of shares on the exercise of employee stock options and ₹134 crore from other receipts. Thus, the company did not raise any significant amount from equity, nor it raised any amount from borrowings during the financial year.

For all three firms – Asian Paints, Avenue Supermarts, and Infosys – net financing cash flows are negative, operating cash flows are positive, and the net change in C&CE is negative. Thus, these firms funded their net investing and financing outflows partly from operating cash flows and the remaining from beginning cash and cash equivalents.

V. Net Change in Cash and Cash Equivalent

Net change in C&CE is ending total C&CE minus beginning total C&CE. This amount is also the same as the sum of the cash flows from operating, investing, and financing activities.

Table 4.4 Net Change in C&CE & Ending Balance of C&CE

Net Change in C&CE		**Asian Paints**		**Avenue Supermarts**		**Infosys**	
₹ crore	31-3-22	2022	2021	2022	2021	2022	2021
Net change C&CE		(1,069)	2,440	(98)	90	(5,329)	4,027
Ending C&CE		2,065	3,134	83	181	12,270	17,612

For all three firms – Asian Paints, Avenue Supermarts, and Infosys – the net change in C&CE is negative in 2021–22. Their C&CE declined during the year, and their operating cash flows were not sufficiently large to cover investing and financing net cash outflows. These firms funded their net cash outflows from investing and financing activities by utilizing net cash inflows from operating activities and their beginning cash and cash equivalents. The pattern of *positive* operating cash flows, *negative* investing cash flows, and *negative* financing cash flows that we see for these three companies is a characteristic of mature companies (Dickinson 2011)[4].

[4] Dickinson, V. (2011). Cash Flow Patterns as a Proxy for Firm Life Cycle. The Accounting Review, 86(6), 1969–1994. http://www.jstor.org/stable/41408043

VI. Free Cash Flows

A healthy company generates positive operating cash flows as well as receives income from investments that, together, are sufficiently large to pay for interest (on borrowings and lease liabilities), dividends (to equity and preference shareholders), and replacement of fixed assets. Any additional cash is the Free Cash Flow to Firm (FCFF) that the company can use to expand its business (through the purchase/construction of fixed assets, mergers & acquisitions), repay borrowings, buyback shares, pay special/additional dividends, or retain it for future use. An adequately positive FCFF is financial strength because it provides the financial power not only to grow but also to sustain difficult times (such as during the COVID-19 pandemic), which is quite valuable to managers, lenders, and investors.

Figure 4.1 PAT, CFOA*, & FCFF across the Four Stages of Company Life Cycle

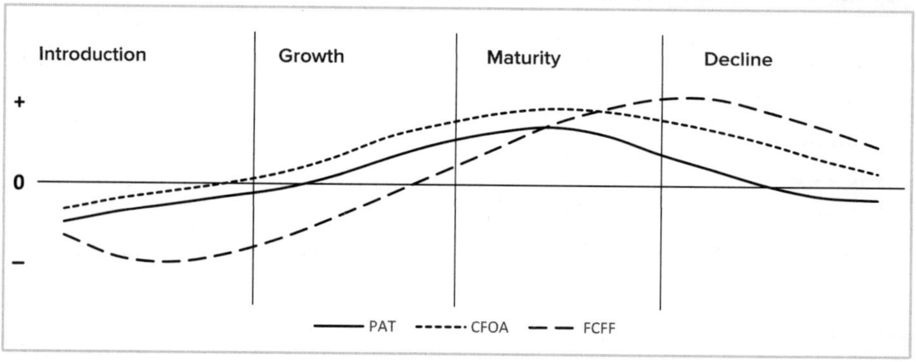

* CFOA is as per U.S. GAAP.

Equity shareholders are also interested in Free Cash Flow to Equity (FCFE). FCFE is free cash flows after including cash inflows from new debts and cash outflows to repay existing debts during the year. FCFE is available for distribution to shareholders as special/additional dividends and share repurchases. Free Cash Flows reveal whether a company can generate sufficient liquidity.

$$FCFF = CFOA + Investment\ Income\ Received - Interest\ Paid - Capital\ Expenditure\ (net)$$

$$FCFE = FCFF + Cash\ inflow\ from\ Debt - Cash\ outflow\ for\ repaying\ Debt$$

Ideally, we should deduct capital expenditure required to maintain the company's productive capacity. However, not only is that information unavailable on the company's cash flow statement but also it may be difficult to split the amounts of capital expenditure into expected/required and excess/shortfall. Therefore, the reported amounts of net capital expenditure are generally deducted for obtaining FCFF.

Let us compute and analyze free cash flows for each of the three companies using information reported on Cash Flow Statements.

Table 4.5 Calculation of Free Cash Flows

Free Cash Flows ₹ crore	Asian Paints 31-3-2022	Avenue Supermarts 31-3-2022	Infosys 31-3-2022
CFOA (reported) (A)	*1,260*	*1,315*	*22,096*
Interest Received	56	39	1,658
Rent Income	–	28	
Dividends from Subsidiaries	0	–	1,218
Dividends Received from Others	15	–	
Investment Income Received (B)	*71*	*67*	*2,876*
Finance Cost (Interest) Paid (C)	*(68)*	*(2)*	*(126)*
US GAAP CFOA (D) = A + B – |C|	*1,263*	*1,380*	*24,846*
Sale of PPE	27	1	–
Purchase of PPE & OIA	–403	–2,283	–1787
Payment to acquire ROU assets	–12	–	–
Capital Expenditure (net) (E)	*(388)*	*(2,282)*	*(1,787)*
FCFF (F) = D – |E|	***875***	***(902)***	***23,059***
Proceeds from borrowings (G)	–	248	–
Acceptances (H)	86	–	–
Repayment of borrowings (I)	–8	–248	–
Repayment of lease liabilities (J) *	–183	–81	–472
FCFE (K) = F + G + H - |I| - |J|	***770***	***(983)***	***22,587***

* For Infosys, Repayment of lease liabilities (principal portion only) = –598 payment of lease liabilities (which is assumed to include both principal portion and interest accrued since its Financing Cash Flows do not have a separate line item for interest paid) + 126 interest accrued on lease liability (included as interest paid to obtain FCFF).

Asian Paints generated a positive FCFF of ₹875 crore and a positive FCFE of ₹770 crore in 2021–22, which indicates that the company generated sufficient free cash flows. Together, its operating cash flows and investment income took care of its capital expenditure and interest payments. Overall, it appears the firm has financially flexibility to grow the business further or sustain difficult times. This is a strength of the firm as revealed by its free cash flows.

Avenue Supermarts also generated a negative FCFF of ₹(902) crore and a negative FCFE of ₹(983) crore in 2021–22. Operating cash flows and investment income together appear to fall short of payment towards capital expenditure and interest. However, when we compare the net Capital expenditure of ₹2,282 crore to the Depreciation & amortization expense of ₹421 crore, it appears that capital expenditure is largely for capacity expansion and much more than the amount needed for maintaining productive capacity, which would be closer to depreciation and amortization expense. Computing FCFF using depreciation & amortization as a proxy for expenditure for maintaining productive capacity indicates a much higher and positive FCFF of ₹959 crore (= –902 + 2282 – 421 depreciation) and FCFE of ₹878 crore (= –983 + 2282 – 421).

Infosys generated a large and positive FCFF of ₹23,059 crore and FCFE of ₹22,587 crore during 2021–22. The company generated cash inflows from operations and investment income, which were large enough to pay for capital expenditure and interest. This indicates good financial health and financial flexibility, which contributes to the financial strength of Infosys. The company was able to use its FCFE to pay large sums of dividend and buy back its equity during the year. Computing FCFF using depreciation & amortization as a proxy for expenditure for maintaining productive capacity would have resulted in a much higher free cash flow.

VII. Analysis of Cash Flow Statement

When analyzing a cash flow statement, we first look at the total cash flows from the three activities and the free cash flows. Next, we look at the principal sources of cash (i.e., inflows) and important uses of cash (i.e., outflows) during a financial year. This information is useful to assess a company's ability to generate liquidity and thus thrive in normal times. In addition, we must look at the total C&CE at the end of the financial year to assess the level of liquidity and check how long the C&CE could last (i.e., support the business operations), which is useful if times go bad as was the case during the COVID-19 pandemic. Thus, both the cash flow and the level of cash are useful information. Now, let us analyze the cash flow statement of each of our three companies.

Table 4.6 Summary of Cash Flows

Obtained from Cash Flow Statement for the year ended March 31, 2022 (amounts in ₹ crore)	Asian Paints	Avenue Supermarts	Infosys
Cash flows from Operating Activities (reported)	1,260	1,315	22,096
Cash flows from Investing Activities (reported)	(340)	(1,292)	(3,150)
Cash flows from Financing Activities (reported)	(1,989)	(121)	(24,275)
Free Cash Flows to Firm (FCFF) (computed)	*875*	*(902)*	*23,059*
Free Cash Flows to Equity (FCFE) (computed)	*770*	*(983)*	*22,587*
Ending Cash & Cash Equivalents (C&CE) (reported)	2,065	83	12,270

In 2021–22, Asian Paints generated ₹1260 crore of net operating cash flows and used ₹(340) crore in investing activities and ₹(1,989) crore in financing activities. The pattern of *positive* operating cash flows, *negative* investing cash flows, and *negative* financing cash flows that we see for this company is a characteristic of mature companies (Dickinson 2011). Asian Paints had a positive FCFF of ₹875 crore and FCFE of ₹770 crore, which indicates the company has financially flexibility to make discretionary expenditures such as capacity augmenting capital expenditure, build cash reserves, buyback shares, or pay dividends. The company's principal source of cash is the operating cash flows before taxes of ₹2,369 crore, whereas the important uses of cash are payment of taxes net of refunds ₹(1,109) crore, capital expenditure net of proceeds from sale of fixed assets ₹(388) crore, and dividends paid ₹(1,741) crore.

During the year, its net C&CE declined ₹1,069 crore to ₹2,065 crore as of 31-3-2022, which is 164% of the operating cash flows during the year 2021–22. This amount would be sufficient to cover one month's cash operating costs (= 12 months × 2,065 Ending C&CE ÷ (25,189 Revenue – 4,868 OPBWCC)) if its business was severely disrupted and all operating cash inflows stopped.[5]

In 2021–22, Avenue Supermarts generated ₹1,315 crore of net cash flows from operating activities and used ₹(1,292) crore in investing activities and ₹(121) crore in financing activities. The pattern of *positive* operating cash flows, *negative* investing cash flows, and *negative* financing cash flows that we see for this company is a characteristic of mature companies (Dickinson 2011). Avenue Supermarts had a negative FCFF of ₹(902) crore and FCFE of ₹(983) crore, which indicates the company is financially stretched. The company's principal sources of cash were the operating cash flows before taxes of ₹1,868 crore and proceeds from fixed deposit ₹1,050, whereas the important uses of cash are payment of taxes net of refunds ₹(553) crore and capital expenditure

[5] Revenue minus OPBWCC is the Expenses incurred in Cash.

net of proceeds from the sale of fixed assets ₹(2,282) crore. During the year, its net C&CE declined ₹(98) crore to ₹83 crore as of 31-3-2022. The company had Other Bank Balances of ₹201 crore on its Balance Sheet. Given the size of its operations and fixed costs, ₹284 crore (=83 + 201) can support 4 days of operations (= 365 days × 284 Ending C&CE ÷ (30,352 Revenue – 2,516 OPBWCC)) if the business were suddenly disrupted.

In 2021–22, Infosys generated ₹22,096 crore of net operating cash flows and used ₹(3,150) crore in investing activities and ₹(24,275) crore from financing activities. The pattern of *positive* operating cash flows, *negative* investing cash flows, and *negative* financing cash flows that we see for this company is a characteristic of mature companies (Dickinson 2011). Infosys had a large and positive FCFF of ₹23,059 crore and FCFE of ₹22,587 crore, which indicates the company has a financial flexibility to make discretionary expenditures such as capacity augmenting capital expenditure, build cash reserves, buyback shares, or pay special dividends. The company generated cash mainly from the operating cash flows before taxes of ₹28,832 crore, whereas its important uses of cash are net payment of taxes ₹(6,736) crore, net capital expenditure ₹(1,787) crore, buyback of shares ₹(11,125) crore, and dividends payment ₹(12,697) crore. During the year, its net C&CE declined ₹(5,329) crore to ₹12,270 crore as of 31-3-2022. This amount appears to be sufficient to support two months of cash operating costs (= 12 months × 12,270 Ending C&CE ÷ (103,940 Revenue – 29,083 OPBWCC)).

Appendix 4A: Assessing a Company's stage in Lifecycle

We can use the sign of the net cash flows from operating, investing, and financing activities to assess the lifecycle stage of a company. The following table is based on Dickinson (2011) study for identifying the lifecycle stage for companies reporting cash flows as per US GAAP:

Table 4A.1 Cash Flow Patterns across Stages of Company Lifecycle

Lifecycle Stage	Operating Cash flows (as per US GAAP)	Investing Cash flows (as per US GAAP)	Financing Cash flows (as per US GAAP)
Introduction stage	–	–	+
Growth stage	+	–	+
Mature stage	+	–	–
Decline stage	–	+	+ or –
Shake-Out stage	–	–	–
	+	+	+ or –

Note that the above cash flows are as per US GAAP. We can easily convert cash flows reported as per Indian GAAP to those as per US GAAP. All income received on investments (such as interest and dividends received) and all interest and finance costs paid should be classified as Operating Cash Flows as per US GAAP. Therefore, (1) reduce net investing cash flows and increase net operating cash flows by all income from investments, and (2) increase net financing cash flows and decrease net operating cash flows by interest paid.

(a) Introduction Stage

In this stage, companies focus on raising money from financing activities and deploying them to build capacity and fund cash needed in operating activities. The 2021–22 Cash Flow Statement of Zomato reveals negative CFOA ₹(509) crore, negative CFIA ₹(8,131) crore, and positive CFFA ₹8,763 crore. The pattern indicates that Zomato is in the introduction phase of the company lifecycle. Note that Zomato received interest of ₹114 crore and paid total interest of ₹(4) crore, which are small in magnitude and, therefore, if we obtained the amounts as per the US GAAP, we would continue to make a similar inference. Another example of a company that shows a similar pattern of cash flows from operating, investing, and financing activities is One 97 Communications (known for the PayTM brand).

Table 4A.2 Cash Flow Pattern of Companies in Introduction Stage of Lifecycle

CFS for year ended 31-3-2022	Zomato	One 97 Communications
Sign of net CFOA (US GAAP)	–	–
Sign of net CFIA (US GAAP)	–	–
Sign of net CFFA (US GAAP)	+	+
Life Cycle Stage	Introduction	Introduction

(b) Growth Stage

Companies in the growth stage generate cash from operating activities, but the amount is not enough to fund expansion. Therefore, they raise resources from financing activities to grow fixed assets. In 2021–22, Adani Wilmar reported a positive CFOA of ₹1,154 crore, negative CFIA of ₹(3,848) crore inclusive of interest received ₹81 crore, and positive CFFA of ₹2,716 crore inclusive of interest paid ₹(304) crore. These amounts suggest that Adani Wilmar is in a growth stage. Dr. Lal Pathlabs is another example of a company showing a similar pattern in its cash flows and therefore can be considered a company in the growth phase.

Table 4A.3 Cash Flow Pattern of Companies in Growth Stage of Lifecycle

CFS for year ended 31-3-2022	Adani Wilmar	Dr. Lal Pathlabs
Sign of net CFOA (US GAAP)	+	+
Sign of net CFIA (US GAAP)	–	–
Sign of net CFFA (US GAAP)	+	+
Life Cycle Stage	Growth	Growth

(c) Mature Stage

Mature companies generate large amounts of cash from operating activities, use these funds to replace fixed assets and build investments (net cash outflows from investing activities) and pay dividends, buyback of shares, repay borrowings, etc. (net cash outflows from financing activities).

We infer that Asian Paints, Avenue Supermarts, and Infosys are in the mature stage of their lifecycle based on the signs of cash flows from operating, investing, and financing sections as per Indian GAAP (i.e., without doing the conversion to US GAAP). Had we done the conversion, we would still reach the same conclusion since the adjustments required are relatively small in magnitude.

Table 4A.4 Cash Flow Pattern of Companies in Mature Stage of Lifecycle

CFS for year ended 31-3-2022	Asian Paints	Avenue Supermarts	Infosys
Sign of net CFOA (US GAAP)	+	+	+
Sign of net CFIA (US GAAP)	–	–	–
Sign of net CFFA (US GAAP)	–	–	–
Life Cycle Stage	Mature	Mature	Mature

(d) Decline Stage

In the decline phase, companies use cash in operating activities (often due to losses) and generate cash from investing activities (often selling investments and/or divisions). Thus, they have a negative U.S. GAAP CFOA and a positive US GAAP CFIA. Their US GAAP CFFA may be either positive or negative. Some companies with negative US GAAP CFOA but positive US GAAP CFIA in 2021–22 are Kirloskar Electric Company (its interest paid ₹61 crore is much larger in magnitude than the positive CFOA reported ₹24 crore and interest & dividend received ₹7 crore is quite small, so although CFOA reported is positive, we get a negative CFOA as per US GAAP), Reliance Home Finance, and Avanti Feeds. Based on the pattern in 2021–22, these companies appear to be in the decline stage.

Table 4A.5 Cash Flow Pattern of Companies in Decline Stage of Lifecycle

CFS for year ended 31-3-2022	Kirloskar Electric	Reliance Home Finance	Avanti Feeds
Sign of net CFOA (US GAAP)	–	–	–
Sign of net CFIA (US GAAP)	+	+	+
Sign of net CFFA (US GAAP)	+	–	–
Life Cycle Stage	Decline	Decline	Decline

Appendix 4B Understanding Reported Cash Flow Statement of Banks

Banks' reported cash flow statements are similar to what we have seen for non-financial firms. The statements have three sections – Operating, Investing, and Financing. Operating Cash Flows are presented by indirect method, whereas Investing and Financing Cash Flows are presented by direct method.

Table 4B.1 SBI's Cash Flows (Summary)

State Bank of India: Cash Flow Statement summarized (Amounts rounded off to nearest ₹ crore)	Year ended 31.03.2022	Year ended 31.03.2021
Net Cash Flows from Operating Activities	58,415	89,866
Net Cash Flows from Investing Activities	(2,613)	(3,354)
Net Cash Flows from Financing Activities	(5,178)	5,633
Effect of Translation Reserve	888	(202)
Net Increase/(Decrease) in Cash & Cash Equivalents	51,514	91,942
Beginning Cash and Cash Equivalents	343,039	251,097
Ending Cash and Cash Equivalents	394,552	343,039

Source: State Bank of India 2021–22, "SBI's Cash Flows (Summary)", www.sbi.co.in

Note that manufacturing, retail, and service firms deduct investment income (such as interest and dividend income) from and add back interest expense to PBT to determine OPBWCC (operating profit before working capital changes). That is not the case with banks. For example, SBI does not add back interest expense and does not deduct income on investments (except dividend income from subsidiaries, joint ventures, and associates). As a result, its cash inflows from interest received on advances and cash outflows for interest paid on deposits are included in its net operating cash flows, and not in their net investing cash flows.

Table 4B.2 SBI's Operating Cash Flows

State Bank of India: Operating Cash Flows summarized from Cash Flow Statement (Amounts rounded off to nearest ₹ crore)	Year ended 31.03.2022	Year ended 31.03.2021
Profit Before Tax	43,422	27,541
OPBWCC	76,149	78,500
Cash Generated from Operations (before taxes)	66,228	92,260
Taxes Paid (net of refunds)	(7,812)	(2,395)
Net CFOA	*58,415*	*89,866*

As noted, a bank's net investing cash flows do *not* include cash inflows from interest & dividends received, cash outflow for purchasing investment securities, and proceeds from selling investments, among others, unless the cash flows are related to the bank's subsidiary, joint venture, or associate. Thus, their investing cash flows include cash flows for purchasing and selling fixed assets and investments in and investment income from subsidiaries, joint ventures, and associates, as can be seen from SBI's investing cash flows reported in 2021–22.

Table 4B.3 SBI's Investing Cash Flows

State Bank of India: Investing Cash Flows summarized from Cash Flow Statement (Amount rounded off to nearest ₹ crore)	Year ended 31.03.2022	Year ended 31.03.2021
Capital Expenditure (net)	(2,521)	(3,336)
Investment in Subsidiaries / JV / Associates (net)	(810)	(661)
Income from Investment in Subsidiaries, JV, Associates	718	643
Net Cash Generated from/(Used in) Investing Activities	*(2,613)*	*(3,354)*

Banks' net financing cash flows do not include cash outflows for interest paid and cash flows related to borrowings *unless* the cash flow is for capital instruments. Such cash flows could be proceeds from issuing capital instruments, payment for redeeming these instruments, or payment of interest on these instruments. Capital instruments are largely bonds and securities issued by banks to meet their capital requirements. For example, SBI's 2021–22 net cash flow from financing activities is comprised of the issue of capital instruments ₹13,974 crore (inflow), redemption of capital instruments ₹10,293 crore (outflow), interest paid on capital instruments ₹5,288 crore (outflow), and dividends paid ₹3,570 crore (outflow).

Table 4B.4 SBI's Financing Cash Flows

State Bank of India: Extracted from Cash Flow Statement (Amount rounded off to nearest ₹ crore)	Year ended 31.03.2022	Year ended 31.03.2021
Cash Flow from Financing Activities:		
Issue of Capital Instruments	13,974	27,431
Redemption of Capital Instruments	(10,293)	(16,848)
Interest Paid on Capital Instruments	(5,288)	(4,951)
Dividend Paid	(3,570)	Nil
Net Cash Generated from/(Used in) Financing Activities	*(5,178)*	*5,633*

CHAPTER FIVE

Financial Ratio Analysis

Financial Ratios are powerful tools to assess the performance, risk, and valuation of companies. Equity analysts use financial ratios to assess the financial strengths and weaknesses of companies they follow and to forecast future financial ratios, earnings, and cash flows. These inputs help an analyst ascertain the intrinsic value of a company. Lenders have debt covenants based on financial ratios. Boards use financial ratios in executive compensation contracting.

In this chapter, we have 25 financial ratios grouped into four categories: profitability, efficiency, liquidity & solvency, and other ratios.[1] It would be useful to understand what causes these ratios to increase or decrease and thus identify how a transaction changes a financial ratio. Each of these ratios has been explained. These ratios are then computed using the data reported on financial statements and notes for Asian Paints, Avenue Supermarts, and Infosys. The ratios for these companies are then analyzed. We also do DuPont Analysis of ROE to understand the drivers of change in ROE. There are three appendices at the end of the chapter. The first appendix presents the value of these ratios for three companies. The second appendix lists the ratios discussed in the text and their numerators and denominators. The third appendix lists 11 key ratios that are required to be reported by listed companies and their formula as per the ICAI guidelines.

Note that there is no *ideal* value for a ratio. A financial ratio is affected by the choices made by a company, which, in turn, is affected by those of its partners and competitors. Therefore, we should assess the strengths and weaknesses of a company by comparing its financial ratios with its industry peers'.

[1] It is important to note that a few ratios can be computed in several ways, each having its own merit and demerit.

I. Profitability Ratios

Profitability ratios help assess the performance of specific portions of a business and the overall business of a company. This section discusses six widely used profitability ratios: Gross Profit Ratio, Operating Profit Ratio, Net Profit Ratio, Return on Assets, Return on Equity, and Return on Capital Employed.

(a) Gross Profit Ratio

$$\textit{Gross Profit Ratio} = \frac{\textit{Gross Profit}}{\textit{Sales}}$$

Gross Profit Ratio is the first measure of profitability on a common-size multi-step income statement. It reveals whether the company has been able to sell its products at a price above the cost incurred to purchase (for a retailer) or produce the product (for a manufacturer) or provide the service (for a service provider). This ratio helps to assess a company's pricing power. A company that enjoys greater goodwill among its customers charges a much higher price than cost and generates a higher gross profit ratio than its competitors (for example, BMW versus Kia, Apple versus Huawei, and Bose versus Boat). A healthy gross profit ratio indicates that the company has sold its products at a price much higher than cost and its product mix is overall profitable. A company's gross profit ratio may be higher than those of its competitors. The higher gross profit indicates that the company performs its manufacturing and procurement activities more efficiently than the competitors. The higher the ratio, the better the performance.

Gross Profit does not appear on the Income Statement of Indian companies. Therefore, we may not be able to compute the gross profit ratio unless a company is a retailer (for example, Avenue Supermarts), provides a multi-step income statement (for example, Infosys), or provides information that we can use to back-calculate Cost of Sales or Gross Profit. See Chapter 3 (Income Statement) for how to obtain gross profits of Avenue Supermarts and Infosys.

Table 5.1 Computation of Gross Profit Ratio

	Asian Paints		Avenue Supermarts		Infosys	
31st March	2022	2021	2022	2021	2022	2021
Gross Profit			4,206	3,373	34,311	30,371
Sales	–	–	30,258	23,729	103,940	85,912
Gross Profit Ratio	–	–	*13.90%*	*14.21%*	*33.01%*	*35.35%*
Change in Ratio	–		*–31 bps*		*–234 bps*	

See Chapter 3 (Income Statements) on how to obtain gross profit of these two companies.

The gross profit ratio of Avenue Supermarts is 13.90% in 2021–22, which is 31 bps lower than the previous year. The lower ratio suggests that the company set low prices for its products (it could be offering discounts to push products) or had difficulty managing its procurement costs and passing on the increases to its customers in 2021–22 than in the year before. Infosys, too, saw a large drop of 234 bps in its gross profit ratio to 33.01% in 2021–22, suggesting difficulty in managing its cost of service during the year.

(b) Operating Profit Ratio

$$\textit{Operating Profit Ratio} = \frac{\textit{Operating Profit}}{\textit{Sales}}$$

The operating profit ratio is the second measure of profitability on a common-size multi-step income statement. It reveals whether a company's sales have been large enough to recover the cost of purchase/production/service and the operating cost. This ratio helps to assess the overall profitability of operations. A healthy operating profit ratio indicates that the company has profitable products in its sales mix, sold products in sufficient volume, priced them above cost, achieved economies of scale, controlled its purchase/production/service costs, and managed its selling, general, and administrative expenses well. The higher the operating profit ratio, the better the operating performance.

Although operating profit does not appear on an income statement of Indian companies, we can easily back-calculate it from the information available on the income statement. See Chapter 3 (Income Statement) for how we obtained the operating profits of Asian Paints, Avenue Supermarts, and Infosys.

Table 5.2 Computation of Operating Profit Ratio

	Asian Paints		Avenue Supermarts		Infosys	
31st March	2022	2021	2022	2021	2022	2021
Operating Profit	3,866	3,796	2,081	1,370	25,399	22,136
Sales	25,003	18,280	30,258	23,729	103,940	85,912
Operating Profit Ratio	*15.46%*	*20.77%*	*6.88%*	*5.77%*	*24.44%*	*25.77%*
Change in the Ratio	*–531 bps*		*111 bps*		*–133 bps*	

See Chapter 3 (Income Statements) on how to obtain operating profit of these three companies.

Asian Paints' operating profit ratio is 15.46% for 2021–22. The company saw a large drop of 531 bps in the operating profit ratio in 2021–22 compared to 2020–21. This suggests that the company struggled to manage its production and operating costs, which resulted in products that were less profit-making during the year. An examination of the expenses (as a percentage of Sales) indicates that the decline in its operating profit ratio is largely driven by an increase of 872 bps in the cost of materials consumed (material cost is 55.35% this year and 46.63% last year), although there was a decrease of 94 bps in employee benefits cost (5.24% vs. 6.18%), 92 bps in depreciation & amortization cost (2.89% vs. 3.81%), and 66 bps in other expenses (14.73% vs. 15.39%). Thus, for Asian Paints, the increase in its material cost overshadowed the savings in other costs. We can do a similar analysis for Avenue Supermarts, Infosys, as well as other companies to ascertain what caused a change in their operating profit ratio.

The operating profit ratio of Avenue Supermarts is 6.88% in 2021–22, which is 111 bps higher than the previous year. This increase (together with 31 bps decline in gross profit ratio) suggests that the company managed its selling, distribution, and administration activities more cost-effectively in 2021–22 than in the year before.

Infosys saw a decline of 133 bps in its operating profit ratio to about 24.44% in 2021–22, suggesting the company faced difficulty in controlling its cost of service and operating expense.

(c) Net Profit Ratio

$$\textit{Net Profit Ratio} = \frac{\textit{Net Profit}}{\textit{Sales}}$$

The net profit ratio, also known as return on sales, is the final and overall measure of profitability on a common-size multi-step income statement. It reveals how effectively a company has generated its operating revenues and non-operating income together and controlled all operating, investing, and financing costs. This ratio helps to assess the overall profitability of a company. A healthy net profit ratio indicates that the company has successfully managed its revenues and effectively controlled its costs. However, as net profit includes other income, operating profit ratio better indicates the operating performance. The higher the net profit ratio, the better the overall performance. As net profit and Sales appear on an income statement of Indian companies, we can easily calculate the net profit ratio.

Table 5.3 Computation of Net Profit Ratio

	Asian Paints		Avenue Supermarts		Infosys	
31st March	2022	2021	2022	2021	2022	2021
Net Profit	3,135	3,052	1,616	1,166	21,235	18,048
Sales	25,003	18,280	30,258	23,729	103,940	85,912
Net Profit Ratio	*12.54%*	*16.70%*	*5.34%*	*4.91%*	*20.43%*	*21.01%*
Change in the ratio	*–416 bps*		*43 bps*		*–58 bps*	

For 2021–22, Asian Paints' net profit ratio is 12.54%, which is 416 basis points lower than the year before. This suggests that the company had difficulty managing its overall costs and selling more profitable products. That is why for every ₹100 sales it was able to generate a net profit of only ₹12.54 in this year as against ₹16.70 last year. Infosys's net profit ratio, too, saw a small decline of 58 basis points to 20.43% in 2021–22, suggesting some difficulty in pricing and managing its overall costs during the year. By contrast, the net profit ratio of Avenue Supermarts, although small at 5.34% in 2021–22, increased by 43 basis points from the previous year. This suggests that the company managed its overall sales and costs more effectively in 2021–22 than in the year before.

(d) Return on Assets

$$\textit{Return on Assets (ROA)} = \frac{\textit{Net Profit}}{\textit{Average Total Assets}}$$

ROA expresses profit as a percentage of average total assets. An ROA of 10% signifies that a company has generated ₹10 in net profit by using ₹100 of total assets. Thus, ROA reveals how effectively a company has utilized its assets to generate profit. It does not consider how assets are financed. A company with a bloated balance sheet (i.e., too many unproductive assets, such as Capital Work-in-Process, that do not currently contribute to increasing profits) is likely to have a lower ROA than a company with fewer unproductive assets. A healthy ROA indicates that the company has done a good job of utilizing assets to generate profit. The higher the ROA, the better the firm's performance.

Table 5.4 Computation of Return on Asset (ROA)

	Asian Paints		Avenue Supermarts		Infosys	
31st March	2022	2021	2022	2021	2022	2021
Net Profit	3,135	3,052	1,616	1,166	21,235	18,048
Ending Total Assets	19,908	17,581	15,404	13,646	99,387	93,939
Beginning Total Assets	17,581	13,588	13,646	12,084	93,939	81,041
Average Total Assets **	18,745	15,585	14,525	12,865	96,663	87,490
ROA	*16.72%*	*19.58%*	*11.13%*	*9.06%*	*21.97%*	*20.63%*
Change in the Ratio	*–286 bps*		*207 bps*		*134 bps*	

** Average Total Assets = [Ending Total Assets (i.e., Total Asset on the current year's balance sheet) + Beginning Total Assets (i.e., Total Assets on the last year's balance sheet)] ÷ 2.

Asian Paints generated a ROA of 16.72% in 2021–22, 286 basis points lower than a year before. For every ₹100 in assets, it was able to generate a net profit of only ₹16.72 in the current year vs. ₹19.58 in the previous year. This suggests that the company utilized its assets less effectively to generate profits in the current year vs. the previous year. By contrast, Avenue Supermarts and Infosys saw an increase in their ROA in 2021–22 as compared to the previous year, suggesting these two companies utilized their assets effectively and produced higher profits. Avenue Supermarts' ROA, although small at 11.13%, increased by a healthy 207 basis points in 2021–22, whereas Infosys' ROA was large 21.97% and the increase was 134 basis points in 2021–22.

(e) Return on Equity

$$Return\ on\ Equity\ (ROE) = \frac{Net\ Profit}{Average\ Equity}$$

ROE expresses earnings available to equity holders (i.e., net profit) as a percentage of average equity.[2] ROE of 20% signifies that a company has generated ₹20 in net profit from using ₹100 of shareholders' equity. Thus, ROE reveals how effectively a company has utilized its total equity to generate profits. Compared to a company with high leverage, an identical company with low leverage (i.e., low levels of total liabilities) has higher equity and lower ROE. A healthy ROE indicates that the company has used a good mix of equity, debt, and operating liability to fund its assets and has done a good job of utilizing equity to generate profits. Investors pay a premium for the equity shares of such companies. The higher the ROE, the better the firm's performance from a shareholder's point of view. Later in the chapter, we will discuss DuPont Analysis to identify the drivers of ROE of companies with no preference shares.

Table 5.5 Computation of Return on Equity (ROE)

	Asian Paints		**Avenue Supermarts**		**Infosys**	
31st March	2022	2021	2022	2021	2022	2021
Net Profit	3,135	3,052	1,616	1,166	21,235	18,048
Ending Equity	13,349	12,089	13,924	12,305	69,306	71,531
Beginning Equity	12,089	9,453	12,305	11,136	71,531	62,234
Average Equity **	12,719	10,771	13,115	11,721	70,419	66,883
ROE	*24.65%*	*28.34%*	*12.32%*	*9.95%*	*30.16%*	*26.98%*
Change in the Ratio	*–369 bps*		*237 bps*		*318 bps*	

** Average Equity = [Ending Equity (i.e., Equity on the current year's balance sheet) + Beginning Equity (i.e., Equity on the last year's balance sheet)] ÷ 2.

[2] Under Ind AS, preference dividend is included in finance cost. Therefore, net profit is reported after deducting preference dividends. Hence, adjustment for preference dividends is no longer required to obtain earnings available to equity shareholders. Thus, a company's net profit is the earnings available to its equity shareholders.

Asian Paints generated an ROE of 24.65% in 2021–22, 369 bps lower than a year before. For every ₹100 in equity, it was able to generate a net profit of only ₹24.65 in the current year vs. ₹28.34 in the previous year. This suggests that the company utilized its equity less effectively to generate profits in the current year vs. the previous year. By contrast, Avenue Supermarts and Infosys saw a healthy increase in their ROE in 2021–22 as compared to the previous year, suggesting these two companies utilized their equity effectively to produce higher profits in the current year than the previous year. Avenue Supermarts' ROE, although small 12.32%, increased by a healthy 237 bps in 2021–22, whereas Infosys has a high ROE of 30.16% and the increase was also a healthy 318 bps in 2021–22. Later in the chapter, using DuPont Analysis, we will identify the drivers of ROE and understand how changes in the drivers affected the ROE of each of the three firms.

(f) Return on Capital Employed

$$\textit{Return on Capital Employed (ROCE)} = \frac{\textit{Profit Before Interest \& Taxes (PBIT)}}{\textit{Average Capital Employed}}$$

ROCE expresses pre-tax profits (available for capital providers) as a percentage of average capital employed. Thus, ROCE reveals how effectively a company has utilized the capital employed in the business to generate profits. A company with high capital employed is likely to have a lower ROCE than another company with less capital employed. A healthy ROCE indicates that the company has used a good mix of equity and debt in its capital employed and has done a good job of utilizing the capital employed for generating profits. Investors pay a premium for such companies. The higher the ROCE, the better the performance.

Table 5.6 Computation of Capital Employed

	Asian Paints			Avenue Supermarts			Infosys		
31st March	2022	2021	2020	2022	2021	2020	2022	2021	2020
B (NC)	16	14	19	0	0	0	0	0	0
+ B (C)	0	8	0	0	0	4	0	0	0
+ LL (C)	519	467	496	320	217	178	3,228	3,367	2,775
+ LL (C)	179	157	142	96	79	64	558	487	390
Total Debt	714	646	657	416	296	246	3,786	3,854	3,165
Add Equity	13,349	12,089	9,453	13,924	12,305	11,136	69,306	71,531	62,234
Capital Employed	14,063	12,735	10,110	14,340	12,601	11,382	73,092	75,385	65,399

B (NC) = Borrowings (Non-Current); B (C) = Borrowings (Current); LL (NC) = Lease Liabilities (Non-Current); LL (C) = Lease Liabilities (Current); Debt = B(NC) + B(C) + LL(NC) + LL(C); Capital Employed = Debt + Equity.

Table 5.7 Computation of Return on Capital Employed

	Asian Paints		Avenue Supermarts		Infosys	
31st March	2022	2021	2022	2021	2022	2021
PBIT	4,264	4,162	2,222	1,579	28,623	24,603
Ending Capital Employed	14,063	12,735	14,340	12,601	73,092	75,385
Beginning Capital Employed	12,735	10,110	12,601	11,382	75,385	65,399
Avg. Capital Employed **	13,399	11,423	13,471	11,992	74,239	70,392
ROCE	*31.82%*	*36.44%*	*16.49%*	*13.17%*	*38.56%*	*34.95%*
Change in the Ratio	*–462 bps*		*332 bps*		*361 bps*	

** Average Capital Employed = (Ending Capital Employed + Beginning Capital Employed) ÷ 2.
Capital Employed = Total Equity + Non-Current Borrowings + Non-Current Lease Liabilities + Current Borrowings + Current Lease Liabilities.

Asian Paints generated ROCE of 31.82% in 2021–22, which is 462 bps lower than the previous year. For every ₹100 in capital employed, it generated PBIT of only ₹31.82 in the current year vs. ₹36.44 in the previous year. This suggests that the company utilized its capital employed less effectively to generate profits in the current year vs. the previous year. By contrast, Avenue Supermarts and Infosys saw a healthy increase in their ROCE in 2021–22 as compared to the previous year, suggesting these two companies utilized their capital effectively to produce higher profits in the current year than the previous year. Avenue Supermarts' ROCE, although small 16.49%, increased by a healthy 332 bps in 2021–22, whereas Infosys has a high ROCE of 38.56% in 2021–22 and the increase, from the year before, was a healthy 360 bps.

II. Efficiency Ratios

Efficiency or turnover ratios help assess how efficiently assets are utilized by a business. Nine widely used efficiency ratios are Asset Turnover, Fixed Asset Turnover, Current Asset Turnover, Working Capital Turnover, Receivable Turnover, Inventory Turnover, Payable Turnover, Operating Cycle, and Cash Cycle.

(a) Asset Turnover Ratio

$$\textit{Asset Turnover Ratio} = \frac{\textit{Sales}}{\textit{Average Total Assets}}$$

Asset turnover ratio assesses how efficiently a firm utilizes its asset to produce sales. An asset turnover ratio of 2 suggests that a firm has generated ₹2 in sales for every ₹1 of assets. The higher the asset turnover, the better the overall efficiency.

A company with bloated balance sheet (too many unproductive assets) is likely to have a lower asset turnover ratio. A manufacturing company with a low-capacity utilization of its factory is also likely to have a lower asset turnover ratio. However, as capacity utilization and sales increase, the asset turnover ratio also improves. This ratio is also affected by a firm's business model and strategy. For example, retailers have high asset turnover ratios. Retailers adopting a cost leadership strategy typically have a higher asset turnover ratio than their competitors pursuing a differentiation strategy. This is also true for low-cost producers versus high-quality producers. This difference arises because differentiation strategy requires additional investments in fixed assets and working capital that increase total assets.

Table 5.8 Computation of Asset Turnover Ratio

	Asian Paints		Avenue Supermarts		Infosys	
31st March	2022	2021	2022	2021	2022	2021
Sales	25,003	18,280	30,258	23,729	103,940	85,912
Ending Total Assets	19,908	17,581	15,404	13,646	99,387	93,939
Beginning Total Assets	17,581	13,588	13,646	12,084	93,939	81,041
Average Total Assets **	18,745	15,585	14,525	12,865	96,663	87,490
Asset Turnover Ratio	*1.33*	*1.17*	*2.08*	*1.84*	*1.08*	*0.98*

** Average Total Assets = (Ending Total Assets + Beginning Total Assets) ÷ 2.

Asian Paints achieved an asset turnover of 1.33 during 2021–22. Thus, for every ₹100 of assets, its Sales is ₹133 in the current year (versus ₹117 in the previous year), suggesting an improvement in its overall efficiency in 2021–22 relative to the year before.

Avenue Supermarts has an asset turnover of 2.08 during 2021–22, which is higher than the ratio 1.84 in the previous year. For a retailer, asset turnover of 2.08 may not be high since most retailers operate in rented stores and have relatively lower levels of PPE (particularly land and building). On the contrary, almost 45% of total assets of Avenue Supermarts is land and building.

Infosys has an asset turnover ratio of 1.08 in 2021–22 and 0.98 in the previous year. The company improved its asset turnover in the current year as compared to the previous year. Still for a service firm, the ratios are too small and have been depressed by huge amounts of current investments and cash & cash equivalents (together 17,737 or about 19% of total assets in 2021–22, and even higher in the previous year). Thus, there is potential for improvement in asset turnover ratio as the company pays back to its shareholders in the form of dividends and share buybacks.

It would be interesting to see how the efficiency (and also profitability, liquidity, and solvency) achieved by these companies compares with those of their competitors over five years.

(b) Fixed Asset Turnover

$$\textit{Fixed Asset Turnover Ratio} = \frac{\textit{Sales}}{\textit{Average Fixed Assets}}$$

Fixed Asset turnover ratio assesses how efficiently a firm utilizes its fixed asset to produce sales. The higher the asset turnover, the better the utilization of fixed assets.

A company with too many unproductive fixed assets is likely to have a lower fixed asset turnover ratio. A manufacturing company with a low-capacity utilization of its factories will have a lower fixed asset turnover ratio. However, as the capacity utilization and sales increase, the fixed asset turnover ratio also improves. Fixed asset turnover ratio is also affected by a firm's business model and strategy. For example, retailers generally have high fixed asset turnover ratios. Retailers adopting a cost leadership strategy typically have a higher fixed asset turnover ratio than their competitors pursuing a differentiation strategy. This is also true for low-cost producers versus high-quality producers. The differentiation strategy requires additional investments in fixed assets that decrease the fixed asset turnover ratio.

Table 5.9 Computation of Fixed Assets

	Asian Paints			Avenue Supermarts			Infosys		
31st March	2022	2021	2020	2022	2021	2020	2022	2021	2020
PPE	3,690	3,972	4,149	7,577	5,773	5,061	11,384	10,930	11,092
+CWIP	225	119	108	1,073	1,006	362	411	906	945
+ROU	786	715	727	1,146	847	647	3,311	3,435	2,805
+IP	0	0	0	96	91	17	0	0	0
+Goodwill	35	35	35	0	0	0	211	167	29
+OIA	43	42	50	10	9	11	32	67	48
+IUD	0	0	0	0	0	0	0	0	0
Total Fixed Assets	4,779	4,883	5,069	9,902	7,727	6,097	15,349	15,505	14,919

PPE = Property, plant, and equipment; CWIP = Capital work-in-progress; ROU = Right-of-use assets; IP = Investment properties; OIA = Other intangible assets; IUD = Intangibles under development. Fixed Assets = PPE + CWIP + ROU + IP + Goodwill + OIA + IUD.

Table 5.10 Computation of Fixed Asset Turnover Ratio

	Asian Paints		Avenue Supermarts		Infosys	
31st March	2022	2021	2022	2021	2022	2021
Sales	25,003	18,280	30,258	23,729	103,940	85,912
Ending Fixed Assets	4,779	4,882	9,902	7,727	15,349	15,505
Beginning Fixed Assets	4,882	5,069	7,727	6,097	15,505	14,919
Average Fixed Assets **	4,831	4,976	8,815	6,912	15,427	15,172
Fixed Asset Turnover	*5.18*	*3.67*	*3.43*	*3.43*	*6.74*	*5.65*

** Average Fixed Assets = (Ending Fixed Assets + Beginning Fixed Assets) ÷ 2. Fixed Assets = Property, plant, and equipment + Capital work-in-progress + Right-of-use assets + Investment properties + Goodwill + Other intangible assets + Intangibles under development. The calculation of fixed assets is shown in the previous table.

Asian Paints achieved an asset turnover of 5.18 during 2021–22. Thus, ₹100 of fixed assets are contributing to ₹518 in Sales during the current year (versus ₹367 in the previous year). The company significantly improved its efficiency of fixed asset in 2021–22 relative to the year before. By contrast, Avenue Supermarts has a fixed asset turnover of 3.43 during 2021–22 as well as 2020–21, which may not be high since most retailers need lower levels of fixed assets. This is because land and building account for about 70% of the company's fixed assets. Infosys has a moderate fixed asset turnover ratio of 6.74 in 2021–22 and 5.65 in the previous year. Thus, it is quite efficient in utilizing its fixed assets.

(c) Current Asset Turnover Ratio

$$\textit{Current Asset Turnover Ratio} = \frac{\textit{Sales}}{\textit{Average Current Assets}}$$

Current asset turnover ratio assesses how efficiently a firm utilizes its current assets to produce sales. The higher the current asset turnover, the better the utilization of these assets. This ratio can be quite volatile across years since current assets fluctuate much more than sales.

Table 5.11 Computation of Current Asset Turnover Ratio

	Asian Paints		Avenue Supermarts		Infosys	
31st March	2022	2021	2022	2021	2022	2021
Sales	25,003	18,280	30,258	23,729	103,940	85,912
Ending Current Assets	12,748	9,947	3,351	3,961	52,437	48,282
Beginning Current Assets	9,947	5,826	3,961	2,292	48,282	43,820
Average Current Assets **	11,348	7,886	3,656	3,127	50,360	46,051
Current Assets Turnover	*2.20*	*2.32*	*8.28*	*7.59*	*2.06*	*1.87*

** Average Current Assets = (Ending Current Assets + Beginning Current Assets) ÷ 2.

Asian Paints had a current asset turnover of 2.20 during 2021–22 (2.32 in the year before). Thus, for every ₹100 of current assets, its Sales is ₹220 in the current year (versus ₹232 in the previous year) indicating improved efficiency of current assets during the current year. That said, the ratio is low due to elevated levels of inventories and current investments.

Avenue Supermarts has a high asset turnover of 8.28 during 2021–22 and 7.59 in the previous year, which suggests that the company is achieving high level of sales from its current assets. The efficiency of current assets has increased in the current year.

Infosys has a low current asset turnover ratio of 2.06 in 2021–22 and 1.87 in the previous year. For a service firm, the ratio is small. It has been depressed by huge amounts of current investments, cash & cash equivalents, and other current assets.

(d) Working Capital Turnover Ratio

$$\text{Working Capital Turnover Ratio} = \frac{\text{Sales}}{\text{Average Working Capital}}$$

Working Capital Turnover ratio shows how efficiently a firm utilizes its working capital to produce sales. By comparing a firm's working capital ratio with its peers', we can also ascertain whether a company has too much or too less working capital. The higher the ratio, the better the utilization of working capital. This ratio can be quite volatile across years given that working capitals fluctuate much more than sales. Working capital fluctuates due to year-to-year variation in current assets and current liabilities.

Table 5.12 Computation of Working Capital

	Asian Paints			Avenue Supermarts			Infosys		
31st March	2022	2021	2020	2022	2021	2020	2022	2021	2020
CA	12,748	9,947	9,957	3,351	3,961	2,292	52,437	48,282	43,820
Less CL	5,647	4,575	4,575	1,094	1,072	722	24,976	17,622	15,220
WC	7,101	5,372	5,381	2,257	2,889	1,570	27,461	30,660	28,600

Amount in crores. CA = Current Assets, CL = Current Liabilities, WC = Working Capital = CA – CL.

Table 5.13 Computation of Working Capital Turnover Ratio

	Asian Paints		Avenue Supermarts		Infosys	
31st March	2022	2021	2022	2021	2022	2021
Sales	25,003	18,280	30,258	23,729	103,940	85,912
Ending Working Capital	7,101	5,372	2,257	2,889	27,461	30,660
Beginning Working Capital	5,372	5,381	2,889	1,570	30,660	28,600
Average Working Capital **	6,236	5,376	2,573	2,230	29,061	29,630
Working Capital Turnover	*4.01*	*3.40*	*11.76*	*10.64*	*3.58*	*2.90*

** Average Working Capital = (Ending Working Capital + Beginning Working Capital) ÷ 2.

Asian Paints had a working capital turnover of 4.01 during 2021–22 (3.40 in the year before). Thus, from ₹100 crore of working capital, it generated Sales of ₹401 crore (versus ₹340 crore in the previous year), which indicates an improved efficiency of working capital during the current year. That said, the ratio would have been higher if the company did not have elevated levels of inventories and current investments. Avenue Supermarts has a high working capital turnover of 11.76 during 2021–22 and 10.64 in the previous year, which suggests that the company is achieving a high level of sales from its working capital, and the efficiency has increased in the current year as compared to the previous year. Infosys has a low working capital turnover ratio of 3.58 in 2021–22 and 2.90 in the previous year. For a service firm, the ratios are too small. The ratio is depressed by huge amounts of current investments and cash & cash equivalents (together 17,737 or three-fifths of average working capital) in 2021–22.

(e) Receivable Turnover Ratio

$$\textit{Trade Receivables Turnover Ratio} = \frac{\textit{Sales}}{\textit{Average Trade Receivables}}$$

$$\textit{Trade Receivables Days} = \frac{365}{\textit{Trade Receivable Turnover}} = \frac{\textit{Average Trade Receivables}}{\left(\dfrac{\textit{Sales}}{365}\right)}$$

Trade Receivables Turnover ratio (receivables turnover in short) assesses how efficiently a firm manages its trade receivables and collects the amounts due from them. The higher the receivable turnover, the faster the company collects its receivables and the greater the efficiency in managing receivables.

We can express receivables turnover in days by dividing 365 by Receivable turnover (alternatively, divide Average trade receivables by Average Sales per day). Trade Receivable Days is also known as Receivable Days (in short), Days of Sales Outstanding, or Average Collection Period. Compared to Receivable Turnover, Receivable days is easier to understand and useful in obtaining the length of Operating Cycle and in financial forecasting.

A decline in receivable days shows that the company is either collecting its receivables faster or the share of cash sales in total sales is rising. An increase in days of receivable indicates a slowdown in the collection speed, which usually happens when a longer credit period is given to customers during a slowdown in sales. A consistent non-trivial rise in receivable days is a sign of not only weakness on the collection front and a possible increase in bad debt and credit losses but also the need for greater working capital in the future.

Table 5.14 Computation of Receivable Turnover Ratio

	Asian Paints		Avenue Supermarts		Infosys	
31st March	2022	2021	2022	2021	2022	2021
Sales (a)	25,003	18,280	30,258	23,729	103,940	85,912
Per Day = (a) ÷ 365	68.50	50.08	82.90	65.01	284.77	235.38
Ending Trade Receivables	2,916	1,810	231	72	18,966	16,394
Beginning Trade Receivables	1,810	1,109	72	49	16,394	15,459
Average Trade Receivables **	2,363	1,459	151	60	17,680	15,927
Trade Receivables Turnover	*10.58*	*12.53*	*200.38*	*395.48*	*5.88*	*5.39*
Trade Receivables Days	*34*	*29*	*2*	*1*	*62*	*68*
Change in days	*5 days*		*1 day*		*–6 days*	

** Average Trade Receivables = (Ending Trade Receivables net + Beginning Trade Receivables net) ÷ 2.

From the receivable days, it appears that Asian Paints gives about 1 month of credit to its customers. However, the current year has seen a 17% increase in receivable days to 34 days from 29 days in the previous year. Thus, the company has reduced the speed of collection of its receivables and is allowing customers to stretch the credit period. This increase may be a sign of weakness. By contrast, Infosys grants about 2 months credit to customers, and the average credit period has declined by 6 days to 62 days in the current year. This reduction is a sign of strength. Being a retailer, Avenue Supermarts has cash sales and a very low Receivable Days. The receivables are mostly for goods sold to its e-commerce subsidiary.

Note that a change of ±3 days is not unusual for measures expressed in days, such as receivable days, inventory days, payable days, operating cycle days, and cash cycle days.

(f) Inventory Turnover Ratio

$$\textit{Inventory Turnover Ratio} = \frac{\textit{Sales}}{\textit{Average Inventory}}$$

$$\textit{Inventory Days} = \frac{365}{\textit{Inventory Turnover}} = \frac{\textit{Average Inventory}}{\left(\frac{\textit{Sales}}{365}\right)}$$

Inventory Turnover ratio indicates the efficiency of inventory management for a retailer and manufacturers. The ratio is not relevant for service firms that usually carry no inventory or carry insignificant inventory. The ratio is usually much higher for retailers than for manufacturers, for firms adopting cost leadership strategy than for firms adopting differentiation strategy, and for firms selling fewer variety of products than for firms selling more heterogenous products.

The longer the waiting time for an inventory (waiting for consumption, transfer, or sale), the higher the inventory days. Inventory days are also affected by the time taken for production and shipment from one place to another (say, one factory to another, a factory to a warehouse, a warehouse to a company store). Any inefficiency in waiting, production, and shipment times is captured by the inventory period. Companies may hold higher levels of inventory to prevent stock-outs when the supply is unreliable. This causes their inventory turnover to rise, though such increases are benign. The higher the inventory turnover, the faster the company produces and/or sells the goods, and the more efficient the inventory management.

We can express inventory turnover in days by dividing 365 by Receivable turnover (alternatively, divide Average inventories by Average Sales per day). The ratio is also known as Inventory Days, Days of Inventory, or Average Inventory Period. When expressed in days, the ratio is easier to understand and useful in obtaining the length of Operating Cycle and in financial forecasting.

A decline in inventory days is a sign of strength since the items are with the company for fewer days and the company is achieving sales sooner. An increase in days of inventory indicates a slowdown in the speed of converting raw material to finished goods and selling finished goods (for a manufacturer) and the speed of selling stock-in-trade (for a retailer). Inventory period increases when companies have purchased or produced more than what they can consume or sell (often due to inefficiencies arising in making consumption and sales forecasts, managing inventories and shipments, and making sales). A consistent non-trivial rise in inventory days is a sign of weakness as it requires greater working capital and increases the risk of inventory obsolescence in the future.

From the inventory days, it appears that Asian Paints keeps 2 months of inventory, and Avenue Supermarts has 1 month of inventory. The efficiency in inventory management has improved for the retailer (by 2 days) but declined for the paint manufacturer (by 2 days). These changes are not unusual as some variation from one year to another is expected.

Table 5.15 Computation of Inventory Turnover Ratio

	Asian Paints		Avenue Supermarts		Infosys	
31st March	2022	2021	2022	2021	2022	2021
Sales (a)	25,003	18,280	30,258	23,729	103,940	85,912
Per Day = (a) ÷ 365	68.50	50.08	82.90	65.01	284.77	235.38
Ending Inventory	5,278	3,125	2,587	2,167	0	0
Beginning Inventory	3,125	2,827	2,167	1,909	0	0
Average Inventory **	4,201	2,976	2,377	2,038	0	0
Inventory Turnover Ratio	*5.95*	*6.14*	*12.73*	*11.64*	–	–
Inventory Days	*61*	*59*	*29*	*31*	*0*	*0*
Change in days	*2 days*		*–2 days*			

** Average Inventory = (Ending Inventory + Beginning Inventory) ÷ 2.

Note that 94% of Asian Paints' inventory comprises raw materials, packing materials, finished goods, and stock-in-trade. Upon further examination, the Days of Raw material & packing materials inventory (= Average inventory of raw material & packing materials ÷ Average cost of material consumed per day) is about 6 weeks (41 days in 2021–22 and 43 days in the previous year), whereas the Days of Finished goods and Stock-in-trade inventory (= Average inventory of finished goods & stock in trade ÷ Average Sales per day) is about 5 weeks (34 days in 2021–22 and 35 days in 2020–21). These two measures shed further light on the paint manufacturer's inventory management policies. It keeps 6 weeks of materials for production and 5 weeks of goods for sale.

Avenue Supermarts' inventory comprises entirely of stock-in-trade; the inventory days indicate that the retailer takes on an average one month to sell its inventory.

(g) Payable Turnover Ratio

$$\textit{Trade Payables Turnover Ratio} = \frac{\textit{Net Credit Purchase}}{\textit{Average Trade Payables}}$$

$$\textit{Trade Payables Days} = \frac{365}{\textit{Trade Payable Turnover}}$$

Suppliers prefer timely payment and offer discounts for early payment. Timely or early payments increase the goodwill of buyers among suppliers. Trade Payables Turnover ratio (payables turnover in short) assesses how timely a firm pays its payables for purchases. The higher the payables turnover, the faster the company pays its suppliers and the greater the efficiency in managing payables.

We can express payables turnover in days by dividing 365 by Payables turnover. Payables Turnover (Days) is known by many names, such as Payables Days or Days of Purchase Outstanding or Average Payment Period. The measure in days is intuitive, easier to understand, and useful in obtaining Operating Cycle and in financial forecasting.

An increase in payable period shows that the company is paying its suppliers more slowly, typically when the liquidity position has deteriorated or when the operating cycle has increased by sales slowdown. A consistent non-trivial rise in payable days is a sign of weakness, the reputation of the company may be adversely affected, and its purchase would become more costly (higher purchase prices due to interest cost for an additional credit period).

Table 5.16 Computation of Payable Turnover Ratio

	Asian Paints		Avenue Supermarts		Infosys	
31st March	2022	2021	2022	2021	2022	2021
Raw Material Purchase	12,596	7,209	0	0	0	0
+ Packing Material Purchase	2,166	1,511	0	0	0	0
+ Stock-in-Trade Purchase	2,979	1,649	26,472	20,614	0	0
+ Purchases of Services	*	*	*	*	*	*
Total Purchases (a)	17,741	10,369	26,472	20,614	*	*
Per Day = (a) ÷ 365	48.61	28.41	72.53	56.48	NA	NA
Ending Trade Payables	3,497	2,814	531	566	2,669	1,562
Beginning Trade Payables	2,814	1,760	566	446	1,562	1,529
Average Trade Payables **	3,156	2,287	549	506	2,116	1,546
Trade Payables Turnover	*5.62*	*4.53*	*48.22*	*40.74*	*11.3****	*9.9****
Trade Payables Days	*65 days*	*81 days*	*8 days*	*9 days*	*32 days*	*37 days*
Change in days	*–16 days*		*–1 day*		*–5 days*	

* Could not ascertain from financial statements & their notes ** Average Trade Payables = (Ending Trade Payables + Beginning Trade Payables) ÷ 2. *** As reported by Infosys in note 2.27 (Page 253 of Infosys 2021-22 annual report).

From the payable days, it appears that Asian Paints takes over 2 months of credit from its suppliers, Avenue Supermarts about 1 week of credit, and Infosys about 1 month. All three companies brought down the number of days they take to pay their suppliers. Being a retailer, Avenue Supermarts has very low receivable days and also low payable days. It collects cash fast and pays its suppliers within a week or so, which is a sign of strength.

Asian Paints was able to cut down its payable days by 16 days, which is noteworthy. Its payable days in 2019–20 and 2018–19 were 72 and 73 days, respectively. Thus, it appears that Asian Paints had taken 9 additional days of credit in 2020–21, and a large part of the reduction in 2021–22 appears to be reversal of the additional credit enjoyed in the previous year 2020–21.

(h) Operating Cycle and Cash Cycle

$$\textit{Operating Cycle (Days)} = \textit{Receivable (Days)} + \textit{Inventory (Days)}$$

$$\textit{Cash Cycle (Days)} = \textit{Operating Cycle (Days)} - \textit{Trade Payable (Days)}$$

Operating cycle is the time between the purchase of raw materials/stock-in-trade and the collection of cash from the sale of finished goods/stock-in-trade. Operating Cycle depends on the strategies and policies of a company, which is influenced by the funds available with the company, uncertainty in its business environment, practices in its industry, and other factors.

The length of the operating cycle is an important metric to assess the joint efficiency of a company's inventory and receivables management. Although we can evaluate inventory days and receivable days separately, these two often affect each other (for example, an increase in demand for products could reduce inventory level and increase trade receivable), which can be mitigated when combined. Thus, evaluating them together for manufacturing and retail firms can be beneficial. Note that for a service firm, inventory days is either zero or close to zero and, therefore, operating cycle is about the same as receivable period.

Cash cycle is the difference between Operating Cycle and Payable Days. It represents the time between when cash is paid to suppliers and when cash is collected from customers. This period requires working capital funding. Cash cycle depends on factors affecting the operating cycle and trade payable. The length of the cash cycle an important metric to assess the joint efficiency of a company's inventory, receivables, and payables management. The longer the cash cycle, the higher the working capital requirement.

Table 5.17 Computation of Operating Cycle & Cash Cycle

	Asian Paints				Avenue Supermarts		Infosys	
31st March	2022	2021	2020	2019	2022	2021	2022	2021
Days of Inventory	61	59	58	54	29	31	–	–
+ Days of Receivable	34	29	25	27	2	1	62	68
= Operating Cycle	*95*	*88*	*83*	*81*	*31*	*32*	*62*	*68*
– Days of Payables	65	81	72	73	8	9	32	37
= Cash Cycle (days)	*30*	*7*	*11*	*8*	*23*	*23*	*30*	*31*
Change in CC (days)	*23*	*–4*	*3*		*0*		*–1*	
Change in OC (days)	*7*	*5*	*2*		*–1*		*–6*	

The operating cycle of Asian Paints consistently increased from 81 days in 2018–19 to 95 days in 2021–22. The 14-day increase in operating cycle is driven by a 7-day surge in inventory and receivable period. Inefficiencies could be creeping in the company's inventory and receivable management, which would be a sign of operating weakness. In 2018–19, the company took 73 days of credit from suppliers, which increased to 81 days in 2020–21. Either the company is taking longer credit from its suppliers, or it is delaying payment to its suppliers in 2020–21. The company was able to reduce its payable period to 65 days in 2021–23. As a result, its cash cycle has significantly increased from 8 days in 2018–19 to 31 days in 2021–22, implying a greater need for working capital investment in its business.

Avenue Supermarts has an operating cycle of about 1 month and pays suppliers in about one week. As a result, its cash cycle is 23 days. Infosys has an operating cycle of 2 months after an improvement of 6 days in 2021–22. The company pays its suppliers in 1 month. As a result, its cash cycle is about a month.

III. Solvency & Liquidity Ratios

A firm is solvent if it has enough assets to meet its current and future (non-current) financial obligations. A firm is said to be insolvent if it is unable to meet its financial obligations. Insolvency leads to organizational distress and increases bankruptcy risk. If its financial position were to deteriorate, the firm could head towards bankruptcy and liquidation, which would be harmful to investors' wealth, employees' careers, as well as to other stakeholders. Six solvency and liquidity ratios are widely used by investors and lenders to assess whether a firm can meet its financial obligations. Current Ratio and Quick Ratios are two such liquidity measures discussed here, followed by four solvency ratios, namely, Debt Equity Ratio, Liability to Equity Ratio, Interest Coverage Ratio, and Debt Service Coverage Ratio.

(a) Current Ratio

$$Current\ Ratio = \frac{Current\ Assets}{Current\ Liabilities}$$

Does a firm have enough short-term assets to cover for its short-term obligations? This question can be answered based on the firm's current ratio. The ratio tells us whether a company has sufficient current assets to pay for its current obligations. Banks and financial institutions use this ratio to assess a borrower's overall liquidity and decide whether to grant short-term credit. A healthy current ratio indicates that current assets are funded using current liabilities and a portion of capital employed, and no long-term assets are funded using current liabilities. The higher the current ratio, the greater the overall liquidity, which is preferable for a lender. But from the shareholders' point of view, a moderate current ratio may be preferable.

How high should a current ratio be for a healthy firm? The answer depends on the supply of cash (i.e., cash inflows) and the demand on cash (i.e., cash outflows). High levels are needed for long operating cycle and when product development cycle is long. Low levels of current ratio may be sufficient for firms with continuous cash inflows (such as retailers, taxi operators, utilities), firms with short operating cycle, and firms with large amounts of liquid assets.

Too high current ratios, unless temporary, may be undesirable as they signal elevated levels of current assets or inadequate use of current liabilities. Thus, such companies may benefit from optimizing the levels of current assets and liabilities. Such an optimization would free capital employed tied in working capital. A current ratio of less than one may be undesirable since it signifies that the current assets are insufficient for current liabilities. The current ratio is less than one when working capital is negative, which happens when current liabilities are used to fund not only the current assets but also a portion of long-term assets. However, short-term liabilities are not a sustainable source of funding of long-term assets. A service firm (for example, airlines such as InterGlobe Aviation) – carrying no inventory, collecting in advance from its customers (i.e., before providing service), but paying in arrears for all goods and services consumed – is likely to have a current ratio that is less than one. For example, on 31-3-2022, InterGlobe Aviation (owner of Indigo Airlines brand) has current assets ₹20,147 crore, current liabilities ₹22,385 crore, a negative working capital, and a current ratio of 0.90.

Table 5.18 Computation of Current Ratio

	Asian Paints		Avenue Supermarts		Infosys	
31st March	2022	2021	2022	2021	2022	2021
Current Assets	12,748	9,947	3,351	3,961	52,437	48,282
Current Liabilities	5,647	4,575	1,094	1,072	24,976	17,622
Current Ratio	*2.26*	*2.17*	*3.06*	*3.70*	*2.10*	*2.74*

(b) Quick Ratio

$$Quick\ Ratio = \frac{Financial\ Assets\ (Current)}{Current\ Liabilities}$$

$$= \frac{Current\ Assets - Inventory - Prepaid\ Expense}{Current\ Liabilities}$$

Quick Ratio tells us whether a company has sufficient financial current assets to quickly pay off its current obligations. This ratio is useful to banks, financial institutions, and creditors to assess liquidity. The higher the quick ratio, the better the liquidity, which is preferable for a lender. However, a moderate quick ratio may be preferable from the shareholders' perspective.

The numerator for the quick ratio is usually total current assets less the sum of inventories and prepaid expenses. Both inventories and prepaid expenses are excluded from quick assets because inventories must be first sold and then cash can be collected after the expiry of any credit period granted to customers, whereas prepaid assets would never be converted into cash. Not only prepaid expenses, but also several items included under the head 'other current asset' may not be recovered in cash (for example, advances to employees are deducted from salaries, advances to suppliers are recovered in goods, etc.). If we remove both inventories and other current assets from total current assets, we get financial current assets.

Table 5.19 Computation of Quick Ratio

	Asian Paints		Avenue Supermarts		Infosys	
31st March	2022	2021	2022	2021	2022	2021
Financial Current Assets **	7,034	6,376	622	1,672	43,502	41,498
Current Liabilities	5,647	4,575	1,094	1,072	24,976	17,622
Quick Ratio	*1.25*	*1.39*	*0.57*	*1.56*	*1.74*	*2.35*

**Financial Current Assets are obtained by deducting from total current assets the sum of inventories and other current assets. Alternatively, we could have added the amounts of all items listed under financial assets within current assets.

Asian Paints has a high quick ratio of 1.25 as on 31-3-2022 (versus an even higher 1.39 on 31-3-2021). Avenue Supermarts has a low quick ratio of 0.57 as on 31-3-2022 (versus a much higher 1.56 a year before). The decline appears to be a result of utilizing cash for purchase of property, plant, and equipment. The quick ratio of Infosys is also very high: 1.74 as on 31-3-2022 versus an even higher 2.35 a year before. The decline in Infosys' quick ratio appears to be a result of utilizing cash for dividends and share buybacks. For these three companies, their high quick ratio suggests elevated levels of liquidity, which is good for their creditors but may not be for the shareholders unless the companies intend to utilize the liquidity productively.

(c) Debt Equity Ratio

$$\textit{Debt Equity Ratio} = \frac{\textit{Total Debt}}{\textit{Total Equity}}$$

Debt Equity Ratio is one of the most important ratios used to examine a firm's solvency. A debt-equity ratio of 0.5 indicates that total debt is half of total equity. Banks and financial institutions examine a borrower's debt equity ratio to assess whether the borrower's existing debt is too high, moderate, or too low, and to decide whether to give a loan or not, how much loan to give, and what should be the terms & conditions of the loan. They consider companies with zero debt-equity ratio, ceteris paribus, as the safest to lend. Higher debt-equity ratio signifies higher financial leverage, lower solvency, and greater risk.

Debt includes preference share capital, borrowings, lease liabilities, notes payable, acceptances, and any other liability on which interest is payable to a third party. A company is contractually obligated to pay interest on debt (dividend in case of preference shares) and repay principal on or before specified dates. Since interest payments are tax deductible, the post-tax cost of debt is lower than the interest expense on debt. Since equity holders bear more risk than debtholders, cost of debt is lower than cost of equity, and having some debt reduces the overall cost of capital of a firm and increases firm value. Therefore, moderate levels of debt may be good for a company.

With too less debt, a company would be missing out on tax-advantage of interest and the opportunity to lower its cost of capital and increase its firm value. However, interest on debt must be paid irrespective of whether a company has made a profit or not and whether a company has enough cash inflows. Thus, the presence of debt increases a firm's fixed costs and thereby increases its financial risk. With too much of debt, a company may be in trouble during bad times (such as Covid-19 pandemic or a recession) and could go bankrupt. That would not only affect the company's shareholders, but it will also harm its lenders as their loan portfolios would suffer losses. That is why, high debt-equity ratio is considered risky.

Table 5.20 Computation of Debt-Equity Ratio

	Asian Paints		Avenue Supermarts		Infosys	
31st March	2022	2021	2022	2021	2022	2021
Borrowings (Non-Current)	16	14	0	0	0	0
+ Borrowings (Current)	0	8	0	0	0	0
+ Lease Liabilities (Non-Current)	519	467	320	217	3,228	3,367
+ Lease Liabilities (Current)	179	157	96	79	558	487
= Total Debt	714	646	416	296	3,786	3,854
Total Equity	13,349	12,089	13,924	12,305	69,306	71,531
Debt-Equity Ratio	*0.05*	*0.05*	*0.03*	*0.02*	*0.05*	*0.05*

With such a low debt-equity ratio (less than 0.05), these three companies are virtually debt free and highly solvent. Such low levels of the ratio indicate that the companies have chosen a conservative financial strategy by avoiding debt in their capital structure and thus are playing safe at the cost of the opportunity to reduce their cost of capital and increase intrinsic value.

(d) Liability to Equity Ratio

$$\textit{Liability to Equity Ratio} = \frac{\textit{Total Liabilities}}{\textit{Total Equity}} = \frac{\textit{Total Assets}}{\textit{Total Equity}} - 1$$

While Debt-Equity ratio signifies financial leverage, the Liability to Equity Ratio signifies total leverage of a company. A liability to equity ratio of 1 would signify that the company has funded its assets using one-part equity and one-part liabilities. Investors examine a company's liabilities to equity ratio to assess whether the company has utilized adequate leverage for funding its asset. A moderate level of this ratio may be more appropriate for most companies. Low levels of this ratio depress ROE, whereas high levels magnify ROE, as we will see when we discuss DuPont Analysis. Higher liability to equity ratio signifies higher leverage, lower solvency, and higher risk.

Total Liabilities include debt and operational liabilities. Thus, Liabilities to Equity Ratio is the sum of debt-equity ratio and operational liabilities to equity ratio. While debt increases financial leverage (as discussed under debt-equity ratio), operational liabilities do not increase financial risk. When companies substitute debt with operational liabilities as a financial strategy, we will see a relatively lower debt-equity ratio but a higher liability to equity ratio.

Table 5.21 Computation of Liability to Equity Ratio

	Asian Paints		Avenue Supermarts		Infosys	
31st March	2022	2021	2022	2021	2022	2021
Total Liabilities	6,559	5,492	1,480	1,341	30,081	22,408
Total Equity	13,349	12,089	13,924	12,305	69,306	71,531
Liabilities to Equity Ratio	*0.49*	*0.45*	*0.11*	*0.11*	*0.43*	*0.31*

The liabilities to equity ratios appear to be low for these companies, especially Avenue Supermarts. The low liabilities to equity ratios signal a reliance on equity by these companies, which is good for the creditors of the company, but not for its shareholders as it depresses ROE (as we will see later when we discuss DuPont Analysis).

(e) Interest Coverage Ratio

$$\textit{Interest Coverage Ratio} = \frac{\textit{Profit Before Interest \& Taxes (PBIT)}}{\textit{Finance Cost}}$$

Interest Coverage Ratio (or Times Interest Earned) evaluates whether a company makes sufficient profits to pay for its interest. For this ratio, a value greater than one indicates that PBIT is more than interest expense. Banks and financial institutions examine a borrower's interest coverage ratio to assess the safety of interest payment by the borrower. Thus, it is one of the key financial ratios used by banks to assess the credit risk of a borrower. Profitable companies with low financial leverage (and thus low interest expense) are likely to have high interest coverage ratios. The higher the coverage ratio, the better is the solvency, and the lower is the credit risk.

Table 5.22 Computation of Interest Coverage Ratio

	Asian Paints		Avenue Supermarts		Infosys	
31st March	2022	2021	2022	2021	2022	2021
PBIT	4,264	4,162	2,222	1,579	28,623	24,603
Finance Cost	70	72	40	34	128	126
Interest Coverage Ratio	*60.91*	*57.81*	*55.55*	*46.44*	*223.62*	*195.26*

The Interest Coverage ratios appear to be quite high for these companies, especially for Infosys, consistent with their very low debt-equity ratios. The high levels of the interest coverage suggest that the companies have much higher levels of profits (before interest and tax) to meet interest expenses. For example, Asian Paints' high interest coverage ratio of 60.91 suggests that even if the company's PBIT in 2021–22 falls by 98.4% (= 1 – 1/60.91), PBIT will still be more than the finance cost, and the company will continue to have positive pre-tax profits and net profit. The likelihood of that happening for Asian Paints is remote. For Infosys, PBIT that can fall by is 99.5%, still the company will have positive PBT and PAT. By contrast, in 2015–16 financial year, Hindalco had an interest coverage ratio of 1.27 (=3041/2390), which is quite low and signals elevated risk. A mere 22% fall in Hindalco's PBIT would result in a negative PBT and PAT. The likelihood of such a decline in PBIT is not remote. Therefore, there is a risk that Hindalco's earnings may fall short of its finance cost.

(f) Debt Service Coverage Ratio

$$\textit{Debt Service Coverage Ratio (DSCR)} = \frac{\textit{Earnings Available for Debt Service}}{\textit{Debt Service}}$$

Debt Service Coverage Ratio (DSCR) evaluates whether a company makes sufficient profits to meet its debt service obligations. For this ratio, a value greater than one indicates that the company has enough earnings available for debt service. Banks and financial institutions examine a borrower's DSCR to assess the safety of the interest and principal payment by a borrower. Thus, it is among the key financial ratios that banks use to assess the credit risk of a borrower and determine the loan amount and interest rate. Profitable companies with low financial leverage (and thus low amounts of interest and principal payments) are likely to have a high DSCR. The higher the ratio, the better the solvency, and the lower the credit risk.

As per the ICAI guidance note, the denominator, Debt service includes lease rental payments, borrowings repayments, and interest on borrowings payments during a year. These can be found under cash flows from financing activities on a cash flow statement. Furthermore, the ICAI guidance note suggests that the numerator, Earnings available for debt service should include Profit after taxes, Non-cash operating expenses (such as Depreciation & amortization expense, bad & doubtful debt expense, etc.), Interest Expenses, and Other adjustments (such as gain/loss on sale of fixed assets, gain/loss on modification/termination of leases, etc.). The inputs needed for the numerator are scattered across notes and difficult to obtain. Hence, we will not obtain the numerators and denominators here, and instead interpret the DSCR reported by the three companies.

Table 5.23 Debt Service Coverage Ratio

	Asian Paints		Avenue Supermarts		Infosys	
	2022	2021	2022	2021	2022	2021
Debt Service Coverage Ratio (reported)	*133.38*	*133.55*	*5.64*	*4.62*	*38.5*	*38.8*

Debt service coverage ratio is very high for Asian Paints, moderate for Avenue Supermarts, and high for Infosys in both financial years, suggesting high/adequate safety. There is a considerable difference in how these companies obtained the numerator and denominator for calculating DSCR (they only reported the formula for and not the value of the earnings available and debt service).

IV. Other Ratios

Here, we discuss four ratios to understand a company's dividend policy and its relative valuation multiples: Payout Ratio, Retention Ratio, Price-Earnings Ratio, and Price-Book Ratio.

(a) Payout and Retention Ratios

$$Payout\ Ratio = \frac{Dividends\ Declared}{Net\ Profit}$$

$$Retention\ Ratio = 1 - Payout\ Ratio = \frac{Net\ Profit - Dividends\ Declared}{Net\ Profit}$$

$$= \frac{Profit\ Retained}{Net\ Profit}$$

Payout and Retention ratios shed light on the dividend policy of a company. Payout ratio reveals what percentage of net profit is being paid as cash dividends during a financial year. The higher the dividend payout ratio, the lower is the retention ratio. Companies with greater need for funds tend to retain profits more and payout dividends less and, therefore, have higher retention and lower payout ratios.

Table 5.24 Computation of Payout & Retention Ratios

	Asian Paints				Avenue Supermarts		Infosys	
31st March	2022	2021	2020	2019	2022	2021	2022	2021
Net Profit	3,135	3,052	2,654	2,132	1,616	1,166	21,235	18,048
Dividends	1,741	465	1,741	854	Nil	Nil	12,700	9,158
Payout Ratio	*56%*	*15%*	*66%*	*40%*	0%	0%	60%	51%
Retention Ratio	*44%*	*85%*	*34%*	*60%*	100%	100%	40%	49%

* Payout Ratio = Dividends Declared ÷ Net Profit; Retention Ratio = 1 – Payout Ratio.

Asian Paints has a payout ratio of 56% in 2021–22, which suggests that the company is paying more than half of its profit as dividends during the year. Its payout ratio has fluctuated over the four years (2018–19 to 2021–22), from a low of 15% in 2020–21 to a high of 66% in 2019–20. Thus, the company does not have a stable payout ratio. Accordingly, its retention ratio has fluctuated. The company could be retaining profits as per its investment needs and paying out the residual as dividends.

Avenue Supermarts has a zero payout ratio and therefore 100% retention ratio in both 2021–22 and 2020–21 financial years. It does not pay any dividends to its shareholders. It retains the entire profit to fund business growth.

Infosys has a payout ratio of 60% in 2021–22 and 51% in 2020–21, suggesting it pays out more than half of its profits as dividends. Effective 2020–21, the company has a policy of returning 85% of its free cash flows over a 5-year period through a combination of semi-annual dividends, share buybacks, special dividends, and taxes applicable on dividends and buybacks.

(b) Price to Earnings and Price to Book Ratios

$$\textit{Price to Earnings (P/E) Ratio} = \frac{\textit{Market Capitalization}}{\textit{Net Profit}} = \frac{\textit{Share Price}}{\left(\frac{\textit{Net Profit}}{\textit{Number of Shares}}\right)}$$

$$\textit{Price to Book (P/B) Ratio} = \frac{\textit{Market Capitalization}}{\textit{Equity}} = \frac{\textit{Share Price}}{\left(\frac{\textit{Equity}}{\textit{Number of Shares}}\right)}$$

P/E and P/B ratios are of considerable interest to investors as they can learn whether the stock market is bullish or bearish on the company's stock. They are useful in relative valuation of stocks.

P/E ratio tells us the price investors are willing to pay for ₹1 of the company's earnings. For this reason, the ratio is also called earnings multiple, whereas its reciprocal (E/P) is called earnings yield. It can be computed for listed companies only. P/E ratio is affected by a company's cost of equity and growth rate of earnings, among others. A rise in earnings growth rate increases the ratio, whereas a rise in cost of equity decreases the ratio. As stock market prices vary across a stock market cycle, so do P/E ratios. A comparison of the P/E ratio of a firm with its peers' can reveal whether the firm's stock is under-valued or over-valued. The higher the P/E ratio, the more bullish the investors are on the company's earnings, the more expensive a stock is, and the more likely the stock is over-valued.

P/B ratio tells us the price investors are willing to pay for ₹1 of the company's equity or book value. For this reason, the ratio is also known as market-to-book ratio. It can be computed for listed companies only. Note we can write P/B = P/E × E/B = P/E Ratio × ROE. Thus, P/B Ratio is affected by ROE, growth rate in earnings, and cost of equity: the ratio increases with ROE and earnings growth rate and decreases with cost of equity. As stock market prices vary across a stock market cycle, so do P/B ratios. A comparison of the P/B ratio of a firm with its peers' can reveal whether the firm's stock is under-valued or over-valued. The higher the P/B ratio, the more bullish the investors are on the company's profits and growth, the more expensive a stock is, and the more likely the stock is over-valued.

Table 5.25 Computation of P/E & P/B Ratios

	Asian Paints		Avenue Supermarts		Infosys	
31st March	2022	2021	2022	2021	2022	2021
Share Price	₹3,079.95	₹2,537.40	₹4,003.35	₹2,859.05	₹1,906.85	₹1,368.05
Number of Shares	95.92	95.92	64.78	64.78	420.67	426.07
Market Cap *	295,428	243,387	259,327	185,202	802,162	582,880
Net Profit	3,135	3,052	1,616	1,166	21,235	18,048
Equity	13,349	12,089	13,924	12,305	69,306	71,531
*P/E Ratio ***	*94.2*	*79.7*	*160.5*	*158.8*	*37.8*	*32.3*
*P/B Ratio ****	*22.1*	*20.1*	*18.6*	*15.1*	*11.6*	*8.1*

* Market Cap (or Capitalization) = Share Price × Number of Shares in crore. ** P/E Ratio = Market Cap ÷ Net Profit. *** P/B Ratio = Market Cap ÷ Equity. Share Prices are from NSE and downloaded on 24-09-2022.

Table 5.26 P/E & P/B Ratios of NSE Nifty50 and Nifty500 Indices

Index	P/E Ratio on 31-03-2022	P/E Ratio on 31-03-2021	P/B Ratio on 31-03-2022	P/B Ratio on 31-03-2021
Nifty50	22.91	33.20	4.56	4.20
Nifty500	23.67	35.89	4.29	3.96

*Index P/E and P/B ratios downloaded on 24-09-2022.

At the end of 2021–22 fiscal year, Asian Paints' P/E ratio is 94.2 and P/B ratio is 22.1, which are much greater than those of the Nifty50 index (P/E 22.91 and P/B 4.56). These valuation ratios have also improved from the previous year. This suggests that the market highly values Asian Paints' profitability and growth. Avenue Supermarts' P/E and P/B ratios are sky-high at 160.5 and 18.6 on 31-3-2022 (and higher than a year before), suggesting the stock enjoys a super-high valuation. By contrast, Infosys has a modest (but still higher than the market index) valuation multiples. All three are well-managed and large companies with stellar performance relative to their peers and command a huge premium.

V. DuPont Analysis of ROE

$$ROE = NPR \times ATO \times LM$$

$$\textit{Net Profit Ratio (NPR)} = \frac{\textit{Net Profit}}{\textit{Net Sales \& Services Revenue}}$$

$$\textit{Asset Turnover (ATO)} = \frac{\textit{Net Sales \& Services Revenue}}{\textit{Average Total Assets}}$$

$$\textit{Leverage Multiplier (LM)} = \frac{\textit{Average Total Assets}}{\textit{Average Equity}}$$

DuPont Analysis is a formidable technique to decompose a performance measure into its various drivers. The idea behind the approach is that if you multiply a ratio (x/y) by 1 or z/z (i.e., $x/y \times z/z$) and rearrange the terms (into $x/z \times z/y$), you can express the ratio x/y as a product of its two drivers (x/z and z/y). While z could be any variable, the two ratios x/z and z/y must be relevant for the analysis to be insightful.

For example, consider Price-to-Book Ratio (i.e., P/B), multiply it by E/E (earnings), rearrange the terms, and we get P/B = P/E × E/B = P/E Ratio × ROE. Thus, P/B is driven by P/E ratio and ROE. Likewise, let us do for ROE (for a company with no preference shares) in three steps:

1. Note that ROE is Net Profit / Average Equity. Let us multiply ROE by Average Assets / Average Assets, rearrange the terms to obtain Net Profit / Average Assets × Average Assets / Average Equity. The first term is ROA as we know. We will call the second term LM or Leverage Multiplier. Thus, ROE = ROA × LM.
2. Let us decompose ROA into two drivers: Net Profit Ratio (NPR) and Asset Turnover (ATO). Multiply ROA, Net Profit / Average Assets, by

Sales / Sales, rearrange the terms, and get Net Profit / Sales (NPR) × Sales / Average Assets (ATO). Thus, ROA = NPR × ATO.

3. Now substitute NPR × ATO for ROA in ROE, and we get ROE = NPR × ATO × LM.

Thus, we have identified three drivers of ROE by DuPont Analysis. An analysis of these three drivers can help us explain the reasons for the change in ROE over time.

Note LM is Average Assets divided by Average Equity, and total assets is the sum of equity and liabilities. Liabilities are either Debt or Operational Liabilities; let us call all liabilities other than debt as operational liabilities, and avoid calling them 'other liabilities' to avoid any confusion since other liabilities is a specific item on the balance sheet. Accordingly, LM can be written as 1 + Average Debt/Average Equity + Average Operational Liabilities/Average Equity. A change in LM indicates a variation in asset funding pattern, i.e., how assets are funded by equity, debt, and operational liabilities.

Let us analyze in detail what caused a decline in the ROE of Asian Paints, and in brief what are the drivers for a rise in the ROE of Avenue Supermarts and Infosys.

Table 5.27 DuPont Analysis of ROE (of companies with no preference share)

DuPont Analysis of ROE	Asian Paints		Avenue Supermarts		Infosys	
	2022	2021	2022	2021	2022	2021
ROE	24.65%	28.34%	12.32%	9.95%	30.16%	26.98%
Change in ROE	–369 bps		237 bps		318 bps	
NPR: Net Profit Ratio	*12.54%*	*16.70%*	*5.34%*	*4.91%*	*20.43%*	*21.01%*
Change in NPR	–416 bps		43 bps		–58 bps	
ATO: Asset Turnover	*1.33*	*1.17*	*2.08*	*1.84*	*1.08*	*0.98*
LM: Leverage Multiplier	*1.47*	*1.45*	*1.11*	*1.10*	*1.37*	*1.31*
NPR × ATO × LM	24.65%	28.34%	12.32%	9.94%	30.16%	26.98%

Asian Paints' ROE is quite high in 2021–22 (24.65%) and 2020–21 (28.34%). However, ROE fell 369 bps in 2021–22 compared to the previous year, and we want to understand what caused this decline. Note that, of the three drivers of ROE, LM is about the same in both years, ATO improved, whereas NPR significantly deteriorated. Thus, ROE declined because the 416-bps deterioration in NPR overshadowed the improvement in ATO. Now, let us delve deeper.

Asian Paints had similar LM in these two years, which suggests that the growth in assets was funded by identical growth in liabilities and equity, i.e., there is no difference in its funding pattern in these two years. Furthermore, its ATO significantly increased, which happens when sales growth rate exceeds asset growth rate. Thus, Asian Paints was more efficient in utilizing assets, and it was able to use existing and new assets more effectively to increase its Sales. However, despite higher sales, its profit margin suffered and NPR fell by 416 bps. Thus, its NPR significantly deteriorated. This happens when profit growth rate is lower than sales growth rate. The company struggled to maintain the profitability of its sales, and its sales growth did not contribute to higher profits. Thus, Asian Paints was unable to translate its higher sales to proportionate increases in its profits. Had it maintained its NPR at the 2020–21 level, its 2021–22 ROE would have been 32.65% (=16.70% × 1.33 × 1.47), about 800 bps higher than what it achieved. That was a missed opportunity for Asian Paints.

If we delve deeper into why NPR declined, we see that its Operating Profit Ratio (OPR) has also decreased by 530 bps indicating weakness in its ability to manage operating costs. During the year, its material cost ratio increased by 703 bps (from 46.37% to 53.40%, see Chapter 3 Section II(b)(i)). Thus, OPR, NPR, ROA, and ROE declined due to a disproportionate rise in material cost and the company absorbed the increase.

Avenue Supermarts' ROE increased by 237 bps in 2021–22 to 12.32%. Of the three drivers, LM is about the same in two years, whereas both ATO and NPR improved. Thus, the company's funding pattern did not change and asset growth was funded by an identical growth in equity and liabilities (particularly operational liabilities). The company was able to deploy additional assets efficiently to grow its sales at a rate higher than that of assets. Furthermore, these sales were more profitable increasing NPR by 43 bps. The company successfully controlled its purchase and operating costs and increased its economies of scale.

Infosys achieved an ROE of 30.16% in 2021–22, which was 318 bps higher than the year before. This increase was a result of improvement in two drivers LM and ATO, which together overshadowed the 58-bps decline in NPR. The company was able to increase the share of liabilities in funding of assets (increasing LM), and was able to deploy assets more efficiently to grow its sales, and its sales growth rate was higher than asset growth rate (thus increasing ATO). However, it could only grow its profits at a rate below its sales growth. Thus, it had difficulty controlling its overall costs and adjusting prices to match cost increases.

Appendix 5A: Value of 25 Ratios at a Glance

Profitability Ratios	Asian Paints		Avenue Supermarts		Infosys	
	2022	2021	2022	2021	2022	2021
Gross Profit Ratio	–	–	13.90%	14.21%	33.01%	35.35%
Operating Profit Ratio	15.46%	20.77%	6.88%	5.77%	24.44%	25.77%
Net Profit Ratio	12.54%	16.70%	5.34%	4.91%	20.43%	21.01%
ROA	16.72%	19.58%	11.13%	9.06%	21.97%	20.63%
ROE	24.65%	28.34%	12.32%	9.95%	30.16%	26.98%
ROCE	31.82%	36.44%	16.49%	13.17%	38.56%	34.95%

DuPont Analysis of ROE	Asian Paints		Avenue Supermarts		Infosys	
	2022	2021	2022	2021	2022	2021
ROE	24.65%	28.34%	12.32%	9.94%	30.16%	26.98%
Change in ROE	–369 bps		238 bps		317 bps	
Net Profit Ratio	12.54%	16.70%	5.34%	4.91%	20.43%	21.01%
Asset Turnover	1.33	1.17	2.08	1.84	1.08	0.98
Leverage Multiplier	1.47	1.45	1.11	1.10	1.37	1.31

Efficiency Ratios	Asian Paints		Avenue Supermarts		infosys	
	2022	2021	2022	2021	2022	2021
Asset Turnover Ratio	1.33	1.17	2.08	1.84	1.08	0.98
Fixed Asset Turnover	5.18	3.67	3.43	3.43	6.74	5.65
Current Assets Turnover	2.20	2.32	8.28	7.59	2.06	1.87
Working Capital Turnover	4.01	3.40	11.76	10.64	3.58	2.90
Trade Receivables Days	34	29	1.8	0.9	62	68
Inventory Days	61	59	29	31	0	0
Operating Cycle Days	95	88	31	32	62	68
Trade Payables Days	65	81	7.6	9.0	32	37
Cash Cycle Days	30	7	23	23	30	31

Liquidity & Solvency Ratios	Asian Paints		Avenue Supermarts		Infosys	
	2022	2021	2022	2021	2022	2021
Current Ratio	2.26	2.17	3.06	3.70	2.10	2.74
Quick Ratio	1.25	1.39	0.57	1.56	1.74	2.35
Debt-Equity Ratio	0.05	0.05	0.03	0.02	0.05	0.05
Liabilities-Equity Ratio	0.49	0.45	0.11	0.11	0.43	0.31
Interest Coverage Ratio	60.91	57.81	55.55	46.44	223.62	195.26
Debt Service Coverage Ratio (reported)	133.38	133.55	5.64	4.62	38.5	38.8

Other Ratios	Asian Paints		Avenue Supermarts		Infosys	
	2022	2021	2022	2021	2022	2021
Payout Ratio	56%	15%	0%	0%	60%	51%
Retention Ratio	44%	85%	100%	100%	40%	49%
P/E Ratio	94.2	79.7	160.5	158.8	37.8	32.3
P/B Ratio	22.1	20.1	18.6	15.1	11.6	8.1

Appendix 5B: Formula for 25 Financial Ratios in this Chapter

Profitability Ratios	Numerator	Denominator
1. Gross Profit Ratio	Gross Profit	Sales
2. Operating Profit Ratio	Operating Profit	Sales
3. Net Profit Ratio	Net Profit	Sales
4. Return on Assets (ROA)	Net Profit	Average Total Assets
5. Return on Equity (ROE)	Net Profit	Average Equity
ROE DuPont Analysis	ROA × Leverage Multiplier = Net Profit Ratio × Asset Turnover × Leverage Multiplier, where Leverage Multiplier = Average Asset ÷ Average Equity	
6. Return on Capital Employed (ROCE)	Profit Before Interest & Taxes (PBIT)	Average Capital Employed (i.e., Equity & Debt)

Efficiency Ratios	Numerator	Denominator
7. Asset Turnover Ratio	Sales	Average Total Assets
8. Fixed Asset Turnover Ratio	Sales	Average Fixed Assets (i.e., PPE, CWIP, ROU, Intangible Assets, & Investment Properties)
9. Current Asset Turnover Ratio	Sales	Average Current Assets
10. Working Capital Turnover Ratio	Sales	Average Working Capital
11. Trade Receivable Turnover	Sales	Average Trade Receivable
Trade Receivable Period (Days)	365	Trade Receivable Turnover
12. Inventory Turnover	Cost of Goods Sold, OR Sales	Average Inventory
Inventory Period (Days)	365	Inventory Turnover
13. Trade Payable Turnover	Purchases of goods and services, OR Sales	Average Trade Payable
Trade Payable Period (Days)	365	Trade Payable Turnover
14. Operating Cycle	Days of Trade Receivable + Days of Inventory	
15. Cash Cycle	Operating Cycle – Days of Trade Payable	

Liquidity & Solvency Ratios	Numerator	Denominator
16. Current Ratio	Current Assets	Current Liabilities
17. Quick Ratio	Financial Assets (Current), OR (Current Assets – Inventories – Prepaid Expenses)	Current Liabilities
18. Debt-Equity Ratio	Debt (preference share capital, borrowings, lease liabilities, acceptances, and any other liability on which interest is payable to a third party)	Equity
19. Liability to Equity	Liabilities	Equity
20. Interest Coverage Ratio	Profit Before Interest & Taxes (PBIT)	Finance Cost
21. Debt Service Coverage Ratio	Earnings available for debt service = Net profit after taxes + Non-cash operating expenses + Interest Expense + Other adjustments like loss on sale of fixed assets, etc.	Debt service (Both debt principal & interest payable during the current year)

Other Ratios	Numerator	Denominator
22. Payout Ratio	Dividends Declared	Net Profit
23. Retention Ratio	1 – Payout Ratio	
24. Price-Earnings Ratio (P/E Ratio)	Market Capitalization = Equity Share Price at the end of the financial year × Number of equity shares outstanding	Net Profit
25. Price to Book Ratio (P/B Ratio)	Market Capitalization	Equity

Appendix 5C: ICAI Guidance Note on the Computation of Key Financial Ratios

An amendment, dated 24-03-2021, made to Division II – Schedule III of the Companies Act, 2013 requires companies to report 11 key financial ratios (listed below) in their notes, mention the items included in the numerator and in the denominator of each ratio, and explain what caused a change in a ratio in the current year if the year-on-year change in the ratio is 25% or more. The amendment notification does not list the formula for a financial ratio. The formula is provided in Annexure B of the Institute of Chartered Accountants of India's (ICAI) Guidance Note (revised on January 2022) on Division II – Schedule III of the Companies Act, 2013. Since guidance notes are recommendatory in nature, companies may use a different numerator and/or denominator to obtain these 11 key ratios. The following table has the required financial ratios and their numerator and denominator as per ICAI's guidance note:

Key Financial Ratios	Numerator	Denominator
1. Current ratio	Current assets	Current liabilities
2. Debt-equity ratio	Total debt	Shareholder's equity
3. Debt service coverage ratio (DSCR)	Earnings available for debt service = PAT + Non-cash operating expenses like depreciation and other amortizations + Interest (Expense) + other adjustments like loss on sale of Fixed assets, etc.	Debt service = Interest & Lease Payments + Principal Repayments
4. Return on equity ratio (ROE)	Net Profits after taxes – Preference Dividend (if any)	Average Shareholder's Equity
5. Inventory turnover ratio	Cost of goods sold OR Sales	Average Inventory
6. Trade receivables turnover ratio	Net Credit Sales = gross credit sales – sales return.	Avg. Accounts Receivable
7. Trade payables turnover ratio	Net Credit Purchases = gross credit purchases – purchase return	Average Trade Payables
8. Net (working) capital turnover ratio	Net Sales	Working Capital
9. Net profit ratio	Net Profit	Net Sales
10. Return on capital employed (ROCE)	Profit Before interest and taxes	Capital Employed = Tangible Net Worth + Total Debt + Deferred Tax Liability
11. Return on investment (ROI)	Income generated from investments (both realized and unrealized)**	Time-weighted average investments**

*As per the guidance note, companies may provide ROI separately for each class of investments (e.g., equity, fixed income, money markets, etc.). In practice, companies report for Quoted and Unquoted investments.

**The numerators and denominators are a simplified description of what is given in the guidance note.

Appendix 5D: Key Financial Ratios Reported by Selected Companies

(a) Key Financial Ratios Reported by Asian Paints

Ratios	Numerator	Denominator	FY 2021–22	FY 2020–21	% Variance
1. Current ratio	Current Assets	Current Liabilities	2.26	2.17	3.83%
2. Debt-equity ratio*	Total Debt (Borrowings)	Total Equity	0	0	–35.24%
3. Debt service coverage ratio	Earning available for Debt Service#	Finance Costs (excluding cost pertaining to lease liabilities) + Repayment of borrowings	133.38	133.55	–0.13%
4. Return on Equity	Profits after tax	Average Total Equity	24.65%	28.33%	–13.02%
5. Inventory turnover ratio	Cost of goods sold	Average Inventory	3.72	3.39	9.67%
6. Trade receivables turnover ratio	Revenue from Sale of Products and Services	Average Trade receivables	10.58	12.53	–15.52%
7. Trade payables turnover ratio	Net Purchases of raw material, packing material and stock-in-trade	Average Trade payables	5.62	4.53	24.00%
8. Net capital turnover ratio	Revenue from Operations	Working Capital (Current Assets – Current Liabilities)	3.55	3.45	2.90%
9. Net profit ratio	Profit after tax	Revenue from Operations	12.44%	16.48%	–24.49%
10. Return on capital employed	Profit before interest (excluding interest on lease liabilities), exceptional items and tax	Average Capital Employed [Total Equity + Total Debt (Borrowings)]	33.50%	38.07%	–12.01%
11. Return on investment	Income during the year	Time weighted average of investment			
(a) Return on Mutual Funds			3.79%	4.41%	–13.93%
(b) Return on Fixed Deposits			5.28%	6.04%	–12.57%
(c) Return on Bonds@			3.88%	10.06%	–61.46%
(d) Return on quoted equity investment^			–11.72%	12.42%	–193.35%

Source: Asian Paints,"Key Financial Ratios Reported by Asian Paints",www.asianpaints.com. *Increase in net worth has led to improved debt equity ratio; @Increase in market yield coupled with higher value of bonds nearing maturity; ^Impact of market dynamics; #Earning available for Debt Service = Profit after tax + Depreciation and Amortization Expense + Finance costs (excluding interest on lease liabilities) – Net gain on sale of property, plant and equipment – Net gain on modification/ termination of leases.

(b) Key Financial Ratios Reported by Avenue Supermarts

	Ratios	Numerator	Denominator	FY 2021–22	FY 2020–21	% Variance
1.	Current Ratio (times)	Current Asset	Current Liability	3.06	3.7	–17%
2.	Debt – Equity Ratio (times)	Total Debt	Shareholder's Equity	0.03	0.02	24%
3.	Debt Service Coverage Ratio (times)	Earnings available for debt service	Debt Service (Finance cost + Lease Payment + Principal Repayment)	5.64	4.62	22%
4.	Return on Equity ratio (%)	Net Profit after tax	Average Shareholder's Equity	12.32%	9.94%	24%
5.	Inventory turnover ratio (times)	Net sales	Avg Inventory	12.77	11.67	9%
6.	Trade receivables turnover ratio (times)*	Net Credit sales	Avg Trade receivable	138.92	261.72	–47%
7.	Trade payables turnover ratio (times)	Net Credit Purchases	Avg Trade payable	48.27	40.76	18%
8.	Net capital turnover ratio (times)@	Net sales	Working Capital	13.45	8.23	63%
9.	Net profit ratio (%)	Net Profit after tax	Net Sales	5.32%	4.90%	9%
10.	Return on Capital employed (%)^	Earnings before interest and taxes	Capital Employed (Tangible Net Worth + Total Debt + Deferred Tax Liability)	17.37%	13.77%	26%
11.	(a) Return on investment (%) (Term Deposits)	Change in market value	Average Investment	3.94%	4.95%	–20%
	(b) Return on investment (%) (Mutual Funds)	Change in market value	Average Investment	3.17%	2.93%	8%

Source: Avenue Supermarts Limited,"Key Financial Ratios Reported by Avenue Supermarts", api.dmartindia.com. *Ratio has reduced due to increase in receivables of credit sales; @The Change is due to increase in Sales and higher maturity of short-term deposits; ^Improved on account of increased earnings

(c) Key Financial Ratios Reported by Infosys

	Ratios	Numerator	Denominator	FY 2021–22	FY 2020–21	% Variance
1.	Current ratio	Current assets	Current liabilities	2.1	2.7	–23.4
2.	Debt – Equity ratio	Total debt (represents only lease liabilities)	Shareholder's equity	0.1	0.1	0.1
3.	Debt service coverage ratio	Earnings available for debt service#	Debt service (Lease payments for the current year)	38.5	38.8	–0.8
4.	Return on Equity (ROE)	Net profits after taxes	Average shareholder's equity	30.20%	27.00%	3.2
5.	Trade receivables turnover ratio	Revenue	Average trade receivable	5.9	5.4	9.0
6.	Trade payables turnover ratio	Purchases of services and other expenses	Average trade payables	11.3	9.9	13.3
7.	Net capital turnover ratio*	Revenue	Working capital	3.8	2.8	35.1
8.	Net profit ratio	Net profit	Revenue	20.40%	21.00%	–0.6
9.	Return on Capital Employed (ROCE)	Earnings before interest and taxes	Capital employed = Tangible net worth + Deferred tax liabilities + Lease liabilities	38.80%	32.50%	6.3
10.	Return on Investment (ROI)	Unquoted Income generated from investments	Time-weighted average investments	8.70%	7.90%	0.9
		Quoted Income generated from investments	Time-weighted average investments	5.90%	6.20%	–0.3

Source: Infosys, "Key Financial Ratios Reported by Infosys",www.infosys.com. *Revenue growth along with higher efficiency on working capital improvement has resulted in an improvement in the ratio. #Earnings available for debt service = Net profit after taxes + Non-cash operating expenses + Interest + Other adjustments like loss on sale of fixed assets, etc.